# OXFORD
## UNIVERSITY PRESS

# Complete
# Economics
## for Cambridge IGCSE® & O Level
# Workbook

D0584474

**Brian Titley**
with Terry Cook and Peter Roscoe

**Oxford excellence for Cambridge IGCSE® & O Level**

OXFORD
UNIVERSITY PRESS

## Your Complete Economics Workbook

The Complete Economics Workbook is designed to help you:

✓ build and strengthen your knowledge and understanding of economics;

✓ prepare for your final examinations;

✓ develop all the key skills you will need to demonstrate to achieve a good grade.

The workbook can be used for study with the 'Complete Economics' student textbook, as well as independently.

Space is provided for you throughout the workbook to write notes and your answers to questions.

Once completed it will provide a valuable resource you can use again to refresh and revise your knowledge and understanding of economics.

Key features of your workbook:

✓ matches the latest Cambridge International Examinations syllabus for IGCSE and O Level Economics;

✓ provides exercises and examination questions, covering all the topics and aims of the Cambridge Economics course;

✓ matches the order of topics in the 'Complete Economics' student textbook;

✓ contains additional sections to support revision and exam preparation, the use of economic vocabulary and terminology and the use and analysis of economic data, diagrams and charts;

✓ provides model answers to all exercises and questions.

## What's in your workbook?

Your workbook is divided into six main parts matching those of the Cambridge IGCSE and O Level syllabus in Economics. These are further sub-divided into a number of sections covering all the topics and aims of the Cambridge Economics course.

**In each section you will find:**

| Content | Key Words | Revision Summary |
|---|---|---|
| These pages cover all the topics and aims of your economics course.<br><br>On each page there is:<br><br>a series of questions to help you develop your knowledge and understanding of at least one key topic and aim<br><br>space under each question for you to write your answer<br><br>an extension exercise to extend your key skills in economics. | An exercise to help you learn, revise and use economic vocabulary and terminology covered in the section.<br><br>The exercise involves matching key terms to the definitions and explanations provided.<br><br>Together, the key word sections in your workbook will build a complete dictionary of all the key economic terms you will need to know and understand by the end of your course. | A full summary of all the key economic facts, definitions, concepts, principles and theories covered in the section.<br><br>You will need to complete the summary with missing economic terms and definitions. Spaces are provided for you to write in your answers.<br><br>Taken together, all the summaries in your workbook will provide a useful revision guide to help refresh and strengthen your knowledge of economics as you prepare for your final exams. |

**At the end of each unit you will find:**

| Working with data and diagrams | Multiple choice questions | Structured questions |
|---|---|---|
| The ability to use data and diagrams to demonstrate economic concepts and changes in economic conditions is an important skill. This section provides practical help and exercises to build your skills of analysis including making calculations with economic data and presenting data in diagrams and charts. | Eight or more multiple choice questions to test your understanding of all the topics covered in the unit and to provide exam practice. | A series of structured questions that require longer written answers. Completing them will test your knowledge and help you to build your skills in presenting economics facts, theories and arguments. |

**At the end of your workbook there are:**

| Answers |
|---|
| Model answers for every question in your workbook, including key word and revision exercises, for you to learn and revise from.<br><br>Compare them with your own answers to check your understanding and to make sure that you have covered the key points. |

You can choose to complete your workbook a topic, section or even unit at a time during the course of your studies.

Alternatively, you can complete the workbook at the end of your studies as you prepare and revise for your final examinations.

## How you will be assessed

This workbook is designed to help you develop and practise the three key skills you will need to demonstrate in your answers to examination questions in order to achieve a good grade.

**KNOWLEDGE AND UNDERSTANDING**　　　(KU)

You will be assessed on how well you:

✓ show knowledge and understanding of definitions, formulas, concepts, principles and theories

✓ use economic vocabulary and terminology.

**ANALYSIS**　　　(An)

The exams will test your ability to:

✓ select, organize and interpret data

✓ use economic information and statistics to recognize patterns in data and to deduce economic relationships

✓ apply economic knowledge and understanding to written, numerical, diagrammatic and graphical data

✓ analyse economic issues and situations, identifying causes and links.

**EVALUATION**　　　(Ev)

You will also be assessed on your ability to:

✓ evaluate economic information and data

✓ distinguish between economic analysis and reasoned statements

✓ recognize uncertainties of the outcomes of economic decisions and events

✓ communicate your economic thinking in a logical and clear manner.

Your skills will be assessed in two examination papers. The key skills assessed in each paper are listed below in order of the importance placed on them.

| Paper | Duration | Types of questions | Key skills assessed | Contribution of paper to final grade |
|---|---|---|---|---|
| 1 Multiple choice | 45 minutes | 30 questions – all must be answered | An KU | 30% |
| 2 Structured questions | 2 hours 15 minutes | 1 compulsory question from Section A plus a choice of 3 questions from Section B | Ev An KU | 70% |

Your answers to all examination questions will be marked and your overall performance graded A to G. The grade you achieve will depend on how well you demonstrate the required skills in each paper.

**Grade A** students must show excellence in all key skills. Answers to more difficult questions should be outstanding and show good use of real world examples.

**Grade C** students must demonstrate they have a good understanding of the course content and some ability to answer the more difficult questions.

**Grade F** students must show some familiarity with the key economic concepts and issues covered in the course. They should be able to answer basic questions correctly and attempt some of the more difficult questions.

To prepare for your final exams it is important that you practise providing answers to many different examination questions throughout your course.

## Answering multiple choice questions

A **multiple choice question** requires you to choose an answer from four possible options. When you have decided on the correct response, you must indicate your choice on the answer sheet. Each right answer to a question is awarded one mark. No marks are deducted for wrong answers.

You have just 45 minutes to answer 30 multiple choice questions in Paper 1. This means you have 1.5 minutes on average to read and answer each question. However, some questions may take more time to read and answer than others.

### Multiple choice 'do's and don'ts'

- Do read through each question carefully. Some questions may appear to have more than one right answer, but only one will be correct. Eliminate all the wrong answers before selecting the best one.

- Don't spend too long on a question. If a question is difficult then move on to the next question and return to the difficult ones later.

- Do try to leave yourself at least 5 minutes before the end of the exam to check your answers and to complete any you may have missed.

- Don't worry if you are unsure about the answer to a question. You have a 25% chance of choosing the right answer to a multiple choice question. So ...

- Do make sure you provide answers to all 30 questions.

1. An entrepreneur is someone who:
   A produces goods and services ✗
   B owns and runs a factory ✗
   C organizes resources in a firm ✓
   D supervises other workers ✗

A is wrong because workers are also producers of goods and services.

B is partially true but not all firms have factories.

C is the best answer.

D refers to labour. A supervisor is a senior worker or manager in a firm organized by an entrepreneur.

## Answering structured questions

A **structured question** is a series of related questions based on some information describing a real economic situation. Some questions may require short, one word answers or a single sentence. Others will require more detailed explanations.

Exam Paper 2 requires you to complete four structured questions.

| Section A | Section B |
|---|---|
| Contains up to a page of information including text, statistical tables and charts on a real economic situation. | Contains six structured questions. You must complete three of these. |
| You must complete the structured question in this section. It will contain a mixture of up to eight short answer questions and more difficult questions about the information presented. | Each structured question contains: <br> • a sentence or short paragraph introducing a real economic situation <br> • four individual questions based on the introduction. |
| A maximum 30 marks are available in this section. | A maximum 60 marks are available in this section, i.e. 20 marks per structured question. |

Here is an example of the type of structured question you may find in Section B.

Developing countries have characteristics that are different from those of more developed countries. One of these is the amount of poverty in such countries.

(a) Define *absolute poverty*. [2]

(b) Explain **two** features of a developing country. [4]

(c) Analyse what is likely to happen to the occupational structure and geographical distribution of the population in a country as it becomes more developed. [6]

(d) Discuss whether government policies will always be successful at reducing poverty in a developing country. [8]

**How much should I write to answer each question?**

You will be provided with an answer booklet in the exam in which to write your answers.

Enough space for you to write a good answer to each question is provided in the booklet. The more space given, the longer and more detailed your answer must be to earn full marks.

This is a short answer question. It only requires a short definition or explanation to be given. Two line spaces will normally be enough.

This question requires you to present arguments for and against the statement to demonstrate critical evaluation skills. Eight or more line spaces will be provided for your answer.

**How do I know what the questions want me to do?**

A command word or phrase, such as 'define', 'explain', 'analyse' or 'discuss' is used at the start of each question to tell you what you need to do. Each command word tells you to answer a question in a particular way in order to assess different key skills.

| Common commands | What you need to do | Key skills assessed |
|---|---|---|
| Analyse | Examine the information provided to identify and describe economic reasons why an outcome may or may not occur. <br><br> *'Analyse the motives that might cause a person to save'* <br><br> *'Analyse three reasons why a market economic system may fail'* | An <br> Ev <br> KU |
| Calculate | Work out a number(s) or percentage(s) from the information provided. <br><br> *'Calculate the reduction in profit between 2007 and 2008'* <br><br> *'Calculate the change in total employment. Show your workings'* | An |
| Define | Give a precise meaning for a key economic term. <br><br> *'Define deflation'* <br><br> *'Define economic growth'* | KU |
| Describe | State key points about a topic or give characteristics or main features. <br><br> *'Describe two reasons why car production is usually undertaken by large multinationals'* <br><br> *'Describe what can influence the demand for smart phones'* | KU |
| Discuss | Explain and contrast, in a structured way, economic reasons or arguments for and against a particular statement or proposal. Where possible, say what arguments or reasons you support and why to gain full marks. These type of questions usually award 8 or more marks. <br><br> *'Discuss why a small food shop might survive when there are very large supermarkets'* <br><br> *'Discuss how firms might achieve a rise in profits'* | KU <br> Ev |
| Explain | Set out why and/or how an economic situation or outcome can occur. Make relationships between different economic variables clear and support your answers with relevant evidence. <br><br> *'Explain why the social costs of car use are greater than the private costs'* <br><br> *'Explain why a reduction in unemployment might increase inflation'* | KU <br> An <br> Ev |
| Give | Provide an answer from recall or memory. <br><br> *'Give an example of an indirect tax'* <br><br> *'Give three ways of measuring the size of a firm'* | KU |
| Identify | Name or select, from information provided, relevant economic facts, characteristics, relationships, measures or factors that may have caused changes in economic conditions to occur. <br><br> *'Identify two functions of money'* <br><br> *'Using information from the extract, identify two characteristics of monopoly'* <br><br> *'Using information from the extract, identify two indicators of improved living standards in Mozambique'* | KU |
| State | Express economic factors, relationships or facts in clear terms. <br><br> *'State four ways in which multinational companies can help a developing country such as Bangladesh'* <br><br> *'State two types of tax'* | KU |

**Structured question 'do's and don'ts'**

- Don't rush. Plan your exam time carefully and make sure you understand what each question is about before you start writing your answers. This means reading each question slowly and in full and re-reading them if necessary.

- Do look out for the command words and economic terms in each question to identify what the question is about and what is expected from your answer.

- Don't try to write down everything you know about the economic concepts, theories or facts in each question. Only write down what the question requires as a response. Writing more than necessary wastes valuable time and is unlikely to gain you any extra marks.

- Do look at the marks for each question to consider how long or detailed your answer should be. The more marks there are, the more is expected.

- Don't forget to correctly label any diagrams you draw.

To help you focus it is good idea to underline or highlight the command words and economic terms in each question.

Initially writing down your answer in note form can help you to focus on the key points you need to make.

Many of the answers at the end of your workbook are much longer and more detailed than you will need to write in your exams. This is because they cover all the possible points or arguments you could make. For example:

[4] marks usually requires only two points or explanations well made; [6] often requires two or three points or arguments to be carefully presented; [8] usually requires two + two opposing arguments to be fully explained ...

Now let's see how well the student below applied these 'do's and don'ts' to the structured question example on page vi.

(a) Define *absolute poverty*. [2]

| Student answer | Examiner's comments |
|---|---|
| Absolute poverty occurs when people cannot meet their basic human needs including food, safe drinking water, sanitation, health, shelter and education. The extent of absolute poverty in a country is usually measured by the number of people living on the equivalent of less than around $2 to $3 per day. Absolute poverty is widespread in a number of countries in Africa but also remains significant in many rapidly developing countries including India and China. | The student has correctly explained what absolute poverty is in the first sentence and this will gain full marks. However, the answer provided is far too long for 2 marks. It provides examples of countries where many people live on less than around $2 or $3 each day. This is not required and will not earn any extra marks. |

(b) <u>Explain</u> **two** features of a <u>developing country</u>. [4]

| Student answer | Examiner's comments |
|---|---|
| A developing country has a relatively low level of economic development and low average income per head. Many people live in poor housing conditions with poor sanitation and have relatively low life expectancy. Birth and death rates are high resulting in rapid population growth. Road, rail and communication networks also tend to be underdeveloped. | The student describes a number of features of a developing economy correctly but only two are required for full marks. Writing more than necessary will have wasted valuable examination time. |

(c) <u>Analyse</u> what is likely to happen to the <u>occupational structure and geographical distribution of the population</u> in a country as it becomes more developed. [6]

| Student answer | Examiner's comments |
|---|---|
| As a country develops it experiences growth in its manufacturing, construction and service industries. Employment and incomes generated by these industries increase. Over time they will account for a larger and larger proportion of jobs and incomes in the country. The share of total employment accounted for by farming and other primary industries falls.<br><br>As incomes and education improve, people also tend to marry later and have less children. As a result the average age of the population tends to increase. This is shown in the diagram. | The student has clearly understood the term occupational distribution for 1 mark and has correctly identified that increased economic development is usually associated with growth in manufacturing, construction and service industries and employment. This will gain a further 2 marks. However, the student has failed to describe the movement of people from rural areas to growing urban areas that also tends to occur with increased development.<br><br>Instead the student wrongly describes what may happen to the age distribution and draws an age–sex population pyramid in an attempt to demonstrate this. The diagram is not required but it is also missing labels that will explain what the diagram shows. |

(d) <u>Discuss</u> whether government policies will always be successful at reducing poverty in a developing country. [8]

| Student answer | Examiner's comments |
|---|---|
| Yes. I believe that government policies designed to reduce poverty will always do so otherwise there would be no point introducing them. For example, lowering taxes and increasing welfare payments will boost the incomes of the poorest people in society. Increasing the minimum wage will also help to increase incomes. The government can also spend more on education to help people get better paid jobs in the future. Policies designed to boost economic growth will help to increase employment and incomes. | The student has only presented economic arguments that support a view that government policies successfully reduce poverty. Reasons why some government policies designed to reduce poverty may fail to do so are not presented. For example, lowering taxes and/or increasing welfare benefits may still leave a lot of people on very low incomes; raising the minimum wage will only benefit those people able to work; not everyone benefits equally from economic growth. Only up to 4 marks can be awarded for a one-sided presentation.<br><br>Many students find questions that require them to present and discuss reasoned arguments difficult. Many will often express their opinions rather than presenting and contrasting different economic theories and evidence. |

**What should I do if I am running out of time in my exam?**

It is always a good idea to prepare your answer to a difficult question, especially one requiring a longer answer, by writing down all the key points you want to make in a series of short notes before you write your answer in full. This will help you think through what the most important points are and to make any corrections before you finalize your answer.

Making notes in your answer booklet will be an especially sensible thing to do if you are running out of time in your final exam and will not be able to answer every question you need to in full. This is because examiners will award marks for your notes if they show you have understood the question and they demonstrate a good knowledge and understanding of the relevant economic ideas, facts and theories.

**Example**

Discuss whether a reduction in agricultural subsidies will be beneficial to employment and the standard of living in a country.

| How to structure your answer | The notes you might make in the exam |
|---|---|
| Give reasons why the action may be beneficial | • Other jobs may be created if the government gives subsidies to other industries instead, invests in new infrastructure projects or cuts taxes<br>• Importing more food may be cheaper than subsidizing domestic farms |
| Suggest reasons why the action may not be beneficial | • Reducing subsidies will increase farm production costs, reduce profits and reduce the supply of food products<br>• Prices of domestic agricultural products are likely to rise – consumers will be worse off, especially those on low incomes<br>• Employment and income may fall significantly if the agricultural sector is a major employer |
| Suggest and justify any alternative actions you can think of | Government could instead:<br>• invest in re-training farm workers to take other jobs<br>• help to train farmers in new farming methods so they become more productive, reduce costs and increase the supply of food |
| Summarize and conclude your arguments | Cutting agricultural subsidies may be beneficial if:<br>• other industries can expand to provide more jobs<br>• farms become more efficient as a result<br>• imported food is cheaper<br>• taxes can be lowered |

## 1.1.1 Finite resources and unlimited wants

1. What problem in economics do the two newspaper headlines below illustrate? [2]

**Extreme weather will triple food shortages**

**Engineering jobs hardest to fill as skills shortage continues**

.............................................................................................................................................

.............................................................................................................................................

2. All countries face economic problems, so choices have to be made. Define *economic problem*. [2]

.............................................................................................................................................

.............................................................................................................................................

3. A factory producing motor vehicles runs out of important component parts and has to stop production. Explain how this illustrates the basic economic problem. [2]

.............................................................................................................................................

.............................................................................................................................................

4. Using examples, explain **two** ways in which human *wants* differ from human *needs*. [4]

.............................................................................................................................................

.............................................................................................................................................

.............................................................................................................................................

.............................................................................................................................................

**E**

Explain why it is impossible to solve the basic economic problem.

## 1.1.2 Economic and free goods

1. Explain why air is an example of a free good in economics. [2]

.....................................................................................................................

.....................................................................................................................

2. Explain why cars are economic goods. [4]

.....................................................................................................................

.....................................................................................................................

.....................................................................................................................

.....................................................................................................................

3. Identify one way in which free goods and economic goods are similar and one way they differ. [4]

.....................................................................................................................

.....................................................................................................................

.....................................................................................................................

.....................................................................................................................

4. Explain how a new idea posted on the internet may be considered a free good. [4]

.....................................................................................................................

.....................................................................................................................

.....................................................................................................................

**E**

Which of the following are examples of free goods and which are economic goods?

| | Free good? | Economic good? |
|---|---|---|
| Pebbles on the beach | | |
| Computers | | |
| Air | | |
| Factories | | |

## 1.2.1 Definitions of the factors of production and their rewards

**1.** Explain the difference between 'labour' and 'enterprise' and how they are rewarded. [4]

..................................................................................................................................

..................................................................................................................................

..................................................................................................................................

..................................................................................................................................

**2.** Explain **two** ways in which labour is different from land. [4]

..................................................................................................................................

..................................................................................................................................

..................................................................................................................................

..................................................................................................................................

**3.** Using examples, explain the factor of production, 'capital'. [4]

..................................................................................................................................

..................................................................................................................................

..................................................................................................................................

..................................................................................................................................

**E**

Factors of production are scarce productive resources. They are organized into firms by entrepreneurs to produce goods and services. We consume or 'use up' goods and services to satisfy our different needs and wants.

Identify **two** examples of labour, land and capital resources that are likely to be used in the production of the following products: (a) clothing (a durable consumer good), (b) milk (a non-durable consumer good), (c) the teaching of educational courses (a service), and (d) a newly constructed office block (a capital good).

## 1.2.2 The mobility of the factors of production

1. Define *factor mobility*. [2]

..........................................................................................................................................................

..........................................................................................................................................................

2. Explain how a lorry is an example of a mobile factor of production. [4]

..........................................................................................................................................................

..........................................................................................................................................................

..........................................................................................................................................................

..........................................................................................................................................................

3. Explain how (a) geographical immobility and (b) occupational immobility may affect the allocation of labour in an economy. [4]

..........................................................................................................................................................

..........................................................................................................................................................

..........................................................................................................................................................

..........................................................................................................................................................

4. Explain the concepts of factor mobility and factor immobility using an area of farmland as an example. [4]

..........................................................................................................................................................

..........................................................................................................................................................

..........................................................................................................................................................

..........................................................................................................................................................

**E**

Describe how a firm may increase the mobility of the labour and capital it uses. What are the potential benefits to the firm of increasing the mobility of the resources it employs?

## 1.2.3 Quantity and quality of the factors of production

1. Using examples, explain the difference between renewable and non-renewable resources. [4]

..................................................................................................................................................

..................................................................................................................................................

..................................................................................................................................................

..................................................................................................................................................

2. Explain **two** ways farmers could improve the quality of their farmland. [4]

..................................................................................................................................................

..................................................................................................................................................

..................................................................................................................................................

..................................................................................................................................................

3. Explain what schools and colleges can do to increase the quality of labour. [4]

..................................................................................................................................................

..................................................................................................................................................

..................................................................................................................................................

..................................................................................................................................................

4. Explain **two** ways the factor of production of land could be increased in an economy. [4]

..................................................................................................................................................

..................................................................................................................................................

..................................................................................................................................................

..................................................................................................................................................

**E**

Using examples, explain how advances in technology have improved both the quantity and quality of different factors of production.

## Key words
*Match economic terms with their definitions*

| | | | |
|---|---|---|---|
| 1 | Human needs **K** | A | Human-made resources including machinery, tools and factory buildings, used in the production of other goods and services |
| 2 | Human wants | B | Skills possessed by successful entrepreneurs: business know-how and the ability to organize productive activities |
| 3 | Production | C | The using up of goods and services by consumers to satisfy their human needs and wants |
| 4 | Free goods | D | The ability to move or reallocate factors of production from one productive task to others |
| 5 | Economic goods | E | All scarce resources used to produce other goods and services. They are the inputs to productive activities |
| 6 | Consumption | F | These are limited in supply. People are therefore willing to pay to obtain them |
| 7 | Goods and services | G | The ability or extent to which factors of production can be moved or reallocated between different productive uses without incurring significant costs or a loss of output |
| 8 | Capital goods | H | Human desires for different goods and services to give them satisfaction. These desires are without limit and increasing |
| 9 | Consumer goods | I | The ability to move or reallocate factors of production from one location to another |
| 10 | Factors of production | J | Human effort used up in productive activities |
| 11 | Land | K | Basic human requirements for life and survival |
| 12 | Labour | L | Goods produced to satisfy consumer needs or wants |
| 13 | Capital | M | Organizations in which entrepreneurs combine and organise factors of production to produce goods and services |
| 14 | Enterprise | N | The outputs (or 'products') of productive activities using scarce resources |
| 15 | Firms | O | Goods produced specifically to make other goods and services and not intended for immediate consumption |
| 16 | Entrepreneur | P | These are goods we may need or want that are without limit |
| 17 | Factor mobility | Q | Using resources to make and deliver goods and services to satisfy the needs and wants of consumers |
| 18 | Occupational mobility | R | All natural resources used to produce other goods and services |
| 19 | Geographic mobility | S | A person with enterprise who is willing to take the risks and decisions necessary to organize scarce resources into firms to produce goods and services |

## Revision summary

*Fill in the missing words and economic terms*

1. _ _ _ _ _ _ _ _ _ of resources is the central problem in economics. Human wants are _ _ _ _ _ _ _ _ _ and there are just not enough resources in the world to produce all the goods and services required to satisfy all our needs and wants.

2. Resources are the inputs to productive activities and economic goods are the outputs of productive activities. Economic goods are therefore _ _ _ _ _ _ _ in supply because the resources used up to produce them are finite.

3. Resources are also known as _ _ _ _ _ _ _ _ _ _ _ _ _ _ _ _ _ _ _ because they are used to produce goods and services.

4. Economists recognize four broad types of factors of production: labour, enterprise, land and capital. Entrepreneurs organize and combine these factors of production into _ _ _ _ _ in order to produce goods and services that will satisfy some of our needs and wants. If they are successful and able to sell the goods or services they produce at a price that exceeds their cost of production, they will be rewarded with _ _ _ _ _.

5. Entrepreneurs possess a factor of production called _ _ _ _ _ _ _ _ _ _. It refers to their willingness and ability to organize production into firms.

6. _ _ _ _ consists of all natural resources, including water, minerals, oils, plants and animals, that are used up in the production of other goods and services.

7. _ _ _ _ _ _ is the mental and physical effort supplied by people to firms to make goods and services, usually in return for _ _ _ _ _ or salaries.

8. _ _ _ _ _ _ _ refers to human-made resources, including machinery, equipment and factory buildings. These _ _ _ _ _ _ _ goods are not intended for immediate consumption but are instead used to produce and supply other goods and services.

9. Increasing both the quantity and _ _ _ _ _ _ _ of factor resources available can help to increase the amount of economic goods and services they are able to produce. As a result, more human needs can be met and more human wants can be _ _ _ _ _ _ _ _ _.

10. For example, increasing the number of skilled workers will increase labour productivity and _ _ _ _ _ _ _ _. This will make it easier to move labour between different productive uses either within a firm or between different firms in different industries.

11. The more mobile factors of production are the easier it is for them to be allocated to their best possible uses so that they are able to produce as many goods and services as they possibly can. However, some factors of production are _ _ _ _ _ _ _. This will make it difficult to move them from one productive use to another as consumer demand for different product changes or technology changes.

12. For example, a factory building cannot be moved. That is, it is _ _ _ _ _ _ _ _ _ _ _ _ _ _ immobile but it could be used to produce computers or car parts. In contrast, while it is possible to move a floating oil platform, it can only be used to drill for oil and gas at sea. Similarly, a bricklayer could not quickly or easily change occupation to become a surgeon. Many workers with limited or very specialist skills are _ _ _ _ _ _ _ _ _ _ _ _ _ immobile.

## 1.3.1 Definition of opportunity cost
## 1.3.2 The influence of opportunity cost on decision making

1. What, according to the definition of 'opportunity cost', is sacrificed when a decision on how to use scarce resources is taken? [2]

..........................................................................................................................................................

..........................................................................................................................................................

2. Explain why the scarcity of resources creates an opportunity cost. [4]

..........................................................................................................................................................

..........................................................................................................................................................

..........................................................................................................................................................

..........................................................................................................................................................

3. Explain why all organizations should consider opportunity cost when deciding how to use their factors of production. [4]

..........................................................................................................................................................

..........................................................................................................................................................

..........................................................................................................................................................

..........................................................................................................................................................

**E**

Explain how the two newspaper headlines below illustrate the economic concepts of scarcity and opportunity cost.

> **Australian government boosts spending on defence and surveillance while continuing to cut funding for health, education and welfare**

> **Increase in demand for land to grow soybeans threatens further deforestation of the Amazon Rainforest**

## 1.4.1 Definition of a PPC
## 1.4.2 Points under, on and beyond a PPC
## 1.4.3 Movements along a PPC

1. The cost of a decision in an economy to use more of its resources to increase the production of consumer goods will be fewer capital goods. Draw a production possibility curve diagram in the space provided to show this impact. [4]

2. Using a diagram, analyse how a production possibility curve can be used to illustrate the concept of opportunity cost. [6]

...........................................................................................................................................................

...........................................................................................................................................................

...........................................................................................................................................................

..................................................................................

..................................................................................

..................................................................................

..................................................................................

..................................................................................

**E**

A firm is able to produce handbags and shoes. The most handbags it can produce per week is 1,000. Alternatively, it can produce up to 600 pairs of shoes per week. Draw and label a diagram to show its production possibility curve.

Currently the firm produces 500 handbags and 300 pairs of shoes each week. Mark this point on your diagram and explain why the firm could produce more output without the need for additional resources. Also explain why it is currently unable to produce 900 handbags and 700 pairs of shoes per week.

## 1.4.4 Shifts in a PPC

1. The diagrams below show what has happened to the production possibility curves for two economies. Which economy has expanded its capacity to produce goods and services and which economy has experienced negative economic growth? [2]

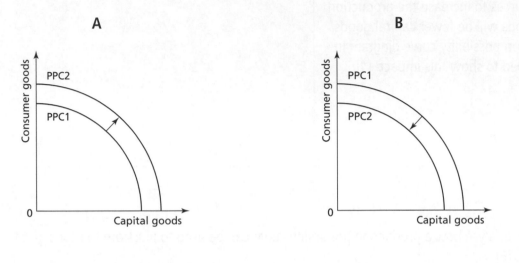

..................................................          ..................................................

2. Explain **two** factors that would cause the production possibility curve of an economy to shift outwards. [4]

..............................................................................................................

..............................................................................................................

..............................................................................................................

..............................................................................................................

3. Explain **two** factors that would cause the production possibility curve of an economy to shift inwards. [4]

..............................................................................................................

..............................................................................................................

..............................................................................................................

..............................................................................................................

**E**

International migration is reducing the supply of labour and enterprise in some countries and increasing it in others. Draw **two** production possibility curve diagrams to show the impact these changes could have on two different national economies.

## Key words

*Match economic terms with their definitions*

| | |
|---|---|
| **1** Opportunity cost      **D** | **A** This is shown by an outward shift in a PPC resulting from an increase in the quantity and/or quality of the resources available either to an individual firm or an entire economy |
| **2** Production possibility curve (PPC) | **B** Any area, such as a nation state, in which the economic activities of production, exchange and consumption take place |
| **3** A decrease in productive capacity | **C** A curved line on a diagram that shows all the possible combinations of two products that a firm or an entire economy is able to produce with its existing resources and know-how if they are fully and efficiently used |
| **4** An inefficient allocation of resources | **D** The benefit that is foregone from choosing one use of scarce resources over the next best use of those same resources |
| **5** An increase in productive capacity | **E** This occurs if factor resources are not fully or effectively used either within a firm or an entire economy. Production will be at a point below its PPC. More output could be produced if existing resources were better utilized |
| **6** An economy | **F** This is shown by an inward shift in a PPC resulting from a decrease in the quantity and/or quality of the resources available either to an individual firm or an entire economy |

## Revision summary

*Fill in the missing words and economic terms*

1.  Because resources are scarce relative to human _ _ _ _ _ , all societies must choose how to allocate them between different uses: what goods and services to produce, how to produce them and which needs and wants to satisfy.

2.  Making a choice between alternative uses of scarce resources therefore always involves a cost in terms of what we have to give up in return. The benefit of the next best alternative foregone is the _ _ _ _ _ _ _ _ _ _ _ _ _ _ _ _ of that decision.

3.  _ _ _ _ _ _ _ _ _ _ _ _ _ _ _ is therefore the cost of choice. Choosing one use for scarce resources will always mean giving up the opportunity to use those same resources in another way, and the loss of other goods and services they might otherwise have produced instead.

4.  A _ _ _ _ _ _ _ _ _ _ _ _ _ _ _ _ _ _ _ _ _ _ _ curve (PPC) diagram provides a simple way of illustrating opportunity cost and the most efficient allocation of resources between the production of two products. Moving along a PPC indicates more of one product can be produced but only at the expense of reducing production of the other product.

5.  An increase in the productive potential of an economy will shift its PPC _ _ _ _ _ _ _ _ _ . This may be the result of an increase in the quantity or quality of resources available.

6.  However, the PPC will shift _ _ _ _ _ _ _ towards the origin if there is a reduction in the resources available to the economy; for example, if workers emigrate, if non-renewable resources become depleted or worn-out capital equipment is not replaced.

Production possibility curve (PPC) diagrams are used to illustrate the economic concept of opportunity cost. Like all diagrams, it is important to label and use them correctly.

1. The diagram below shows the production possibility curve for a firm producing bicycles and skateboards. It shows the firm is able to produce a maximum of either 500 skateboards or 400 bicycles each week with its factors resources. However, important labels are missing from the diagram. From the list provided, add the correct labels to the correct places on the diagram.

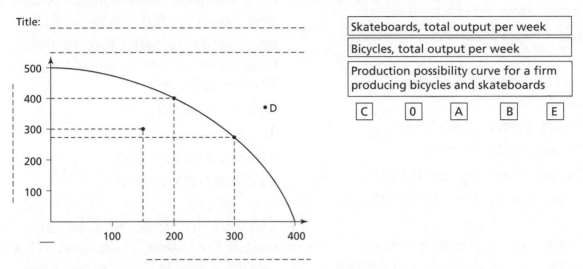

Title: _____

Skateboards, total output per week

Bicycles, total output per week

Production possibility curve for a firm producing bicycles and skateboards

| C | | 0 | | A | | B | | E |

2. The firm in the diagram above is currently producing 400 skateboards and 200 bicycles each week at point A on its production possibility curve. Using the diagram, calculate the opportunity cost of a decision to increase the production of bicycles to 300 each week (point B). [2]

.................................................................................................................................

.................................................................................................................................

3. What would be the opportunity cost of a decision to only produce bicycles (point C)? [2]

.................................................................................................................................

.................................................................................................................................

4. Explain why the firm is unable at present to produce the combination of outputs at point D. [2]

.................................................................................................................................

.................................................................................................................................

5. Imagine that the firm is currently only producing 300 skateboards and 150 bicycles each week (point E). What advice, if any, would you give the owners of the firm? [2]

.................................................................................................................................

.................................................................................................................................

## Multiple choice questions (Paper 1)

*Tick or circle the correct answers*

1. The basic economic problem is:

    (a) Destruction of the natural environment

    (b) Increasing prices

    (c) Underemployment of scarce resources

    (d) Human wants exceed available resources

2. Which of the following is a factor of production?

    (a) The bread produced in a bakery

    (b) The oven used in a bakery

    (c) The wages paid to bakery workers

    (d) The profit received by the bakery owner

3. Parvin runs a small business. She has just completed a course to learn how to start and run a successful business. Which factor of production is most likely to have increased as a result?

    (a) Capital

    (b) Enterprise

    (c) Labour

    (d) Land

4. Which of the following resources used in the production of glass would an economist classify as land?

    (a) A kiln

    (b) Skilled glass workers

    (c) Sand

    (d) Safety goggles

5. What, according to the definition of opportunity cost, is given up when a decision is taken?

    (a) An identical alternative

    (b) The next best alternative

    (c) All possible alternatives

    (d) The least desirable alternative

6. A firm produces 1,000 units of a good X and 600 units of a good Y each week using its resources. It wants to increase output of X to 1,200 units per week. To do so it must cut production of Y to 500 units per week.

    What will be the opportunity cost of the decision to increase the output of good X by 200 units each week?

    (a) 200 units of Y per week

    (b) 500 units of Y per week

    (c) 100 units of Y per week

    (d) 250 units of Y per week

7. A firm making smart phones and tablet computers operates its two factories 24 hours each day in order to maximize production at point X on its production possibility curve. However, a problem at one of its suppliers of component parts causes the firm to close one of its factories temporarily.

    Which point on the diagram could represent its new position?

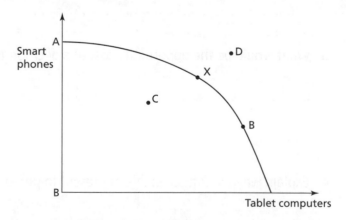

8. A farmer uses one of his fields to plant corn. What could be the opportunity cost of this decision?

    (a) The cost of the seeds

    (b) Wages paid to his farm workers

    (c) The water used to irrigate the field

    (d) Using the field to grow potatoes

1.

# Boeing ramps up production of its Dreamliner

US aircraft maker Boeing is ramping up production rates for two of its most popular planes, the 737 and the 787 Dreamliner. The Boeing Vice President of product development said that increasing automation has been key to achieving higher production rates including retraining its workforce to operate more advanced machinery and industrial robots.

During the first three quarters of this year, Boeing delivered 101 Dreamliners, a 29 percent increase over the same period last year. Boeing in the third quarter also delivered 126 model 737s, compared to 120 in the third quarter of last year. In contrast, production of its 767, 747 and 777 plane models has reduced.

The recent announcement by Boeing's Chief Executive that the company plans to open a 737 completion plant in China could boost production rates for the model further in the future. The planned facility would install seats, in-flight entertainment systems, and some galleys and lavatories, as well as completing the custom paint job for each airline. However, engineers and machinists in Boeing's US factories fear the move could mean some of their jobs being transferred to Chinese workers.

a) Give an example of opportunity cost from the extract. [2]

b) Using examples from the extract, identify **three** factors of production used to make and supply aircraft. [6]

c) Using a production possibility curve, analyse how Boeing may allocate its resources between its 787 Dreamliner and other aircraft models. [6]

2. All economic decisions involve an opportunity cost.

   a) Define *opportunity cost*. [2]

   b) Explain why economic decisions will involve an opportunity cost. [4]

   c) Using a production possibility curve diagram, analyse how it can demonstrate the concept of opportunity cost. [6]

   d) Discuss the extent to which the concept of opportunity cost is relevant only to government spending decisions. [8]

3. All countries face the economic problem and must choose how to allocate their factors of production.

   a) Define *the economic problem*. [2]

   b) Using appropriate examples, explain the **four** factors of production. [4]

   c) Analyse how a production possibility curve can be used to show the consequences of a change in the allocation of resources between the production of two goods. [6]

   d) Discuss whether more factors of production should be used to build roads. [8]

## 2.1.1 Microeconomics
## 2.1.2 Macroeconomics

1. Explain the difference between microeconomics and macroeconomics. [4]

..........................................................................................................................................

..........................................................................................................................................

..........................................................................................................................................

2. Identify the **three** main groups of decision makers involved in the study of microeconomics. [4]

..........................................................................................................................................

..........................................................................................................................................

..........................................................................................................................................

3. Describe **three** key macroeconomic issues. [6]

..........................................................................................................................................

..........................................................................................................................................

..........................................................................................................................................

..........................................................................................................................................

**E**

Identify the macro or microeconomic issues and decision makers described in each news article.

The Czech central bank has raised interest rates for the fourth time in just under a year, as the country's economy continues to accelerate and record-low unemployment pushes up wages fuelling fears of rising price inflation.

Car maker Porsche axes all diesel cars from its range due to 'falling consumer demand' for the fuel type.

Demand for gold jewellery in India fell by as much as 30% in the run-up to the Diwali festival due to heavy rains in October and an increase in gold bullion prices after the introduction of the new goods and services tax.

## 2.2.1 Key resource allocation decisions
## 2.2.2 The market system
## 2.2.3 The price mechanism

1. What **three** questions can be used to define the problem of resource allocation in an economy? [3]

   ..............................................................................................................................................

   ..............................................................................................................................................

2. Explain the difference between market equilibrium and market disequilibrium in a market economy. [4]

   ..............................................................................................................................................

   ..............................................................................................................................................

   ..............................................................................................................................................

   ..............................................................................................................................................

3. Analyse the role of the price mechanism in a market economy. [6]

   ..............................................................................................................................................

   ..............................................................................................................................................

   ..............................................................................................................................................

   ..............................................................................................................................................

   ..............................................................................................................................................

**E**

How are producers in a market economy likely to respond to the following changes in market conditions?

A new consumer report confirms that demand for plant-based food is on the rise. The report states that the sales growth of vegan food and produce is outpacing total food and beverage sales in supermarkets.

UK manufacturers feel the pinch as raw material costs rise

The sales and profitability of hard disk computer drives has been on the decline this year because of slow demand for personal computers and tough competition from solid-state drives.

## Key words

*Match economic terms with their definitions*

| | | | | |
|---|---|---|---|---|
| 1 | Microeconomics | **E** | **A** | This occurs in a market when consumer demand for the product is exactly equal to the amount producers are willing and able to supply each period. As a result, the market price and quantity traded will be stable from period to period |
| 2 | Macroeconomics | | **B** | The means by which decisions are made about what goods and services are produced, how they are produced and who they are produced for in a free market economy |
| 3 | Macroeconomy | | **C** | The distribution of scarce productive resources among different uses |
| 4 | Resource allocation | | **D** | Any set of arrangements that brings together all the producers and consumers of a good or service so they may engage in trade or exchange |
| 5 | Market economic system | | **E** | The study of the economic decisions and actions of individual consumers, producers and households and how they interact to determine different market outcomes |
| 6 | Mixed economic system | | **F** | The state of a market when the quantity producers are willing and able to supply each period differs from the quantity consumers are willing and able to buy |
| 7 | Market | | **G** | The study of major economics issues and conditions that affect a national economy |
| 8 | Market equilibrium | | **H** | An economic system that combines free markets with government planning to allocate its scarce resources and distribute goods and services |
| 9 | Market disequilibrium | | **I** | The means by which the decisions of many different consumers and producers interact and cause changes in market prices which in turn help to determine how scarce resources should be allocated within a market economy |
| 10 | Price mechanism | | **J** | A national economy |

## Revision summary

*Fill in the missing words and economic terms*

1. The problem of _ _ _ _ _ _ _ _ _  _ _ _ _ _ _ _ _ _ _ involves finding solutions to three key questions: what goods and services to produce; how to produce them; and who to produce them for. Who decides and how they decide the 'answers' to these questions in an economy is referred to as its

   _ _ _ _ _ _ _ _  _ _ _ _ _ _ .

2. The decisions of many individual consumers, producers and households will determine what goods and services are produced and who they are produced for in a _ _ _ _ _ _ economic system.

3. The _ _ _ _ _ mechanism in a market economy ensures that scarce resources are allocated to their most profitable uses. Changes in _ _ _ _ _ _ prices provide signals to producers about what goods and services consumers want and will earn the most _ _ _ _ _ _ .

4. _ _ _ _ _economics involves studying what influences the economic decisions of consumers, producers and households, how their decisions interact and the impact they can have on different market outcomes (market prices and quantities exchanged).

5. In contrast, _ _ _ _ _economics involves the study of major economic issues and actions, including those taken by a government in a _ _ _ _ _ economic system, that affect the national economy.

**2.3.1 Definition of demand**
**2.3.2 Price and demand**
**2.3.3 Individual and market demand**

1. Define *demand*. [2]

   ........................................................................................................................................

   ........................................................................................................................................

2. Explain the difference between a 'human want' for a product and an 'effective demand' for a product. [3]

   ........................................................................................................................................

   ........................................................................................................................................

   ........................................................................................................................................

3. If you plot the market demand curve for a product on a graph, what units would you measure (a) on the vertical axis, and (b) on the horizontal axis? [4]

   ........................................................................................................................................

   ........................................................................................................................................

   ........................................................................................................................................

   ........................................................................................................................................

4. Explain why market demand curves for most products are 'downward sloping'. [4]

   ........................................................................................................................................

   ........................................................................................................................................

   ........................................................................................................................................

   ........................................................................................................................................

5. Explain the difference between a 'movement along a demand curve' and a 'shift in a demand curve'. [4]

   ........................................................................................................................................

   ........................................................................................................................................

   ........................................................................................................................................

   ........................................................................................................................................

## 2.3.4 Conditions of demand

1. What is the difference between complementary products and products that are substitutes in demand? [4]

.................................................................................................................................

.................................................................................................................................

.................................................................................................................................

.................................................................................................................................

2. Using examples, explain what is likely to happen to the demand for (a) a normal good, and (b) an inferior good following an increase in the disposable incomes of consumers. [4]

.................................................................................................................................

.................................................................................................................................

.................................................................................................................................

.................................................................................................................................

3. State **three** factors that may have caused the shift in the market demand curve from D1 to D2 in diagram (a) and **three** different factors that may have caused the shift in the market demand curve from D1 to D2 shown in diagram (b). [6]

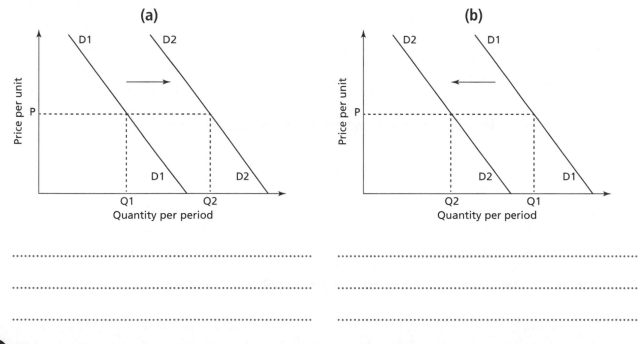

.......................................................................        .......................................................................

.......................................................................        .......................................................................

.......................................................................        .......................................................................

**E**

A rise in the price of product A results in a fall in demand for product B and a rise in demand for product C. Which **two** of these products are in joint demand and which **two** are products that can satisfy the same consumer demand?

**2.4.1 Definition of supply**
**2.4.2 Price and supply**
**2.4.3 Individual and market supply**

1. Define *supply*. [2]

..................................................................................................................................................

..................................................................................................................................................

2. Explain how the supply curve of a product of an individual firm and the market supply curve for the same product are related. [4]

..................................................................................................................................................

..................................................................................................................................................

..................................................................................................................................................

3. If you plot the market supply curve for a product on a graph, what units would you measure (a) on the vertical axis, and (b) on the horizontal axis? [4]

..................................................................................................................................................

..................................................................................................................................................

..................................................................................................................................................

..................................................................................................................................................

4. Explain why the market supply curves for most products are 'upward sloping'. [4]

..................................................................................................................................................

..................................................................................................................................................

..................................................................................................................................................

5. Explain the difference between a 'movement along a supply curve' and a 'shift in a supply curve'. [4]

..................................................................................................................................................

..................................................................................................................................................

..................................................................................................................................................

## 2.4.4 Conditions of supply

1. The profitability of producing a product A has increased due to technical advance, reducing its cost of production. In contrast, new regulations have increased the cost of producing a product B. Explain the impact these changes are likely to have on the allocation of resources between product A and B and the amount of each product producers are willing to supply to consumers. [4]

........................................................................................................................................................................

........................................................................................................................................................................

........................................................................................................................................................................

........................................................................................................................................................................

2. State **three** factors that may have caused the shift in the market supply curve from S1 to S2 in diagram (a) and three different factors that may have caused the shift in the market supply curve from S1 to S2 shown in diagram (b). [6]

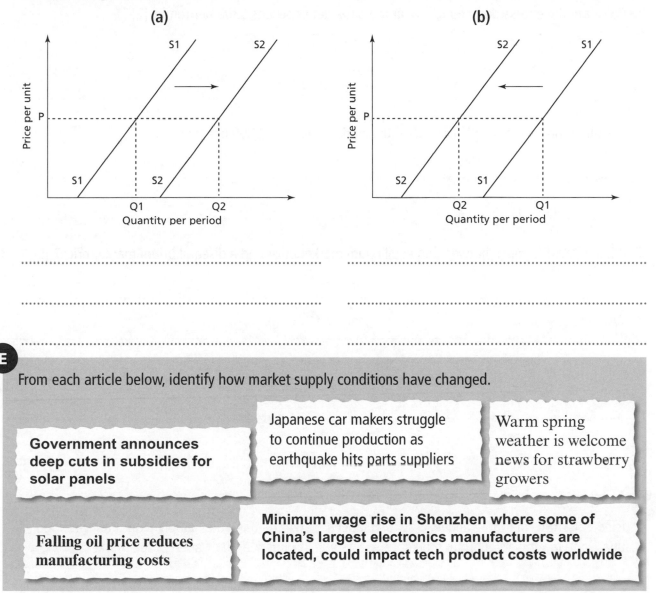

........................................................................    ........................................................................

........................................................................    ........................................................................

........................................................................    ........................................................................

**E**

From each article below, identify how market supply conditions have changed.

**Government announces deep cuts in subsidies for solar panels**

Japanese car makers struggle to continue production as earthquake hits parts suppliers

Warm spring weather is welcome news for strawberry growers

**Falling oil price reduces manufacturing costs**

**Minimum wage rise in Shenzhen where some of China's largest electronics manufacturers are located, could impact tech product costs worldwide**

## 2.5.1 Market equilibrium
## 2.5.2 Market disequilibrium

The table below records the market demand and supply schedules for refined sugar.

| Price ($ per tonne) | Market demand (million tonnes per month) | Market supply (million tonnes per month) |
|---|---|---|
| $200 | 20 | 5 |
| $300 | 18 | 8 |
| $400 | 16 | 11 |
| $500 | 14 | 14 |
| $600 | 12 | 17 |
| $700 | 10 | 20 |
| $800 | 8 | 23 |

1. At what price will the market be in equilibrium? [2]

    ....................................................................................................................................................

2. Calculate the excess demand for sugar if the market price was $300 per tonne. [2]

    ....................................................................................................................................................

    ....................................................................................................................................................

3. Calculate the excess supply of sugar if the market price was $800 per tonne. [2]

    ....................................................................................................................................................

    ....................................................................................................................................................

4. What is the difference between an equilibrium market price and a disequilibrium market price? [5]

    ....................................................................................................................................................

    ....................................................................................................................................................

    ....................................................................................................................................................

    ....................................................................................................................................................

    ....................................................................................................................................................

**E**

Using data from the table above, draw and label a market demand and supply diagram for refined sugar showing the equilibrium market price and equilibrium quantity traded in the market.

## 2.6.1 Causes of price changes
## 2.6.2 Consequences of price changes

1. The diagrams below show the impact of changes in demand and supply conditions in two markets. For each one fill in the missing words below to describe what has changed and the effect it has had on the equilibrium price and equilibrium quantity traded. [6]

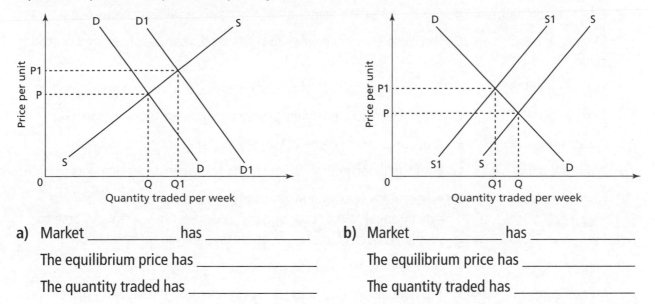

a)  Market _____ has _____

The equilibrium price has _____

The quantity traded has _____

b)  Market _____ has _____

The equilibrium price has _____

The quantity traded has _____

2. Using a demand and supply diagram, analyse the likely impact of an increase in advertising on the equilibrium price and equilibrium quantity traded of a product in a market. [6]

..........................................................................................

..........................................................................................

..........................................................................................

..........................................................................................

..........................................................................................

..........................................................................................

**E**

For each of the newspaper headlines below, identify how market conditions have changed and the impact this had on market prices.

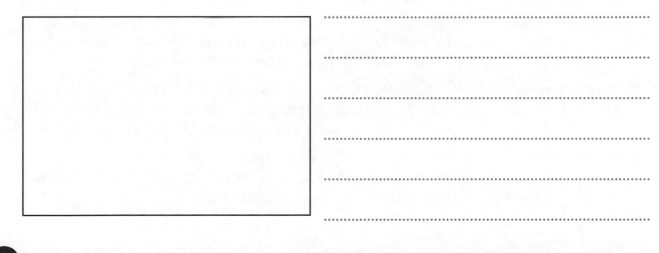

Avocado prices set to rise due to a combination of high demand and bad weather

Slump in China auto sales results in deep price cuts

Iron ore prices fall below $50 per tonne as Australia increases supply

Retailers are expected to raise prices to pay for the increase in minimum wages

## Key words

*Match economic terms with their correct definitions*

| | | |
|---|---|---|
| **1** Demand     i | **A** | An economic situation in which a market is in disequilibrium because demand for the product exceeds its supply. As a result, there will be pressure on the market price to rise |
| **2** Effective demand | **B** | A good for which demand will rise as disposable incomes rise |
| **3** Market demand curve | **C** | The willingness and ability to buy a product to satisfy a need or want |
| **4** Joint demand | **D** | The desire and ability of producers to make and sell a given product |
| **5** Complements | **E** | The price at which demand will exactly match supply in a market |
| **6** Substitutes | **F** | A good for which demand will fall as disposable incomes rise |
| **7** A normal good | **G** | Products that compete to satisfy the same consumer demand |
| **8** An inferior good | **H** | An economic situation in which the market demand for a product is exactly equal to the total amount producers are willing and able to supply. As a result, there will be no pressure on the market price |
| **9** Supply | **I** | The desire to buy and use a product to satisfy a need or want |
| **10** Market supply curve | **J** | The demand for one product is dependent on the demand for another because they are consumed together, e.g. razors and razor blades |
| **11** Market equilibrium | **K** | A good or service that is in joint demand with another, for example, cars and petrol/gasoline |
| **12** Equilibrium price | **L** | A line drawn on a diagram to show how the total quantity demanded for a product varies with its price. The line is the sum of the individual demand curves of all the consumers of that product |
| **13** Excess demand | **M** | An economic situation in which a market is in disequilibrium because the supply of the product exceeds the amount consumers are willing and able to purchase. As a result, there will be pressure on market price |
| **14** Excess supply | **N** | A line drawn on a diagram to show how the total quantity supplied of a product varies with its price. The line is the sum of the individual supply curves of all the producers of that product |

## Revision summary

*Fill in the missing words and economic terms*

1.  The market demand for a good or service is the total _ _ _ _ _ _ _ _ _ _ demand of all consumers willing and able to buy that product. Market demand curves are _ _ _ _ _ _ _ _ sloping. As the price of a product increases, consumer demand for the product will _ _ _ _ _ _ _ _.

2.  Consumer demand for a product may increase following a rise in _ _ _ _ _ _ _ _ _ _ incomes, a fall in the price of a complementary good or a rise in the price of a _ _ _ _ _ _ _ _ _ _ , increased advertising or as consumer tastes and fashions change. Population and seasonal factors can also affect demand.

3.  An increase in demand for a product will cause its market demand curve to shift to the _ _ _ _ _. In contrast, a decrease in demand for a product will result in its market demand curve shifting inwards to the left.

4.  The market supply of a good or service is the total quantity producers of that product are willing and able to produce and sell to consumers. Market supply curves are _ _ _ _ _ _ sloping. As the price of a product rises, it becomes more profitable so producers will be willing to supply more of it.

5.  Producers may be willing to increase the supply of a product even if its selling price is unchanged if their costs of production _ _ _ _ or if the production and sale of other products become less profitable. Other factors such as weather conditions, natural disaster and changes in business optimism can also affect the supply of different products.

6.  An increase in the market supply of a product will cause its market supply curve to shift to the _ _ _ _ _. A decrease in the market supply of a product will cause its market supply curve to shift to the _ _ _ _.

7.  When the market demand for a product is equal to its market supply, the market will be in a state of _ _ _ _ _ _ _ _ _ _ _. The market price will be stable because consumers are willing and able to buy exactly the same amount of the product that producers are willing and able to supply.

8.  However, if market demand does not match supply, the market will be in _ _ _ _ _ _ _ _ _ _ _ _ _ _. If demand exceeds supply, the market price will _ _ _ _ _ _ _ _ to reduce the excess demand. If supply exceeds demand, then the market price will fall to sell off the excess supply.

9.  Changes in market demand and supply conditions for a product will affect its equilibrium market price and the quantity exchanged. An increase in market demand or fall in market supply will _ _ _ _ _ _ _ _ the equilibrium market price. A decrease in market demand or an increase in market supply will _ _ _ _ _ _ the equilibrium market price.

**2.7.1 Definition of PED**
**2.7.2 Calculation of PED**

1. Explain, using an example, what is meant by 'price elasticity of demand'. [4]

   ................................................................................................................................................

   ................................................................................................................................................

   ................................................................................................................................................

   ................................................................................................................................................

2. Explain why different products have different price elasticities of demand. [4]

   ................................................................................................................................................

   ................................................................................................................................................

   ................................................................................................................................................

   ................................................................................................................................................

3. The owners of a local supermarket have observed that reducing the price of tomatoes from $5 to $4.50 per kilogram (kg) during winter months increased weekly sales from 200 kg to 240 kg.

   Use this information to calculate the price elasticity of demand for tomatoes at the supermarket. Show your calculations in full. [4]

   ................................................................................................................................................

   ................................................................................................................................................

   ................................................................................................................................................

   ................................................................................................................................................

4. Which of the following statements applies to the local market conditions described above? [2]

   | (a) Demand for tomatoes at the supermarket is relatively price elastic. The rise in the quantity demanded per week is proportionally greater than the 10% cut in price. As a result, revenue from the sale of tomatoes will have increased. | (b) Demand for tomatoes at the supermarket is relatively price inelastic. The rise in the quantity demanded per week is proportionally less than the 10% cut in price. As a result, revenue from the sale of tomatoes will have decreased. |
   |---|---|

## 2.7.3 PED and total spending on a product and revenue
## 2.7.4 Significance of PED

1. Previously a firm sold 1,000 units of its product each week at a price of $5 per unit. After raising the price of its product to $5.10, the quantity sold fell to 900 units per week. Calculate:

   **(a)** the elasticity of demand for the product [2]

   ..............................................................................................................................................................

   ..............................................................................................................................................................

   **(b)** total revenue from the sale of its product before and after the change in its price. [2]

   ..............................................................................................................................................................

   ..............................................................................................................................................................

   **(c)** Do you think raising the price of the product was a good decision? Explain your answer. [4]

   ..............................................................................................................................................................

   ..............................................................................................................................................................

   ..............................................................................................................................................................

   ..............................................................................................................................................................

2. Complete the following table. [6]

| Change in product price | Change in quantity demanded each period | Is demand price elastic or inelastic? | Will total revenue each period increase or decrease? |
|---|---|---|---|
| Increase by 2% | Decrease by 4% | Price elastic | Revenue will fall |
| Increase by 2% | Decrease by 1% | | |
| Decrease by 5% | Increase by 10% | | |
| Decrease by 5% | Increase by 3% | | |
| Increase by 1% | Unchanged | | |

**E**

The answer to the following question is given below. Complete the missing words and terms.

*How useful do you think the concept of price elasticity of demand is to the supermarket and why?*

The concept is useful because it will help the supermarket owners think about the impact on sales _____ of changing prices. For example, cutting the prices of products for which demand is price _____ will increase revenue, but if demand is price inelastic, a reduction in price will _____ revenue. However, the owners of the supermarket may not be able to calculate price elasticities accurately. Price elasticities can also change with _____ ; for example, if demand for a product is seasonal. In addition, demand may not respond to a price cut as predicted if competitors also _____ their prices.

## 2.8.1 Definition of PES
## 2.8.2 Calculation of PES

1. Define *price elasticity of supply*. [2]

..................................................................................................................................................

..................................................................................................................................................

2. Explain why different products can have different price elasticities of supply. [4]

..................................................................................................................................................

..................................................................................................................................................

..................................................................................................................................................

..................................................................................................................................................

Sprint Sports Ltd. manufactures racing bicycles. Its bicycles currently sell for $250 each. The owners of the company have stated that if the average price was to rise to $275 they could increase production immediately from 1,000 to 1,200 per week using existing resources. If the market price remains at $275, thereafter the company would invest in additonal capacity over the next 12 months allowing it to increase production from 1,000 to 1,400 per week.

3. Calculate the initial price elasticity of supply at Sprint Sports Ltd. [2]

..................................................................................................................................................

..................................................................................................................................................

4. Calculate what the company's price elasticity of supply could be after 12 months. [2]

..................................................................................................................................................

..................................................................................................................................................

5. Explain why the price elasticity of supply at the company could be different next year. [4]

..................................................................................................................................................

..................................................................................................................................................

..................................................................................................................................................

..................................................................................................................................................

## 2.8.3 Determinants of PES
## 2.8.4 Significance of PES

1. The diagrams below show an increase in demand in two different product markets. For each one, show and explain the impact it will have on the market price and quantity supplied and why. [4]

.......................................................................  .......................................................................

.......................................................................  .......................................................................

.......................................................................  .......................................................................

.......................................................................  .......................................................................

2. Analyse the reasons why a firm may want to increase the price elasticity of supply of its product and suggest ways it may be able to do this. [6]

.................................................................................................................................................

.................................................................................................................................................

.................................................................................................................................................

.................................................................................................................................................

.................................................................................................................................................

.................................................................................................................................................

**E**

How do you think the price elasticities of supply of the following products compare? Give reasons for your views.

| Natural rubber | Synthetic rubber | Cars | Cruise ships |

## Key words

*Match economic terms with their correct definitions*

| | | | |
|---|---|---|---|
| 1 | Price elasticity of demand (PED) **E** | A | Demand for a product is sensitive to changes in its price. A small percentage change in price will result in a larger percentage change in quantity demanded |
| 2 | Price elastic demand | B | A measure of the responsiveness of the quantity supplied of a product to a change in its price |
| 3 | Price inelastic demand | C | At any given moment in time, the quantity supplied of a product will be fixed and unable to respond to change in demand and price |
| 4 | Price elasticity of supply (PES) | D | Demand for a product is relatively insensitive to changes in its price. A small percentage change in price will result in a smaller percentage change in quantity demanded |
| 5 | Perfectly price inelastic supply | E | A measure of the responsiveness of consumer demand for a product to a change in its price |

## Revision summary

*Fill in the missing words and economic terms*

1. Knowledge of the price _ _ _ _ _ _ _ _ _ _ _ of demand for different products can help firms to forecast the effect on their _ _ _ _ _ _ _ _ of changes in market prices.

2. If demand for a product is price _ _ _ _ _ _ _ _ , a small increase in its price will result in proportionately larger reduction in the quantity demanded each period. As a result, revenue from its sale will decrease. However, lowering the price of the product could boost demand and revenue significantly

3. If demand for a product is price _ _ _ _ _ _ _ _ _ _, a small increase in its price will result in a proportionately smaller reduction in the quantity demanded each period. As a result, revenue from its sale will rise. Cutting price will therefore reduce revenue because it will have relatively little effect on the quantity demanded.

4. The greater the number of substitutes a product has and the more time consumers have to shop around to buy alternatives, the _ _ _ _ price elastic consumer demand for that product will be.

5. Price elasticity of supply measures the responsiveness of the supply of a product to changes in price. The supply of many products is fixed or price _ _ _ _ _ _ _ _ _ in the very short term but over time producers can respond to an increase in their prices by allocating additional resources to their production. That is, the supply of many products becomes more price _ _ _ _ _ _ _ with time.

## 2.9.1 Definition of market economic system
## 2.9.2 Advantages and disadvantages of the market economic system

1. Explain how resources are allocated in a market economic system. [4]

..............................................................................................................................................

..............................................................................................................................................

..............................................................................................................................................

..............................................................................................................................................

2. Explain **two** advantages of the market economic system. [4]

..............................................................................................................................................

..............................................................................................................................................

..............................................................................................................................................

..............................................................................................................................................

3. Explain **two** disadvantages of the market economic system. [4]

..............................................................................................................................................

..............................................................................................................................................

..............................................................................................................................................

..............................................................................................................................................

**E**

What do the two articles reveal about how resources are allocated in a market economy and who benefits?

### Agri firm expands as demand from Europe increases

Rising demand from European consumers has driven the expansion of Andas Foods, a local agri-products company, which employs 100 staff at its 70,000 sq ft site.

Last year the company completed a $2 million expansion and is now investing an additional $1m to increase production.

### Sales growth in Asia boosts profits at UK fashion brand Burberry

Profits rose by a better-than-expected 14% to £428m ($652m).

Revenue in China increased by 20% following the opening of 11 new stores during the past financial year.

The company plans to spend a further £200m in the next year opening up to 25 new stores including in China and Latin America.

## 2.10.1 Definition of market failure
## 2.10.2–3 Causes and consequences of market failure

1. Define the term *market failure*. [2]

........................................................................................................

........................................................................................................

2. Explain how a market economic system may result in some goods and services being overconsumed and others being underconsumed. [6]

........................................................................................................

........................................................................................................

........................................................................................................

........................................................................................................

........................................................................................................

........................................................................................................

3. Describe **two** ways a market economic system can fail to produce desirable outcomes. [4]

........................................................................................................

........................................................................................................

........................................................................................................

........................................................................................................

**E**

What market failures do the following articles suggest may occur in market economies?

**Tesco has been fined £300,000 after admitting it misled customers over whether strawberries on sale were genuinely "half price".**

**Thousands protest against lack of affordable housing**

Factory workers in Bangladesh making fashion clothes for some of the biggest global retailers have testified to shocking conditions and poverty pay. Many workers are paid so little that an entire month's wages would not buy a single item they produce.

The largest Coca-Cola plant in India has been accused of putting thousands of farmers out of work by draining the water that feeds their wells, and poisoning the land with waste sludge that the company claims is fertilizer.

**2.11.1 Definition of the mixed economic system**
**2.11.2 Government intervention to address market failure**

1. Explain the difference between a 'market economy' and a 'mixed economy'. [4]

......................................................................................................................................

......................................................................................................................................

......................................................................................................................................

......................................................................................................................................

2. Explain **two** ways a government may intervene in a market to ensure production decisions reflect the external costs and benefits they create. [4]

......................................................................................................................................

......................................................................................................................................

......................................................................................................................................

......................................................................................................................................

3. Discuss, using the concepts of social costs and social benefits, why a government might wish to subsidize the provision of bus and rail services but tax the use of cars. [8]

......................................................................................................................................

......................................................................................................................................

......................................................................................................................................

......................................................................................................................................

......................................................................................................................................

......................................................................................................................................

......................................................................................................................................

......................................................................................................................................

4. Explain **two** reasons why a government might set a legal minimum price in a market. [4]

......................................................................................................................................

......................................................................................................................................

......................................................................................................................................

......................................................................................................................................

5. The diagrams below show the market demand and supply curves for two different products. The government has set a maximum price (Pmax) for each product. Explain the impacts the price controls will have in each market. [4]

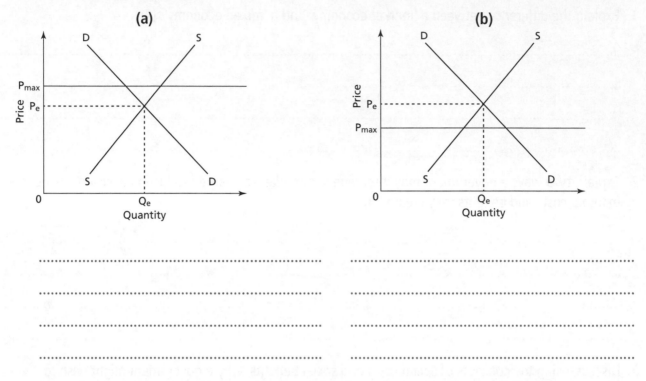

(a)

(b)

........................................................          ........................................................

........................................................          ........................................................

........................................................          ........................................................

........................................................          ........................................................

6. To encourage people to stop smoking, the government of a country introduces an indirect tax of 20% on the price of cigarettes (currently $10 per packet). The price elasticity of demand for cigarettes in the country is estimated to be 0.6. Describe the likely impact the tax will have on (a) the demand for cigarettes, and (b) government revenue. [4]

........................................................................................................................................

........................................................................................................................................

........................................................................................................................................

........................................................................................................................................

7. Which of the following demand and supply diagrams shows (a) the effect of an indirect tax on market supply and price, (b) the effect of a subsidy on market supply and price? [2]

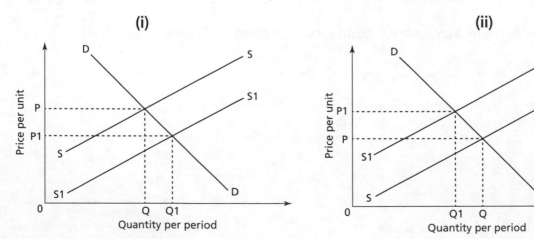

(i)

(ii)

**8.** Discuss whether it is desirable for a government to act as a producer of goods or services. [8]

..................................................................................................................................................

..................................................................................................................................................

..................................................................................................................................................

..................................................................................................................................................

..................................................................................................................................................

..................................................................................................................................................

..................................................................................................................................................

..................................................................................................................................................

..................................................................................................................................................

..................................................................................................................................................

..................................................................................................................................................

..................................................................................................................................................

..................................................................................................................................................

..................................................................................................................................................

..................................................................................................................................................

..................................................................................................................................................

**E**

Government policies or interventions may aim to correct market failures but can also result in unintended and undesirable consequences. Identify those suggested by the headlines and articles.

**High taxes forcing companies to relocate overseas**

The cost of complying with employment laws and other regulations is reducing enterprise and job opportunities, argues a new report.

**Subsidies paid to farmers in North East China have resulted in an excess supply of corn causing prices and farm incomes to collapse. "The original purpose of government support for the corn industry was to help farmers, but now it is hurting them," said an official from the China National Association of the Grain Sector. "It has also damaged the grain structure of the region as many farmers switched to corn from growing soybeans and rice".**

**The allocation of resources**

**2.9 Market economic system**
**2.10 Market failure**
**2.11 Mixed economic system**

## Key words

*Match economic terms with their correct definitions*

| | | | |
|---|---|---|---|
| 1 | Market failures **M** | A | A cost created by an economic activity that is imposed on people or organizations who have no control over the activity. For example, pollution created by firms from the burning or dumping of waste materials from their production processes |
| 2 | Public goods | B | An activity or use of resources that reduces economic welfare because it generates a social cost that exceeds its social benefit |
| 3 | Merit goods | C | The total benefit to a society of an economic activity or use of resources, including both the private and external benefits it creates |
| 4 | Demerit goods | D | The transfer of public sector activities and state-owned enterprises to private sector firms |
| 5 | External cost | E | Goods that have a negative impact on consumer health or welfare. They are likely to be overproduced and consumed in a free market |
| 6 | External benefit | F | Legal rules used by a government to limit, control or even ban some private sector activities and behaviours that are considered socially or economically undesirable |
| 7 | Private costs and benefits | G | A type of economy in which free markets coexist with government intervention and public sector ownership and control of some resources |
| 8 | Social cost | H | Goods and services provided by a government that no private firm would be willing to supply. This is because private firms could not prevent consumers from benefiting from such products regardless of whether they have paid for them or not. Examples include street-lighting and national defence |
| 9 | Social benefit | I | Taxes imposed on goods and services |
| 10 | An uneconomic use of resources | J | Legal minimum or maximum prices set by a government in some markets |
| 11 | Mixed economy | K | A benefit created by an economic activity that is received by people or organizations not directly involved in that activity. For example, a person who is vaccinated against an infectious disease will protect other people from the disease spreading |
| 12 | Microeconomic policy measures | L | The transfer of ownership and control of private sector activities, firms or industries to the public sector |
| 13 | Regulations | M | These occur when the price mechanism in free markets fails to produce outcomes that are socially and economically desirable |
| 14 | Price controls | N | The total cost to a society of an economic activity or use of resources including both the private and external costs it creates |
| 15 | Indirect taxes | O | Goods and services that are socially and economically beneficial, such as education and healthcare, that people will underconsume if they have to pay the full cost of their provision |
| 16 | Subsidies | P | The financial costs and benefits of individual consumption and production decisions, such as the cost of buying a product and the enjoyment a consumer receives from it, and the revenue a firm receives from its sale |
| 17 | Nationalization | Q | Financial supports or grants provided by a government to private firms to encourage them to produce and supply more socially or economically desirable products |
| 18 | Privatization | R | Government interventions in different markets aimed at correcting or reducing market failures. They include public sector provision of goods and services that may be underprovided or consumed in free markets; and the use of price controls, indirect taxes and subsidies |

**The allocation of resources**

**2.9 Market economic system**
**2.10 Market failure**
**2.11 Mixed economic system**

## Revision summary

*Fill in the missing words and economic terms*

1. The price mechanism may fail to produce equilibrium _ _ _ _ _ or quantities in some markets that are socially or economically desirable. The prices of some beneficial goods and services may be too high and this will discourage their consumption. In contrast, too many _ _ _ _ _ _ _ and other harmful goods may be produced and supplied by private sector firms simply because it is profitable for them to do so.

2. Market _ _ _ _ _ _ _ _ _ result in a misallocation of resources. Other uses of resources and market outcomes will be more efficient and worthwhile but a _ _ _ _ _ _ economic system will not achieve them without government intervention.

3. A government can intervene in markets in a _ _ _ _ _ economy in an attempt to correct market failures. It can use its resources to provide public goods and merit goods that would otherwise be _ _ _ _ _ provided by private sector firms. It can also introduce legal rules known as _ _ _ _ _ _ _ _ _ _ _ to control or even ban undesirable activities and behaviours.

4. If a product is underconsumed because its market price is too high, a government may set a legal maximum price for the product that is _ _ _ _ _ its market price. However, private sector producers are likely to contract supply. As a result, there will be _ _ _ _ _ _ demand in the market. The available supply may have to be rationed. It may also encourage smuggling.

5. Demerit and other harmful goods are likely to be _ _ _ _ supplied and consumed in a free market economy. To reduce their sale and consumption, a government may set maximum prices for these products _ _ _ _ _ their equilibrium market prices. However, this would create an excess _ _ _ _ _ _ _. Some producers may attempt to sell this off illegally at lower prices.

6. A large powerful firm may use its market power to overcharge consumers in order to earn excessive profits. If the product it supplies is essential and has few close substitutes, consumers will be forced to pay the high price and will therefore have less disposable income to spend on other goods and services. To prevent this, a government may impose a _ _ _ _ _ _ _ price on the product of the firm that is _ _ _ _ _ its market price.

7. The production and consumption of some goods and services create significant external costs. However, market prices only need to exceed the _ _ _ _ _ _ _ costs of their production for firms to make a profit. Indirect _ _ _ _ _ may be imposed on such products to _ _ _ _ _ _ _ their market prices and reduce demand for them.

8. In contrast, government subsidies may be paid to private firms to _ _ _ _ _ _ _ _ the supply of some worthwhile goods and services that are underconsumed. This should _ _ _ _ _ _ their market prices, making them more affordable for more people to buy and consume.

9. However, government interventions may also have unintended effects. For example, if taxes are too high, they can reduce incentives to work and for enterprise, while some regulations increase production costs and market prices above socially desirable levels. In addition, public sector organizations may be inefficient and produce poor quality goods and services because they are under less pressure than private firms to control their _ _ _ _ _ and make profits.

Demand, supply and their price elasticities are the most important concepts you can learn and use in economics. They can be applied to many areas of study including how wages (the price of labour) and exchange rates (the price of one currency in terms of another) are determined and what causes them to change. The ability to draw and use demand and supply diagrams to analyse the impact of changes in market conditions on prices, quantities and revenues is therefore an essential skill.

1. The following diagram shows the impact of a decrease in demand for umbrellas during summer months. That is, market conditions have changed as shown by the movement between a number of points marked on the diagram. Match the labels to these movements. The first one has been completed for you. [3]

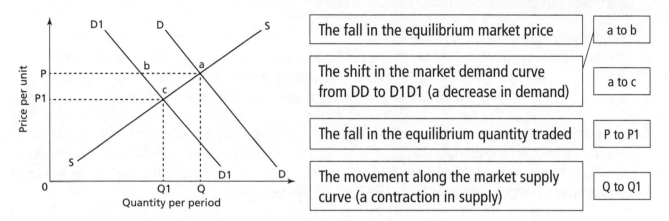

| | |
|---|---|
| The fall in the equilibrium market price | a to b |
| The shift in the market demand curve from DD to D1D1 (a decrease in demand) | a to c |
| The fall in the equilibrium quantity traded | P to P1 |
| The movement along the market supply curve (a contraction in supply) | Q to Q1 |

2. Complete the following equation used to calculate price elasticity of demand. [2]

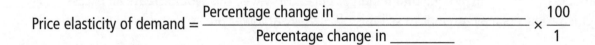

$$\text{Price elasticity of demand} = \frac{\text{Percentage change in} \underline{\hspace{2cm}} \underline{\hspace{2cm}}}{\text{Percentage change in} \underline{\hspace{1.5cm}}} \times \frac{100}{1}$$

3. A window cleaner estimates that raising his charges by 5% will reduce demand for his services by 8%.

   a) Calculate the price elasticity of demand for his window cleaning services. [2]

   .........................................................................................................................................

   .........................................................................................................................................

   b) Explain **one** possible reason for the degree of price elasticity you have calculated. [2]

   .........................................................................................................................................

   .........................................................................................................................................

   c) What will happen to the window cleaner's revenue if he was to increase his charges by 5%? [2]

   .........................................................................................................................................

   .........................................................................................................................................

**40**

4. The following diagram shows the impact of a decrease in the supply of strawberries during the winter. That is, market conditions have changed as shown by the movement between a number of points marked on the diagram. Match the labels to these movements in the table below. [4]

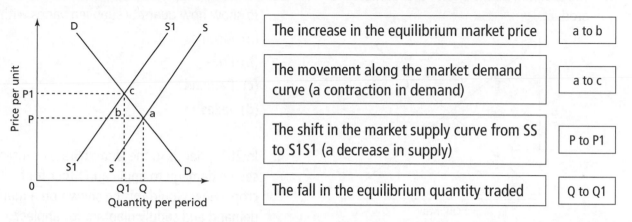

| The increase in the equilibrium market price | a to b |
| The movement along the market demand curve (a contraction in demand) | a to c |
| The shift in the market supply curve from SS to S1S1 (a decrease in supply) | P to P1 |
| The fall in the equilibrium quantity traded | Q to Q1 |

5. Complete the following equation used to calculate price elasticity of supply. [2]

$$\text{Price elasticity of demand} = \frac{\text{Percentage change in } \underline{\hspace{2cm}} \quad \underline{\hspace{2cm}}}{\text{Percentage change in } \underline{\hspace{2cm}}} \times \frac{100}{1}$$

6. The government want farmers to grow more wheat. Annual output is currently 10,000 tonnes and the market price of wheat is $200 per tonne. The government estimates that paying a subsidy of $50 per tonne will expand supply by 2,000 tonnes over the next year and by 3,000 tonnes in the following year.

a) Calculate the price elasticity of supply of wheat in the country for each of the next **two** years. [4]

..................................................................................................................................................................

..................................................................................................................................................................

..................................................................................................................................................................

..................................................................................................................................................................

b) Is supply relatively price elastic or inelastic? [2]

..................................................................................................................................................................

..................................................................................................................................................................

c) What might explain the difference in the two price elasticities you have calculated? [3]

..................................................................................................................................................................

..................................................................................................................................................................

..................................................................................................................................................................

## Multiple choice questions (Paper 1)

**1.** The diagram below shows the market for a product.

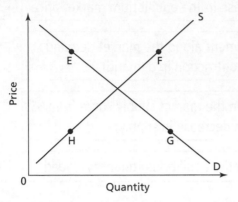

Which statement about the diagram is correct?

**(a)** The distance between E and F is an excess demand for the product

**(b)** The distance between H and G is an excess supply for the product

**(c)** The movement from F to H is a contraction in the quantity of the product supplied

**(d)** The movement from E to G is a contraction in the quantity of the product demanded

**2.** The diagram below shows the market demand for ice cream.

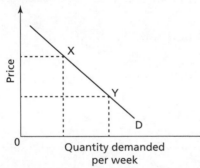

What would cause the movement from point X to point Y?

**(a)** A fall in the price of ice cream

**(b)** A change in tastes

**(c)** Hot weather

**(d)** A fall in incomes

**3.** A market supply curve for a product is drawn to show how quantity supplied varies with:

**(a)** Income

**(b)** Price

**(c)** Demand

**(d)** Taxes

**4.** In 2015, floods in the United States caused severe damage to apple and other fruit crops. How would this be shown on a market demand and supply diagram for apples?

|  | Demand curve | Supply curve |
|---|---|---|
| **(a)** | shift to the left | shift to the right |
| **(b)** | shift to the right | shift to the left |
| **(c)** | no change | shift to the left |
| **(d)** | shift to the left | no change |

**5.** A market is in equilibrium at point X. What changes in market conditions would result in a new equilibrium at point Y?

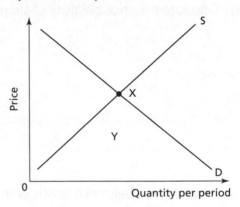

**(a)** A fall in demand with an increase in supply

**(b)** A fall in demand with a fall in supply

**(c)** An increase in demand with a fall in supply

**(d)** A fall in demand with an increase in supply

**6.** A market is in disequilibrium. There is excess demand. What is required to return the market to an equilibrium?

(a) A reduction in the market price

(b) A reduction in market supply

(c) An increase in the market price

(d) An increase in market demand

**7.** The diagram below shows a range of outcomes in the market for a normal good. The market was in equilibrium at point X, but the government has since imposed an excise duty on the product and also raised the basic rate of income tax in the economy. Which point represents the new market equilibrium following these changes?

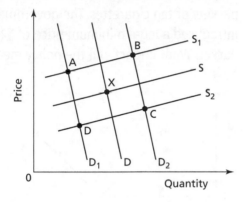

**8.** The United States is the world's largest exporter of corn. What change is most likely to lead to a fall in the global market price of a metric tonne of corn?

(a) An increase in the quantity demanded by 5% with no change in the quantity supplied

(b) An increase in the quantity demanded by 5% with an increase in the quantity supplied by 5%

(c) No change in the quantity demanded but with a 5% decrease in the quantity supplied

(d) No change in the quantity demanded but with a 5% increase in the quantity supplied

**9.** A large electrical store sells microwave ovens. When it cut the price of its microwave ovens from $100 to $80, demand for them expanded from 100 to 140 per week.

What is the price elasticity of demand for microwaves?

(a) Zero

(b) Less than 1

(c) Unitary

(d) Greater than 1

**10.** The price of a product is doubled. As a result, the quantity demanded contracts by less than half and the revenue received by the seller increases.

What might this suggest about the product?

(a) It has many substitutes

(b) It is an essential product

(c) It is an inferior good

(d) Demand is highly price elastic

**11.** What is found in a mixed economy but not a free market economy?

(a) Planning laws

(b) Specialization

(c) Tertiary industries

(d) A profit motive

**12.** A mixed economy has:

(a) A primary sector and a secondary sector

(b) Consumer goods and capital goods

(c) A financial sector and an industrial sector

(d) A private sector and a public sector

**13.** Which of the following is a type of market failure?

(a) Increased air fares during busy public holidays

(b) Increased travel times due to traffic congestion

(c) An increase in food prices due to bad weather

(d) Falling sales due to a change in consumer tastes

**14.** An explosion on the Deepwater Horizon oil platform in the Gulf of Mexico in 2010 caused the largest oil spill in history. Many people were badly affected.

What type of market failure did they experience?

(a) Underprovision of socially desirable items

(b) Tax distortions

(c) Negative externalities

(d) Anti-competitive behaviour by a monopoly

**15.** In 2015, a milk processing plant in Ottawa, Canada was fined by the Government's Environment Agency for dumping toxic chemicals into the local river and killing many fish.

What was the external cost of this incident?

(a) The cost of disposing of toxic chemicals

(b) The cost of the fine

(c) The loss of revenue by the local fishing industry

(d) The possible loss of reputation and revenue by the milk processing plant

**16.** A country needs more doctors. How could an increase in the supply of doctors be encouraged in a mixed economy but not in a market economy?

(a) Private medical colleges can offer more courses

(b) Increased statutory minimum pay for doctors

(c) Course fees for medical students could be raised

(d) Subsidies paid to teaching hospitals could be cut

**17.** Why do the governments of many countries subsidize the research and development (R&D) of renewable energy technologies?

(a) Private sector firms may overestimate the external benefits and ignore the private benefits of renewable energy

(b) Private sector firms may overestimate the external costs and ignore the private costs of renewable energy

(c) Private sector firms may underestimate the private costs and ignore the external costs of renewable energy

(d) Private sector firms may underestimate the private benefits and ignore the external benefits of renewable energy

**18.** The diagram below shows the market for packets of ten cigarettes. The government has introduced a legal minimum price of $12 per packet. What impact will the policy measure have?

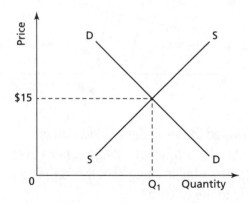

(a) It will reduce the external costs of cigarette consumption

(b) It will create an excess demand of cigarettes

(c) It will contract the demand for cigarettes

(d) It will have no effect on the market equilibrium

**19.** The diagram below shows the market for plastic carrier bags. The market is currently in equilibrium at point X. The government wants to place an indirect tax on the bags to reduce their use and production. Which point will represent the new market equilibrium following the imposition of the tax?

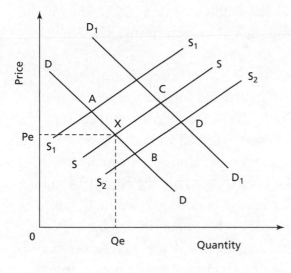

**20.** The government of China has decided that the Chinese economy should make more use of the market economic system.

Which policy will contribute to this objective?

(a) Increasing controls on imported goods

(b) Reducing tax free allowances

(c) Reducing government ownership of resources

(d) Introducing minimum wage laws

1.

# Mixing it up in Cuba

Cuba's economy is dominated by government-run enterprises. Most of the means of production are owned and run by the government and most of the labour force is employed by the government, although in recent years the government has encouraged the formation of cooperatives and self-employment. In 1981, the public sector employed 91% of all Cuban workers and the private sector just 8%. Now, private sector employment is around 28% and growing.

Following the break-up of the Soviet Union in 1991, Cuba's economy shrank by over 30% between 1990 and 1993. This was partly because the Cuban government used to receive generous subsidies from the Soviet Union to help cover its costs of production and to pay for imported products. These stopped when the Soviet Union came to an end. However, the economic collapse was also due to a steep decline in global sugar prices around the same time. As a result, over half the country's sugar mills were forced to close during the 1990s. For many years, sugar production and processing had been the largest industry, employer and exporter in Cuba.

The rapid growth in tourism has since overtaken sugar as Cuba's largest industry and source of foreign earnings. In response, significant resources are now being devoted to building new tourist facilities and renovating historic structures for use in the tourism sector. However, even the sugar industry is once again growing in Cuba. Rising demand for sugar since 2009 has stimulated new investment in modern sugar processing facilities.

In 2011, new economic reforms were introduced by the Cuban government, effectively creating a new economic system. Since then, many Cubans have signed up to run their own businesses.

The economic system in Cuba now operates more like a market economic system. However, many companies remain government owned, including those providing essential services such as water and electricity and other socially beneficial services including education and healthcare.

a) How are resources allocated in a 'market economic system'? [2]

b) What evidence is there in the extract that Cuba is moving to a more mixed economic system? [4]

c) Explain **two** economic factors that may have influenced the decision of the Cuban government to allow a greater role for the private sector in the economy? [4]

d) Using a production possibility curve diagram, explain why choices will have to be made in Cuba about how to allocate resources between the public sector and the private sector. [5]

e) Draw a demand and supply diagram to show what is likely to have happened in the global sugar market after 2009. [4]

f) Explain why the social benefit of healthcare exceeds its private benefit. [3]

g) Discuss whether other economies would benefit from an increase in the public sector provision of healthcare. [8]

2. Prices in a market economy are determined by demand and supply conditions and these conditions can change for many different reasons.
   a) Define the term *market economy*. [2]
   b) Explain the concept of price elasticity of demand. [4]
   c) Using a demand and supply diagram, analyse the likely effect of an increase in the average income of consumers on the equilibrium price and equilibrium quantity of a product in a market. [6]
   d) Discuss how useful knowledge of price elasticity of demand is to a business. [8]

3. A government announces it will impose an indirect tax on the price of petrol because it wants to discourage travel by car and encourage the use of bus and rail services instead. This, it believes, will help to reduce traffic congestion and harmful exhaust emissions.
   a) Define the term *social cost*. [2]
   b) Explain why the social costs of car use are greater than the private costs. [4]
   c) Using a demand and supply diagram, analyse the effect of the tax on the market for petrol. [6]
   d) Discuss whether public transport services should be provided by the public sector or the private sector in an economy. [8]

4. Many governments want people to adopt healthier lifestyles by eating more fresh fruit and vegetables, taking regular exercise and reducing their consumption of fatty foods, alcohol and cigarettes. They are concerned about the health effects of consuming too many unhealthy products.
   a) Define the term *mixed economy*. [2]
   b) Explain **two** factors that may affect the demand for fresh fruit and vegetables. [4]
   c) Analyse how a government could use the concept of price elasticity of demand to decide whether or not to impose a tax on the price of cigarettes. [6]
   d) Discuss whether the price mechanism is less important in a mixed economy than a market economy. [8]

## 3.1.1 Money

**1.** What is a 'money'? [2]

.......................................................................................................................

.......................................................................................................................

**2.** Explain **two** functions of money. [4]

.......................................................................................................................

.......................................................................................................................

.......................................................................................................................

.......................................................................................................................

**3.** Explain **three** characteristics of a good money. [6]

.......................................................................................................................

.......................................................................................................................

.......................................................................................................................

.......................................................................................................................

.......................................................................................................................

.......................................................................................................................

**4.** Explain why there is a need for exchange in a modern economy. [6]

.......................................................................................................................

.......................................................................................................................

.......................................................................................................................

.......................................................................................................................

.......................................................................................................................

.......................................................................................................................

**E**

Explain why using money to pay for goods and services is preferable to bartering.

## 3.1.2 Banking

1. What makes up the supply of money in a modern economy? [2]

........................................................................................................................................

........................................................................................................................................

2. Explain **two** reasons why most banks charge customers interest rates to borrow money. [4]

........................................................................................................................................

........................................................................................................................................

........................................................................................................................................

........................................................................................................................................

3. Explain **two** main functions of a commercial bank. [4]

........................................................................................................................................

........................................................................................................................................

........................................................................................................................................

........................................................................................................................................

4. Explain **two** functions of the central bank in a country. [4]

........................................................................................................................................

........................................................................................................................................

........................................................................................................................................

........................................................................................................................................

**E**

Research your own economy. Explain how the role of the central bank differs from that of a commercial bank in your country.

## Key words

*Match economic terms with their definitions*

| | | | |
|---|---|---|---|
| 1 | Self-sufficiency **L** | **A** | The total value of all notes, coins and deposits with banks and other financial institutions in an economy |
| 2 | Specialization (by an individual) | **B** | A market consisting of all those people and organizations willing and able to supply money to people and organizations who want to borrow it |
| 3 | Barter | **C** | The direct exchange of goods or services for other goods or services without the use of money |
| 4 | Double coincidence of wants | **D** | A bank that supplies financial services to many businesses and members of the general public |
| 5 | Money | **E** | A financial institution, such as a bank, that brings together savers and borrowers |
| 6 | Token money | **F** | The national bank within a macroeconomy with responsibilities for supervising the banking system, managing the national debt and operating the government's monetary policy and finances |
| 7 | Money supply | **G** | When a person concentrates their productive efforts on producing a limited range of goods or services, or focuses on building expertise in a limited number of skills or tasks that they are individually best able to do |
| 8 | Liquid assets | **H** | Any item that is a generally accepted means of exchange or accepted method of payment for all other goods and services |
| 9 | Velocity of circulation | **I** | The cost of borrowing money (and the reward for saving) expressed as a % of the total monetary value of a loan (or amount of savings) |
| 10 | Money market | **J** | A necessary condition for exchange between two people, where each one wants the good or service the other has to offer |
| 11 | Financial intermediary | **K** | A term used to describe modern-day money because the face values printed on different notes and coins are far greater than the value of the paper or metal used in them |
| 12 | Interest rate | **L** | The ability of individuals or communities to produce everything they need and want for themselves |
| 13 | Commercial bank | **M** | The number of times notes and coins are exchanged each day, week or year in an economy |
| 14 | Central bank | **N** | Financial assets, such as money held in savings accounts, that can be converted into cash quickly and easily |

## Revision summary

*Fill in the missing words and economic terms*

1. _ _ _ _ _ is any item that is generally accepted by people and firms as a medium of exchange. Without it, people would need to _ _ _ _ _ _ or swap their services or any surplus goods they produced themselves or others they could not.

2. Money must also perform a number of other functions in a modern economy. It must also hold its value over time and provide a _ _ _ _ _ _ _ _ _ _ _ _ _ that can be used to express and compare the prices of all other goods and services in a common measure of value.

3. In order to perform its functions, a money must be acceptable, durable, portable, _ _ _ _ _ _ _ _ _ and _ _ _ _ _ _ .

4. Money enables specialization and trade. Without money, people and firms would need to _ _ _ _ _ _ with each other to obtain the goods and services they need and want.

5. The money supply in a modern economy consists of _ _ _ _ _, _ _ _ _ _ and bank _ _ _ _ _ _ _ _ .

6. Banks are financial intermediaries because they bring together customers who want to _ _ _ _ money with customers who want to _ _ _ _ _ _ money.

7. There are several different types of bank in a modern economy. They all offer very similar services, but each type tends to specialize in particular financial products and groups of consumers. For example, _ _ _ _ _ _ _ _ _ _ banks provide financial services including loans to businesses and members of the public.

8. The _ _ _ _ _ _ _ bank in an economy maintains the stability of the national currency and money supply on behalf of that country's government. It also regulates the banking sector and ensures it has sufficient funds to continue its activities.

## 3.2.1 (i) Spending

1. Define *disposable income*. [2]

........................................................................................................................

........................................................................................................................

2. Explain why richer people are able to spend more than poorer people. [6]

........................................................................................................................

........................................................................................................................

........................................................................................................................

........................................................................................................................

........................................................................................................................

........................................................................................................................

3. Analyse the main motives for spending. [8]

........................................................................................................................

........................................................................................................................

........................................................................................................................

........................................................................................................................

........................................................................................................................

........................................................................................................................

........................................................................................................................

........................................................................................................................

**E**

Think about what you have spent your money on in the last year. Consider the main factors affecting your spending decisions.

## 3.2.2 (ii) The influences on saving

1. Explain why people earning approximately the same amount of money may differ in the proportion of income that they save. [4]

   .......................................................................................................................................

   .......................................................................................................................................

   .......................................................................................................................................

   .......................................................................................................................................

2. Explain why poorer people are able to save less than richer people. [6]

   .......................................................................................................................................

   .......................................................................................................................................

   .......................................................................................................................................

   .......................................................................................................................................

   .......................................................................................................................................

   .......................................................................................................................................

3. Explain why interest rates are a major influence, but not the only influence, on savings decisions. [8]

   .......................................................................................................................................

   .......................................................................................................................................

   .......................................................................................................................................

   .......................................................................................................................................

   .......................................................................................................................................

   .......................................................................................................................................

   .......................................................................................................................................

   .......................................................................................................................................

**E**

Consider why poorer people may find it difficult to save.

## 3.2.1 (iii) The influences on borrowing

**1.** Analyse the different motives that people may have for borrowing. [4]

..............................................................................................................................

..............................................................................................................................

..............................................................................................................................

..............................................................................................................................

**2.** Why are poorer people more likely to borrow than richer people? [6]

..............................................................................................................................

..............................................................................................................................

..............................................................................................................................

..............................................................................................................................

..............................................................................................................................

..............................................................................................................................

**3.** Explain how high levels of borrowing could become a serious economic problem. [8]

..............................................................................................................................

..............................................................................................................................

..............................................................................................................................

..............................................................................................................................

..............................................................................................................................

..............................................................................................................................

..............................................................................................................................

**E**

Why is an older, skilled worker's pattern of spending, saving and borrowing likely to be different from that of a younger, unskilled worker?

## Key words

*Match economic terms with their definitions*

| | | | | |
|---|---|---|---|---|
| 1 | Disposable income | **L** | A | The satisfaction consumers enjoy from the consumption of goods or services |
| 2 | Consumer expenditure | | B | Failure to repay a loan |
| 3 | Real disposable income | | C | The total amount spent each period by consumers on goods and services |
| 4 | Propensity to consume | | D | The proportion of the total disposable income in an economy that is saved |
| 5 | Utility | | E | The total amount of accumulated borrowing by private individuals or households |
| 6 | Experience good (or service) | | F | The value of disposable income or the amount of goods and services it can purchase after allowing for the impact of inflation on prices |
| 7 | Wealth | | G | A product with characteristics, such as quality or taste, that are difficult to judge or observe in advance – they can only be judged once the product has been consumed |
| 8 | Saving | | H | A stock of assets that have a monetary value |
| 9 | Savings ratio | | I | Something of value that a person or company can offer a lender as security against failure to repay a loan |
| 10 | Dissaving | | J | A term used to describe the situation when a person is declared bankrupt |
| 11 | Personal debt | | K | Withdrawing savings to meet day-to-day living expenses |
| 12 | Default | | L | Income available to save or spend once all income related taxes have been deducted or paid |
| 13 | Collateral | | M | The portion of disposable income not immediately spent on the consumption of consumer goods and services; alternatively, the process of setting aside a proportion of current income for future use (known as delayed consumption) |
| 14 | Insolvency | | N | The proportion of disposable income a person or household spends on goods and services. The proportion tends to decline as disposable income increases |

1. The greater the _ _ _ _ _ _ _ _ _ _ income and wealth of a person, the greater their ability to spend and _ _ _ _.

2. People will choose to spend and save their disposable incomes in ways that will maximize their _ _ _ _ _ _ _.

3. _ _ _ _ _ _ _ _ _ _ goods and services, such as a meal at a restaurant or a holiday, have product characteristics that are difficult to observe before they are consumed. It is therefore difficult for consumers to judge how much _ _ _ _ _ _ _ they will enjoy from their consumption.

4. Rising prices will reduce the amount people are able to buy with their disposable incomes. That is, _ _ _ _ _ _ _ _ _ will reduce the purchasing power of their incomes and also their savings. People may increase their current spending if they think prices will rise in the future.

5. People with _ _ _ incomes tend to spend all or most of their disposable incomes meeting their basic _ _ _ _ _ for food, clothing and housing. They may not be able to afford to save any money from their incomes or to borrow any money from a bank.

6. In contrast, people with high incomes can spend far more than people on low incomes satisfying their _ _ _ _ _ and will still have enough money left over to save. That is, people on high incomes may spend more in total but overall they will spend a lower proportion of their disposable incomes than people with low incomes.

7. _ _ _ _ _ _ _ involves delaying consumption. As interest rates rise, people may save _ _ _ _ and spend _ _ _ _.

8. Borrowing, from a bank or by using a credit card, allows a person to increase their current _ _ _ _ _ _ _ _ _ _ _ of goods and services. As interest rates rise, people tend to borrow _ _ _ _. This is because it increases the _ _ _ _ of borrowing and people may no longer be able to afford to repay loans from their incomes.

9. Young adults may borrow _ _ _ _ than older people, to fund their further education or to buy their first car or home, for example. Older people may have paid off all their loans and are able to save more and spend more on holidays and other leisure activities. Young families may also spend a much larger proportion of their household income than other households.

10. _ _ _ _ _ _ is in held physical assets, such as gold and property, and in financial assets, including savings accounts and company shares. These will earn income from interest and dividends. Banks will often lend more to wealthy people because they can offer their assets as _ _ _ _ _ _ _ _ _ _ or security against their loans. If necessary, these assets can be sold to pay off their loans.

## 3.3.1 Factors affecting an individual's choice of occupation

1. Explain **two** reasons why someone may be prepared to work for a low wage. [4]

........................................................................................................................

........................................................................................................................

........................................................................................................................

........................................................................................................................

2. Explain **two** ways in which a wage can be paid to an employee. [4]

........................................................................................................................

........................................................................................................................

........................................................................................................................

........................................................................................................................

3. Explain, with the use of examples, what is meant by 'non-wage factors'. [4]

........................................................................................................................

........................................................................................................................

........................................................................................................................

........................................................................................................................

**E**

### Bookshop Assistant Required

An opportunity to work in a lively and expanding bookshop. Salary is $10,000 p.a. Flexible hours of work. Generous holiday entitlement. Good promotion prospects and job security. Extensive training opportunities. Good working conditions. Interesting and varied work.

If interested, please telephone 01234 987654.

(a) To what extent do you think non-wage factors will be more important than wage factors in influencing a person to apply for this job?

(b) Suggest why the successful applicant for the job of bookshop assistant may be more motivated in their work than a worker in a factory carrying out a repetitive job.

## 3.3.2 Wage determination

**1.** Define *equilibrium or market wage rate*. [2]

........................................................................................................................................................

........................................................................................................................................................

**2.** The diagram below shows the labour market for petrochemical engineers. Use the diagram to **(a)** mark the equilibrium market wage and number employed, and **(b)** show the impact of a fall in demand for petrochemical engineers in the space provided below. [4]

**3.** Explain **two** factors that may have caused the fall in demand for petrochemical engineers. [4]

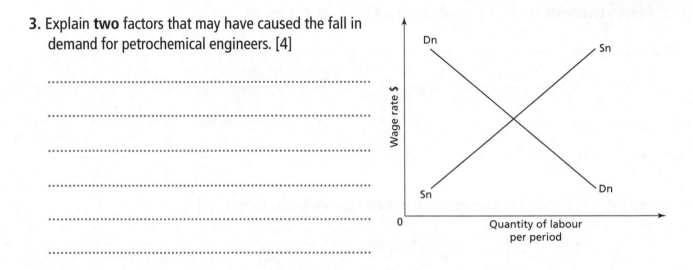

........................................................................................

........................................................................................

........................................................................................

........................................................................................

........................................................................................

........................................................................................

**4.** Explain **two** ways in which training could help an employee to earn a higher wage. [4]

........................................................................................................................................................

........................................................................................................................................................

........................................................................................................................................................

........................................................................................................................................................

**E**

The articles describe a number of changes in conditions in different labour markets. For each one, suggest how it could affect the market wages of employees.

> UK manufacturing businesses are facing a shortage of factory workers as the number of EU workers in the UK falls.

> Economists fear falling productivity will prevent rise in living standards.

> US unemployment falls to lowest level for 18 years

> Demand for organic food and drink products soars

## 3.3.3 Reasons for differences in earnings

**1.** What are 'wage differentials'? [2]

........................................................................................................................

........................................................................................................................

**2.** Explain **two** factors that could explain occupational wage differentials. [4]

........................................................................................................................

........................................................................................................................

........................................................................................................................

........................................................................................................................

**3.** Explain **two** reasons why an individual's earnings are likely to increase over time. [4]

........................................................................................................................

........................................................................................................................

........................................................................................................................

........................................................................................................................

**4.** Analyse the reasons why male workers often earn more on average than female workers. [4]

........................................................................................................................

........................................................................................................................

........................................................................................................................

........................................................................................................................

........................................................................................................................

........................................................................................................................

5. Describe the likely differences in earnings between skilled and unskilled workers. [4]

..................................................................................................................................................

..................................................................................................................................................

..................................................................................................................................................

..................................................................................................................................................

6. Describe the likely difference in earnings you would expect to see between workers in the private sector and those employed in the public sector of an economy. [4]

..................................................................................................................................................

..................................................................................................................................................

..................................................................................................................................................

..................................................................................................................................................

7. What are likely to be the differences in earnings between those who work in the agricultural, manufacturing and services sectors of the economy? [4]

..................................................................................................................................................

..................................................................................................................................................

..................................................................................................................................................

..................................................................................................................................................

8. Explain why a legal minimum wage needs to be set above the equilibrium wage in a labour market if it is to be effective. [4]

..................................................................................................................................................

..................................................................................................................................................

..................................................................................................................................................

..................................................................................................................................................

**E**

Think of an occupation that might interest you when you leave school or college. Research this occupation and find out how your earnings could change over time; for example, in your first year, after five to ten years, and eventually as you near retirement. Find out what you will need to do to increase your earnings over time, such as going on appropriate training courses, studying for additional qualifications and gaining promotions.

## 3.3.4 Division of labour and specialization

**1.** What is the 'division of labour' in production? [2]

..................................................................................................................................................

..................................................................................................................................................

**2.** Analyse the advantages and disadvantages of the division of labour for firms and their employees. [6]

..................................................................................................................................................

..................................................................................................................................................

..................................................................................................................................................

..................................................................................................................................................

..................................................................................................................................................

..................................................................................................................................................

**3.** Explain **two** benefits of occupational specialization for the individual. [4]

..................................................................................................................................................

..................................................................................................................................................

..................................................................................................................................................

..................................................................................................................................................

**4.** Explain **two** disadvantages of occupational specialization for the individual. [4]

..................................................................................................................................................

..................................................................................................................................................

..................................................................................................................................................

..................................................................................................................................................

**E**

Suggest ways in which firms could try to overcome some of the problems associated with the division of labour in production and overspecialization of their workers.

## 3.4.1 Definition of a trade union
## 3.4.2 The role of trade unions in the economy
## 3.4.3 The advantages and disadvantages of trade union activity

1. Explain why a worker might decide to join a trade union. [4]

   .........................................................................................................................................
   .........................................................................................................................................
   .........................................................................................................................................
   .........................................................................................................................................

2. Analyse the factors that could improve the bargaining strength of a trade union in negotiations for improved wages. [6]

   .........................................................................................................................................
   .........................................................................................................................................
   .........................................................................................................................................
   .........................................................................................................................................
   .........................................................................................................................................
   .........................................................................................................................................

3. Discuss whether trade unions play a positive role in an economy. [8]

   .........................................................................................................................................
   .........................................................................................................................................
   .........................................................................................................................................
   .........................................................................................................................................
   .........................................................................................................................................
   .........................................................................................................................................
   .........................................................................................................................................

**E**

Research the economy in your own country. Select three trade unions that exist in your country. Try to find out the purpose of these trade unions and how they attempt to achieve their objectives.

## Key words

*Match economic terms with their definitions*

| | | | |
|---|---|---|---|
| 1 | Trade union | C | **A** A refusal by employees to continue their work |
| 2 | Collective bargaining | | **B** When workers deliberately slow down production by making sure they comply fully with every rule and regulation in their workplace |
| 3 | Closed shop | | **C** An organization that represents the interests of workers and whose members are workers – also called a labour union |
| 4 | Single union agreement | | **D** A process used to settle industrial disputes |
| 5 | Industrial action | | **E** A union requirement that makes trade union membership compulsory for all employees in a particular workplace and prevents the employer from hiring non-union labour |
| 6 | Work to rule | | **F** A beneficial agreement between an employer and a trade union that means employees in the workplace are only able to join that particular union |
| 7 | Go-slow | | **G** The process of negotiating pay and working conditions between trade unions and employers |
| 8 | Strike | | **H** Any act taken by trade union members to disrupt productive activities in response to a dispute over pay and/or working conditions with one or more employers |
| 9 | Arbitration | | **I** When workers deliberately carry out tasks slowly in order to reduce the rate of production |

## Revision summary

*Fill in the missing words and economic terms*

1. Trade unions aim to promote and protect the interests of workers. This involves seeking improvements in the _ _ _ _ _ and working conditions of their members, as well as defending the rights and jobs of employees.

2. There are many different types of trade union. A general union will represent workers from many different industries and occupations while an _ _ _ _ _ _ _ _ _ _ union will only represent workers in one particular industry, such as mining or the automotive industry.

3. Unions that represent people employed in banks and offices, or as teachers or police, are called _ _ _ - _ _ _ _ _ _ unions.

4. Negotiations between trade unions and employers over pay and working conditions are called _ _ _ _ _ _ _ _ _ _ _ _ _ _ _ _ _ _ _ _. When this fails to reach agreement, a trade union may take industrial action.

5. Industrial action, such as a ban on _ _ _ _ _ _ _ _ working or an all-out _ _ _ _ _ _, aims to put pressure on employers to agree to improvements in wages or other working conditions by disrupting production. This can increase costs and reduce sales and revenues. However, workers will not be paid if they are on strike.

## 3.5.1 Classification of firms

1. Productive activities in an economy are classified into three broad industrial sectors. Using examples, explain the difference between primary, secondary and tertiary sector industries. [4]

........................................................................................................................................................

........................................................................................................................................................

........................................................................................................................................................

........................................................................................................................................................

2. Explain why a government may take over the ownership of private sector enterprises. [6]

........................................................................................................................................................

........................................................................................................................................................

........................................................................................................................................................

........................................................................................................................................................

........................................................................................................................................................

........................................................................................................................................................

3. Explain why a state-owned enterprise might be moved from the public sector to the private sector. [6]

........................................................................................................................................................

........................................................................................................................................................

........................................................................................................................................................

........................................................................................................................................................

........................................................................................................................................................

........................................................................................................................................................

**E**

To which industrial sectors of an economy do the following industries belong?

| Industry | Sector? | Industry | Sector? | Industry | Sector? |
|---|---|---|---|---|---|
| Retailing | *Tertiary* | Construction | | Coal mining | |
| Oil extraction | | Advertising | | Insurance | |
| Ship building | | Textiles | | Car production | |
| Farming | | Fishing | | Food processing | |

## 3.5.1 Classification of firms
## 3.5.2 Small firms

1. Explain **two** methods that can be used to measure the size of a firm. [4]

..................................................................................................................................................

..................................................................................................................................................

..................................................................................................................................................

..................................................................................................................................................

2. An international trading company employs over $500 million worth of capital, yet employs only 40 full-time workers, and has a global market share of 3% worth around $1.5 billion in revenue each year. Analyse whether the company should be considered small or large. [6]

..................................................................................................................................................

..................................................................................................................................................

..................................................................................................................................................

..................................................................................................................................................

..................................................................................................................................................

..................................................................................................................................................

3. Analyse the reasons why most firms in an economy remain small. [6]

..................................................................................................................................................

..................................................................................................................................................

..................................................................................................................................................

..................................................................................................................................................

..................................................................................................................................................

..................................................................................................................................................

## 3.5.3–4 Mergers and the causes and forms of the growth of firms

1. Explain the difference between internal growth and external growth in the size of firms. [4]

..................................................................................................................................................

..................................................................................................................................................

..................................................................................................................................................

..................................................................................................................................................

2. Explain **two** reasons why two firms producing the same or similar products in the same industry may choose to merge into a single organization. [4]

..................................................................................................................................................

..................................................................................................................................................

..................................................................................................................................................

..................................................................................................................................................

3. Explain **two** reasons why two firms in different industries may choose to merge into a single organization. [4]

..................................................................................................................................................

..................................................................................................................................................

..................................................................................................................................................

..................................................................................................................................................

**E**

What types of merger (vertical backwards, vertical forwards, horizontal or conglomerate) do the following describe?

| Description | Type of merger? |
| --- | --- |
| A clothes manufacturer takes over a chain of clothing shops | |
| An investment company takes over a solar energy supplier | |
| A restaurant chain merges with a food wholesaler | |
| Two internet service providers merge | |

## 3.5.5 Economies and diseconomies of scale

1. The following describe different examples of cost advantages that large firms may enjoy compared to smaller firms. For each one, state whether it is an example of a purchasing, marketing, technical or financial economy of scale. [4]

| Cost advantage | Type of economy of scale? |
|---|---|
| Large firms can afford to employ their own specialist staff and equipment | |
| Banks are willing to lend more money to large firms and often at lower interest rates because they are less likely to fail than smaller firms and have assets they can offer as security | |
| Suppliers will often offer price discounts for bulk purchases of items | |
| Large firms can spread the high fixed costs of distribution and advertising over a much larger output | |

2. What type of economy of scale does the following situation describe? [2]

'A large firm may be able to diversify its product range and sell its products into different consumer markets at home and overseas. This will reduce the impact on the business of a fall in demand for any one of its products or in any one of its markets.'

.............................................................................................................................

.............................................................................................................................

3. Explain **two** ways an increase in the size of an industry can benefit firms within that industry. [4]

.............................................................................................................................

.............................................................................................................................

.............................................................................................................................

.............................................................................................................................

4. Explain **two** diseconomies of scale a firm could experience as it continues to expand its scale of production. [4]

.............................................................................................................................

.............................................................................................................................

.............................................................................................................................

.............................................................................................................................

## Key words

*Match economic terms with their correct definitions*

| | | | |
|---|---|---|---|
| 1 | Industry    J | A | Growth in the size of a firm through the purchase or hire of additional productive assets |
| 2 | Primary sector | B | Coordination and other problems that occur in a firm that expands in size beyond its maximum efficient scale causing its average production costs to increase |
| 3 | Secondary sector | C | This occurs when a firm merges with a distributor of its products or a major business customer. For example, the takeover of a retail chain by a manufacturer |
| 4 | Manufacturing | D | Industries in this sector of an economy process natural and human-made materials and components to produce other goods |
| 5 | Tertiary sector | E | Growth in the size of a firm through mergers |
| 6 | State-owned enterprise | F | The time period in economics in which all factors of production including capital can be varied by firms. Only in this period can firms expand their scale of production through the deployment of additional capital |
| 7 | Internal growth | G | This occurs when two or more firms producing the same or similar products in the same industry and at the same stage of production combine to form a single, larger firm |
| 8 | External growth | H | Cost advantages associated with increasing the scale of production within an entire industry. As a result, all firms in the industry can benefit from lower average production costs |
| 9 | Capital employed | I | A trading organization wholly or partially owned and operated within the public sector of an economy |
| 10 | Market share | J | A group of firms that use similar production processes or specialize in a similar range of products |
| 11 | Long run | K | The name given to the production process and also to the group of industries that process natural resources and other unfinished goods to make other finished and semi-finished goods |
| 12 | Short run | L | Firms within industries in this sector of an economy specialize in the production or extraction of natural resources |
| 13 | Horizontal merger | M | This occurs when a firm merges with one or more firms in its supply chain. For example, the merger of a food processor with a farm |
| 14 | Forward vertical merger | N | The time period in economics in which firms can only increase production by hiring more labour because capital is a fixed factor of production |
| 15 | Backward vertical merger | O | Firms in this sector of an economy provide services |
| 16 | Conglomerate merger | P | The proportion of total sales recorded in a specific market or industry in a given period of time that has been earned by a single firm or supplier |
| 17 | Internal economies of scale | Q | The value of all the productive assets or capital equipment employed within a firm |
| 18 | External economies of scale | R | Cost advantages associated with increasing the scale of production within a firm. They result in a reduction in average production costs |
| 19 | Diseconomies of scale | S | A merger between two or more firms in different industrial sectors |

## Revision summary                    *Fill in the missing words and economic terms*

1.  Firms using similar production processes producing similar products are grouped together into
    different industrial sectors. Industries including farming, fishing and mining in the _ _ _ _ _ _ _
    sector of an economy, produce or extract natural resources. Industries in the _ _ _ _ _ _ _ _ _ sector
    process natural resources and human-made materials or parts to make other goods and services.
    _ _ _ _ _ _ _ _ sector industries supply services.

2.  Firms may also be classified according to their size and whether they are privately owned and
    controlled or state-owned enterprises in the _ _ _ _ _ _ sector of an economy.

3.  A firm may grow in size by employing more labour and capital to increase its scale of production
    (known as _ _ _ _ _ _ _ _ growth) or by combining with one or more other firms (referred to as
    _ _ _ _ _ _ _ _ growth).

4.  Most mergers are _ _ _ _ _ _ _ _ _ _ _ because they occur between firms engaged in the production
    of the same or similar goods or services. This type of merger can benefit the firms involved by
    _ _ _ _ _ _ _ _ _ _ the market share of the combined business and reducing competition.

5.  Firms may also combine vertically with their suppliers, distributors and major customers. For example,
    a manufacturer may increase control over the supply and cost of the materials and parts it needs
    for production through a _ _ _ _ _ _ _ _ vertical merger with a key supplier. It may also seek a
    _ _ _ _ _ _ _ vertical merger with a major retailer to better promote and sell its products.

6.  Larger firms often enjoy substantial cost advantages over their smaller competitors. These cost
    advantages or _ _ _ _ _ _ _ _ _ _ of _ _ _ _ _ arise because larger firms are able to buy the supplies
    they need in bulk at discounted prices from their suppliers and because they are able to secure low
    cost loans or finance from banks and other investors more easily than smaller, more risky firms.

7.  Large firms may also benefit from _ _ _ _ _ _ _ _ _ economies because their large scale of
    production justifies the use of more capital-intensive production methods using modern, specialized
    machinery and equipment.

8.  These and other cost reductions associated with large-scale production will reduce the _ _ _ _ _ _ _ _
    cost of producing each unit of output in large firms below the unit costs of smaller firms.

9.  Additionally, firms within an industry may enjoy _ _ _ _ _ _ _ _ economies of scale as their industry
    expands. This is because a larger industry will create a larger pool of skilled labour to hire from.
    Firms may also benefit from shared infrastructure and shared equipment and service providers able
    to supply the specific needs of firms within the industry; for example, for specialized equipment,
    transportation, marketing, etc.

10. A firm that expands beyond its maximum efficient scale will experience _ _ _ _ _ _ _ _ _ _ _ _ _ of
    scale. These will cause its average costs to _ _ _ _ _ _ _ _ _. This is because a very large firm can be
    difficult to manage effectively and may find it difficult to recruit all the workers it needs. It may also
    run short of supplies.

11. However, most firms in any national economy are small and remain small because they serve small
    local markets and lack the _ _ _ _ _ _ _ they need to expand their scale of production.

## 3.6.1 Production and productivity

**1.** Explain the difference between 'productivity' and 'production'. [4]

.......................................................................................................................................

.......................................................................................................................................

.......................................................................................................................................

.......................................................................................................................................

**2.** Explain **two** ways the productivity of labour can be measured. [4]

.......................................................................................................................................

.......................................................................................................................................

.......................................................................................................................................

.......................................................................................................................................

**3.** Explain **two** ways a firm could increase the productivity of its workforce. [4]

.......................................................................................................................................

.......................................................................................................................................

.......................................................................................................................................

.......................................................................................................................................

.......................................................................................................................................

.......................................................................................................................................

.......................................................................................................................................

.......................................................................................................................................

.......................................................................................................................................

**E**

You have been appointed Production Manager in a large factory and it has been made clear to you that your main job is to improve the level of productivity in the factory. Consider what you could do to achieve this objective.

## 3.6.2 Labour-intensive and capital-intensive production
## 3.6.3 Demand for factors of production

1. Distinguish between 'labour-intensive' and 'capital-intensive production'. [4]

...............................................................................................................................

...............................................................................................................................

...............................................................................................................................

...............................................................................................................................

2. Analyse the reasons why a firm may increase its demand for different factors of production. [8]

...............................................................................................................................

...............................................................................................................................

...............................................................................................................................

...............................................................................................................................

3. Analyse the reasons why a firm may replace labour with capital in its production process. [6]

...............................................................................................................................

...............................................................................................................................

...............................................................................................................................

...............................................................................................................................

...............................................................................................................................

...............................................................................................................................

**E**

What impacts are the following factors likely to have on the demand for different factors of production by firms?

**Small Firms Association argues increase in legal minimum wage will hurt economy**

**Real wages falling as inflation accelerates while wage growth stagnates**

**Increase in government subsidies to help firms invest in new equipment**

Profits slump as consumer spending continues to fall

**Government announces 2% increase in payroll taxes on employers**

**New smart technologies boost productivity**

## 3.7.1–2 Definition and calculation of costs of production
## 3.7.3–4 Definition and calculation of revenues

1. Distinguish between a 'fixed cost' and a 'variable cost' of production. [4]

   ....................................................................................................................................................

   ....................................................................................................................................................

   ....................................................................................................................................................

   ....................................................................................................................................................

2. Distinguish between the 'total cost' of producing a given level of output and the 'average cost' of production. [4]

   ....................................................................................................................................................

   ....................................................................................................................................................

   ....................................................................................................................................................

   ....................................................................................................................................................

3. A young entrepreneur is about to set up a new firm producing protective cases for sunglasses. She calculates that the variable cost of producing each case will be $4.00 and that the total fixed costs of production will be $3,000 each month regardless of how many cases (or 'units') produced each month.

   Complete columns (a), (b) and (c) in the table below to show the total fixed costs, total variable costs and total costs of producing each possible level of output. [10]

| | (a) | (b) | (c) | (d) | (e) | (f) |
|---|---|---|---|---|---|---|
| Total output (units per month) | Total fixed costs ($) | Total variable costs ($) | Total cost ($) | Average cost per unit ($) | Total revenue ($) | Profit or loss ($) |
| 0 | 3,000 | 0 | 3,000 | – | 0 | –3,000 (loss) |
| 1,000 | | | | | | |
| 2,000 | | | | | | |
| 3,000 | | | | | | |
| 4,000 | | | | | | |
| 5,000 | | | | | | |

4. From the table in question 3 above, explain why the total costs of producing the sunglasses cases will be $3,000 per month even if the total monthly output of the new firm is zero. [2]

...................................................................................................................................................

...................................................................................................................................................

5. Complete column (d) in the table above by calculating the average cost per unit at each possible level of output. [5]

...................................................................................................................................................

...................................................................................................................................................

...................................................................................................................................................

...................................................................................................................................................

...................................................................................................................................................

6. From the table you have completed, explain what will happen to the average cost of producing each unit as the total monthly output of cases is increased and why. [4]

...................................................................................................................................................

...................................................................................................................................................

...................................................................................................................................................

...................................................................................................................................................

7. The young entrepreneur estimates she will be able to sell each glass case for $5.00 if she produces no more than 4,000 cases each month. Using this information, calculate the total revenue she will receive from the sale of her glasses cases in column (e) of the table at every possible level of output up to 4,000 units per month. [4]

...................................................................................................................................................

...................................................................................................................................................

...................................................................................................................................................

...................................................................................................................................................

8. If the firm produces and supplies more than 4,000 cases each month, the entrepreneur estimates she will have to lower her price to $4.50 per case in order to sell them all. Calculate the total revenue of selling 5,000 cases priced at $4.50 each and use this information to complete column (e) in the table.

9. From the table:
   a) calculate the average revenue per unit if the firm is able to sell 4,000 units each month and the average revenue per unit from the sale of 5,000 units each month. [2]

   ..............................................................................................................................................

   ..............................................................................................................................................

   b) Explain what has happened to average revenue and why. [2]

   ..............................................................................................................................................

   ..............................................................................................................................................

10. Using the information on total costs and total revenue from the table, calculate the amount of profit or loss the new firm will make each month at each possible level of output and complete column (f). [5]

    ..............................................................................................................................................

    ..............................................................................................................................................

    ..............................................................................................................................................

    ..............................................................................................................................................

    ..............................................................................................................................................

11. At what level of output will the firm:

    a) make the biggest loss? [2]

    ..............................................................................................................................................

    ..............................................................................................................................................

    b) earn the most profit? [2]

    ..............................................................................................................................................

    ..............................................................................................................................................

    c) break even? [2]

    ..............................................................................................................................................

    ..............................................................................................................................................

## 3.7.5 Objectives of firms

1. Define *profit*. [2]

..............................................................................................................................

..............................................................................................................................

2. Describe the 'principle of profit maximization'. [4]

..............................................................................................................................

..............................................................................................................................

..............................................................................................................................

..............................................................................................................................

3. Explain why some business organizations have objectives other than profit maximization. [6]

..............................................................................................................................

..............................................................................................................................

..............................................................................................................................

..............................................................................................................................

..............................................................................................................................

..............................................................................................................................

**E**

What are the objectives of the organizations in the articles?

US aircraft manufacturer Boeing has laid out an ambitious, five-year strategy to increase its revenue and profits and secure the company's future for the next 100 years, promising to boost efficiency, return cash to shareholders and expand its after-market services and parts business.

BORDER Biscuits is adding a new production line at its factory in Scotland. The investment is part of the biscuit manufacturer's plans to increase its sales and market share south of the border and overseas.

## Key words

*Match economic terms with their definitions*

| | | | |
|---|---|---|---|
| 1 | Productivity **P** | A | Swapping one factor input for another in a production process usually in response to a change in their relative prices. For example, a firm may swap capital for labour if wages rise or the cost of new capital equipment falls |
| 2 | Labour productivity | B | A cost of production that does not vary directly with the amount produced |
| 3 | Mass production | C | The production of large quantities of standardized products at a low unit or average cost |
| 4 | Labour intensive production | D | The revenue generated per unit of output sold |
| 5 | Capital intensive production | E | The volume or value of output produced per unit of labour input, i.e. by each worker or for each hour worked |
| 6 | Factor substitution | F | Also known as turnover, it is the total amount of money raised by a firm from the sale of its output in a given period |
| 7 | Fixed cost | G | The sum of fixed costs and variable costs incurred in the production of a given level of output |
| 8 | Variable cost | H | The reward for successful enterprise. It is the surplus remaining after total costs are deducted from total revenue |
| 9 | Total cost | I | An organization that does not aim to make a profit from its activities |
| 10 | Average cost | J | Production that requires proportionally more capital inputs than labour |
| 11 | Total revenue | K | That level of output at which a firm will cover its total cost of production and earn zero profit if it sells all the output in full |
| 12 | Average revenue | L | The process by which a firm determines the price and output level that will return it the biggest profit where the difference between its total revenue and total costs is greatest |
| 13 | Break-even level of output | M | The cost of producing each unit of output. It is equal to the total cost of production divided by total output |
| 14 | Profit | N | Production that requires proportionally more labour input than capital |
| 15 | Profit maximization | O | A cost of production that varies directly with the amount produced |
| 16 | Not-for-profit organization | P | A measure of the average efficiency of production. It involves comparing the amount of output that is produced by a given amount of land, labour and capital inputs |

## Revision summary

*Fill in the missing words and economic terms*

1. Most firms will aim to increase the productivity of the factors of production they employ. This involves _ _ _ _ _ _ _ _ _ the total output they can produce each period without increasing total costs or producing the same amount of output with fewer resources. Increasing productivity therefore results in lower average costs.

2. _ _ _ _ _ _ productivity is the most common measure of factor productivity. It is calculated by dividing total output over a given period of time by the total number of employees to give the average output per period per worker.

3. Moving from labour-intensive production to more _ _ _ _ _ _ _-intensive production methods may help to increase productivity in some firms because they will be able to mass produce their products. However, machinery and other equipment can be expensive to install and maintain.

4. The use of _ _ _ _ _ _ _ - _ _ _ _ _ _ _ _ _ _ production methods is more suitable for smaller firms supplying personalized services or bespoke handmade items. Labour can often be used more flexibly than immobile machinery and other equipment. However, wage costs can be high and some firms may find it difficult to recruit employees with the skills they require.

5. As consumer demand increases, a firm may increase its demand for all factors of production so it can increase output. However, labour may be replaced with capital equipment if wages _ _ _ _ _ _ _ _ or if the productivity of labour _ _ _ _ _ relative to capital equipment.

6. Buying and installing additional capital equipment will increase the _ _ _ _ _ costs of a firm. However, running the equipment for longer and longer periods each day to increase output will require additional power and this will increase _ _ _ _ _ _ _ _ costs.

7. To maximize profit a firm will need to maximize the difference between its total _ _ _ _ _ _ _ and total fixed and variable costs of production each period. However, if the average revenue per unit sold is less than the average cost of producing each unit sold, the firm will make a _ _ _ _ on each sale.

8. Many new firms are not expected to make a profit in the first few months or even years of operation as they attempt to build-up their numbers of customers and levels of sales. Start-up costs for a new business are high and the best that many new firms can hope for in their first year is to _ _ _ _ _ - _ _ _ _ which requires each firm to generate total revenues equal to its total costs.

9. Many private sector firms therefore aim to achieve _ _ _ _ _ _ _ profit maximization, after a period of growth, to earn a significant and sustained profit each year thereafter from its resources.

10. Some firms may instead aim to make more modest or satisfactory profits, preferring instead to attain social welfare and environmental objectives. Achieving these can be expensive and reduce _ _ _ _ _ _.

## 3.8.1 Competitive markets
## 3.8.2 Monopoly markets

1. Explain what is meant by 'market structure'. [4]

   ............................................................................................................................

   ............................................................................................................................

   ............................................................................................................................

   ............................................................................................................................

2. The following are characteristics of different market structures. Which set of characteristics describes perfect competition and which set describes monopoly? [4]

| Market characteristics (a) | Market characteristics (b) |
|---|---|
| There are a large number of firms supplying the market | One firm or a small number of firms acting together dominate the market |
| All firms are price takers | Firm(s) are price makers, i.e. they can determine the price at which they will sell their products |
| All firms sell the same 'homogenous' product | Advertising and branding will often be used to differentiate products |
| New firms are able to enter the market easily | There are barriers to entry to new firms |
| All firms have access to the same technical knowledge and equipment | Existing firms may be able to restrict access to new firms of technical knowledge and equipment |
| Firms aim to maximize their profits by selling as much as they can at the market price | Firms are able to earn excess or abnormal profits by restricting competition and market supply to keep prices high |
| Type of market structure? ........................................ | Type of market structure? ........................................ |

3. Explain why firms in a perfectly competitive market are referred to as 'price takers'. [4]

   ............................................................................................................................

   ............................................................................................................................

   ............................................................................................................................

   ............................................................................................................................

4. Suggest and explain a pricing strategy each of the following firms could use in the situations described:

   (a) A firm wanting to avoid a price war with its major competitors. [4]

   ........................................................................................................................................

   ........................................................................................................................................

   ........................................................................................................................................

   ........................................................................................................................................

   (b) A monopoly that risks losing sales and profits to new competitors seeking to enter its market. [4]

   ........................................................................................................................................

   ........................................................................................................................................

   ........................................................................................................................................

   ........................................................................................................................................

5. Discuss whether the price of a product supplied by a monopoly is likely to be higher or lower than it would be if firms in a competitive market had supplied it. [8]

   ........................................................................................................................................

   ........................................................................................................................................

   ........................................................................................................................................

   ........................................................................................................................................

   ........................................................................................................................................

   ........................................................................................................................................

   ........................................................................................................................................

   ........................................................................................................................................

**E**

Suggest ways a government may be able to prevent or stop a monopoly from restricting competition and earning excess or 'abnormal profits'.

## 3.8.2 Monopoly markets

**1.** Distinguish between 'natural' and 'artificial' barriers to entry. [4]

.......................................................................................................................................

.......................................................................................................................................

.......................................................................................................................................

.......................................................................................................................................

**2** Explain **two** artificial barriers to entry a monopoly may use to restrict competition and protect its market position. [4]

.......................................................................................................................................

.......................................................................................................................................

.......................................................................................................................................

.......................................................................................................................................

**3.** Explain **two** potential disadvantages for consumers of a monopoly market structure. [4]

.......................................................................................................................................

.......................................................................................................................................

.......................................................................................................................................

.......................................................................................................................................

**E**

### Creation of a new monopoly!

In one country, there have only been two firms involved in running passenger rail services. It was always believed that the existence of the two firms provided competition that was in the interest of the customers.

However, the two firms have been finding it very difficult to be profitable and so they have decided to merge to be able to benefit from the large size of the single firm that will be created.

This could be in the interests of consumers, but it is also possible that the creation of the monopoly will act against the public interest, giving the firm too much power and influence.

What are likely to be the main advantages and disadvantages of the creation of this monopoly rail company?

## Key words

*Match economic terms with their definitions*

| | | | |
|---|---|---|---|
| 1 | Market structure **L** | A | A market structure in which one firm is the sole supplier of the product |
| 2 | Perfect competition | B | Laws and regulations designed to promote competition and to prevent or reduce anti-competitive behaviours |
| 3 | Product differentiation | C | A market which has no or low barriers to entry so that new firms can come into the market to compete with existing firms |
| 4 | Pure monopoly | D | A pricing strategy in which firms competing to supply a market avoid price competition by setting their prices at or close to those set by the market leader |
| 5 | Abnormal profit | E | Competing firms working together, often illegally, to control or fix their prices usually at artificially high levels |
| 6 | Cartel | F | This occurs when the most efficient number of firms supplying a market is one |
| 7 | Collusion | G | A period of fierce competition in which competing firms repeatedly try to undercut their rivals' prices in an attempt to increase their shares of the market |
| 8 | X-inefficiency | H | Making minor changes to a product's features other than price, such as brand name, image, colour, shape, packaging and warranty periods, in order to distinguish it from very similar competing products and attract and retain customers |
| 9 | Natural barriers to entry | I | These obstacles to new competition occur when existing firms in a market enjoy significant economies of scale |
| 10 | Natural monopoly | J | An organisation that has the exclusive legal right to provide a particular product, for example, due to having a patent |
| 11 | Legal monopoly | K | A strategy used by one or more firms in a market to eliminate or prevent competition by cutting prices to a very low level, often below the average costs of competing firms |
| 12 | Price war | L | The organisational and other characteristics of a market such as the degree of competition or collusion between firms |
| 13 | Destruction pricing | M | A market structure in which numerous firms compete to supply the market with an identical product and have no control over the market price |
| 14 | Follow-the-leader pricing | N | An agreement between competing firms to control market supply and price |
| 15 | Competition policy | O | This occurs when a monopoly has little incentive to control its costs because it does not have to compete with other firms. This causes its average cost of production to be higher than necessary |
| 16 | Contestable market | P | An excessive or monopoly profit above that level of profit firms would normally earn if the market was a competitive one instead |

## Revision summary

*Fill in the missing words and economic terms*

1. Firms will compete with each other on prices and product features in an attempt to out sell each other, increase their market shares and earn more profits. How many firms compete with each other in a market, how they compete and how much control they each have over the market price determines the market _ _ _ _ _ _ _ _ _ .

2. In a perfectly competitive market, so many firms compete to supply an identical product that no one firm is able to influence the market price. That is, all firms in a perfectly competitive market are price _ _ _ _ _ _ .

3. In contrast, in a pure _ _ _ _ _ _ _ _ market structure a single firm controls the total market supply and is therefore able to set the market price. As a result, the market price charged by a monopoly firm and the profit it is able to earn is likely to be _ _ _ _ _ _ than in a highly competitive market.

4. In reality, there are very few perfectly competitive markets or pure private sector monopolies, but there are many markets with similar features to one or other of these two extremes. Competition between firms will often result in _ _ _ _ _ prices and improved product features as firms try to innovate, cut their costs and take sales away from each other. As a result, the market shares and profits of competing firms will often change over time.

5. For example, prices, product features and the market shares and profits of individual firms will often change in a _ _ _ _ _ _ _ _ _ _ _ market as they try to innovate, reduce their costs below those of their rivals and take sales away from each other.

6. In a monopoly market, one or more firms acting together can control the market supply. By restricting the market supply they can _ _ _ _ _ _ _ _ _ the market price and earn _ _ _ _ _ _ _ _ profits. Consumer choice and product quality may also be lower than in competitive markets.

7. Powerful monopolies may be able to protect their market positions and profits from new competitors by using artificial _ _ _ _ _ _ _ _ _ to _ _ _ _ _ . These may include cutting the market price to below the average costs of smaller rivals so they make a loss and have to exit the market. This strategy is called destruction or _ _ _ _ _ _ _ _ _ pricing.

8. However, some firms naturally grow to become monopolies because they are able to enjoy significant economies of scale and are far more efficient than smaller firms. If a single firm is able to produce the entire market supply of a product at a lower average cost than a number of smaller competing firms together, then it has a _ _ _ _ _ _ _ _  _ _ _ _ _ _ _ _ .

9. A monopoly need not be bad for consumers. Without _ _ _ _ _ _ _ _ _ profits many monopolies would not have the incentive or the money they need to fund large, risky investments in new inventions and the development of better products.

10. A monopoly may also offer competitive prices and high quality products to protect its dominant market position if its market is _ _ _ _ _ _ _ _ _ _ _ . This means its market is open to competition because barriers to market entry are _ _ _ .

The ability to calculate costs, revenues and profit is as important in economics as it is in business. Equally important is the ability to analyse how changes in different costs and market conditions can affect the profitability of different firms and their output decisions. This can also be achieved by plotting information on costs and revenues on graphs.

A firm can produce any level of output up to 8,000 units each month with its existing workforce and equipment. Its fixed costs are $4,000 each month and the variable cost of producing each unit is $10.

| Output per month | Total fixed costs ($) | Total variable costs ($) | Total cost ($) | Total revenue ($) | Profit or loss ($) |
|---|---|---|---|---|---|
| 0 | | | | | |
| 2,000 | | | | | |
| 4,000 | | | | | |
| 6,000 | | | | | |
| 8,000 | | | | | |

1.  Complete the table above assuming (a) that the average price at which each unit is sold is $12 and (b) that no output is left unsold. [8]

2.  Use data from the table to plot and label the total cost and total revenue of producing and selling each possible level of output. On the graph show and label the area between these two curves that represents profit and the area that represents loss. Also show and label the level of output at which the firm will break even assuming it is able to sell its output in full. [8]

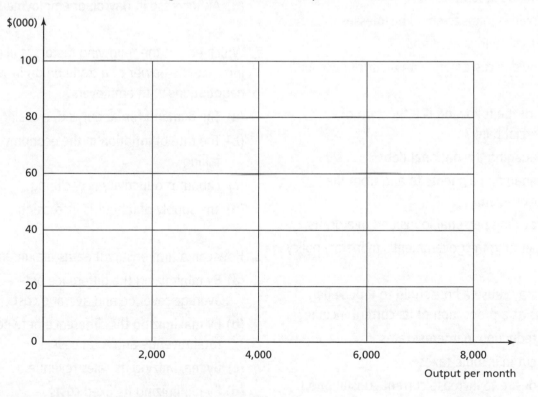

3.  On the same graph, show the effect of a decrease in the variable cost of producing each unit to $9, assuming all other things remain unchanged. [6]

## Multiple choice questions (Paper 1)

1. Which characteristic must a commodity possess if it is to be used as money?
   (a) It is generally acceptable
   (b) It is not easily divisible
   (c) Its value never changes
   (d) It has an unlimited supply

2. Which function of money is most appropriate for buying goods on credit?
   (a) A measure of value
   (b) A means of deferred payment
   (c) A medium of exchange
   (d) A store of value

3. Which of the following is a function of a central bank?
   (a) Acts as a lender of last resort to the banking system
   (b) Provides loans to small businesses
   (c) Offers savings accounts
   (d) Provides customers with a current account

4. Which of the following is a function of a commercial bank?
   (a) Managing the national debt
   (b) Managing payments to and from the government
   (c) Providing personal loans and overdrafts
   (d) Operating the government's monetary policy

5. What may cause a household to reduce its savings as a proportion of its current income?
   (a) A reduction in interest rates
   (b) A cut in income taxes
   (c) A desire to increase current consumption
   (d) Increased economic uncertainty

6. The diagram below shows the labour market for manufacturing workers. What is likely to have caused the increase in demand for their labour from DnDn to Dn1Dn1?

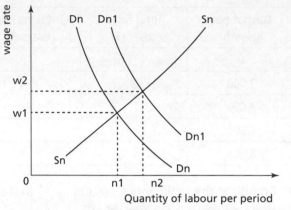

   (a) A fall in demand for manufactured goods
   (b) An increase in labour productivity
   (c) A fall in the wages of manufacturing workers
   (d) An increase in payroll or employment taxes

7. Which one of the following factors is likely to increase the power of a trade union in wage negotiations with employers?
   (a) The demand for labour is decreasing
   (b) The rate of inflation in the economy is falling
   (c) Labour productivity is declining
   (d) The supply of labour is increasing

8. How can a firm ensure it earns maximum profit?
   (a) By minimizing the difference between its average revenue and average cost
   (b) By maximizing the difference between its total revenue and total cost
   (c) By maximizing its sales revenue
   (d) By minimizing its fixed costs

9. What is a variable cost to a firm producing cakes?
   (a) The ingredients of its cakes
   (b) The interest on money it has borrowed
   (c) The monthly rent of its factory
   (d) The salaries of its managers

10. In 2016, loss-making airline Thai Airways stated it would defer delivery of a number of new aircraft it had ordered.

    Which of its costs were directly affected by this decision?
    (a) Fixed costs
    (b) External costs
    (c) Opportunity costs
    (d) Variable costs

11. Which of the following statements about total fixed costs is correct?
    (a) It falls as output increases
    (b) It is calculated by dividing total cost by output
    (c) It increases with output
    (d) It must be paid even when output is zero

12. The table contains information on the production costs of a firm.

| Units of output | Total variable costs ($) | Total costs ($) |
|---|---|---|
| 100 | 200 | 290 |
| 200 | 390 | 480 |
| 300 | 550 | 640 |
| 400 | 720 | 810 |

    What are the total fixed costs of the firm?
    (a) 0
    (b) $90
    (c) $100
    (d) $290

13. Wheat and sugar are used in a factory to produce biscuits. What is a fixed cost in the production of biscuits?
    (a) Wheat
    (b) Electricity
    (c) Rent
    (d) Sugar

14. When is a firm considered more capital-intensive than other firms?
    (a) When it has a lower ratio of workers to machinery and equipment than other firms
    (b) When it has fewer workers than the other firms
    (c) When it has lower average costs than the other firms
    (d) When it employs more machinery and equipment than other firms

15. A large sugar refinery expands by taking over a sugar plantation. What type of merger does this represent?
    (a) Horizontal
    (b) Conglomerate
    (c) Forward vertical
    (d) Backward vertical

16. Which of the following is an external economy of scale?
    (a) Skills training courses are provided in local colleges
    (b) Increased labour productivity
    (c) Increased availability of low cost credit from banks
    (d) Price discounts from bulk buying

17. What would indicate that a firm is experiencing diseconomies of scale?
    (a) Average costs begin to fall
    (b) Average variable costs begin to fall
    (c) Average costs begin to rise
    (d) Average revenue begins to rise

18. Unilever, a British-Dutch multinational with interests in food, beverages, cleaning agents and personal care products, has recently taken over a number of foreign companies.

    What is the most likely objective of this action?

    **(a)** To achieve a domestic monopoly position

    **(b)** To increase its level of specialization

    **(c)** To reduce its fixed costs

    **(d)** To spread risks through diversification

19. Prices tend to be lower in a competitive industry than in a monopoly. Why is this?

    **(a)** Profits are usually lower in a monopoly

    **(b)** A monopoly is a price taker

    **(c)** A competitive industry enjoys more economies of scale

    **(d)** New firms are free to enter the competitive industry

20. What will definitely happen when a monopoly takes over an industry from competitive firms?

    **(a)** The monopoly will earn less profit

    **(b)** The monopoly will increase the market price

    **(c)** The monopoly will increase consumer choice

    **(d)** The monopoly will operate a larger scale of production

## Structured questions (Paper 2, Section A)

1.

# US Federal Reserve raises interest rates

In June 2018, the Federal Reserve, the US central bank, decided to increase its benchmark interest rate by 0.25%, raising its funding rate from 1.75% to 2% – its highest level since 2008.

The Federal Reserve Chair said falling unemployment had boosted disposable income and confidence in the US economy, leading to strong growth and increased spending. However, there was a risk the rise in spending would pull inflation up to harmful levels.

However, some consumer groups are worried about the impact the decision could have on households as commercial banks pass on the increase in the funding rate to their customers. Indebted households, especially those with low-incomes, may struggle to repay the higher interest charges on their debts but those with savings accounts could benefit from higher rates. However, new research shows that people on low wages tend not to hold savings accounts but often have large loans to manage.

a) Define *disposable income*. [2]

b) Explain **two** functions, other than taking decisions on interest rates, that a central bank performs. [4]

c) Explain how price inflation can affect the functions of money. [4]

d) Analyse the motives people have for saving rather than spending. [6]

e) Analyse the reasons why some workers are prepared to work for low wages. [6]

f) Discuss the extent to which household spending is influenced by the rate of interest. [8]

## Structured questions (Paper 2, Section B)

2. a) Define *trade union*. [2]

   b) Explain what is meant by 'collective bargaining'. [4]

   c) Analyse how a firm may respond to a request by its workers to increase their wages. [6]

   d) Discuss how two workers in the same country doing very similar jobs can be paid different amounts. [8]

3. a) Define *market structure*. [2]

   b) Explain the main features of a competitive market. [4]

   c) Analyse why two firms in completely distinct industries might decide to merge. [6]

   d) Discuss whether a monopoly is always against the interests of consumers. [8]

4. a) Define *social enterprise*. [2]

   b) Explain the difference between labour-intensive production and capital-intensive production. [4]

   c) Analyse why some firms do not have short-term profit maximization as their main objective. [6]

   d) Discuss whether or not average costs will continue to fall as a firm continues to expand its scale of production. [8]

## 4.1.1 The role of government
## 4.2.1 The macroeconomics aims of government

1. Describe how a government can act as a producer of goods and services in an economy. [4]

.......................................................................................................................

.......................................................................................................................

.......................................................................................................................

.......................................................................................................................

2. Describe how a government can act as an employer in an economy. [4]

.......................................................................................................................

.......................................................................................................................

.......................................................................................................................

.......................................................................................................................

3. Explain the difference between current expenditure and capital expenditure by a government. [2]

.......................................................................................................................

.......................................................................................................................

4. State the **four** main macroeconomic aims of government. [4]

.......................................................................................................................

.......................................................................................................................

.......................................................................................................................

.......................................................................................................................

5. State **two** other objectives a government may have. [2]

.......................................................................................................................

.......................................................................................................................

**E**

Research your own economy. What are the main economic objectives of your government?

## 4.2.2 Possible conflicts between macroeconomic aims

1. Discuss possible conflicts between a government's objectives of increasing employment and keeping the rate of inflation relatively low. [8]

..................................................................................................................

..................................................................................................................

..................................................................................................................

..................................................................................................................

..................................................................................................................

..................................................................................................................

..................................................................................................................

..................................................................................................................

2. Discuss possible conflicts between a government's objectives of reducing inequalities in incomes and encouraging economic growth. [8]

..................................................................................................................

..................................................................................................................

..................................................................................................................

..................................................................................................................

..................................................................................................................

..................................................................................................................

..................................................................................................................

..................................................................................................................

**E**

The government has announced a number of initiatives in an attempt to bring down the level of unemployment in the economy. These include a reduction in both income tax and sales tax and a lowering of interest rates. The aim of these policy measures is to increase the level of total demand in the economy, although the government recognises that there will be a delay in increasing total supply to meet this increased level of demand.

Read this newspaper article and consider if there is likely to be a conflict between the reduction in unemployment and the achievement of other government objectives.

## Key words

*Match economic terms with their definitions*

| | | | | |
|---|---|---|---|---|
| 1 | Public expenditure **D** | A | The sum of consumer expenditure, investment expenditure, public sector expenditure and spending on exports |
| 2 | Current expenditure (by the public sector) | B | Measures used by a government to help it achieve its policy aims |
| 3 | Capital expenditure (by the public sector) | C | Government policy measures that aim to boost the productive capacity and total output of a macroeconomy |
| 4 | Central government | D | Total spending by all government or public sector organizations within a macroeconomy |
| 5 | Gross domestic product | E | Recurrent government spending on consumable items and services within each financial year. It also includes the wages and salaries of public sector workers and transfer payments such as state pensions and welfare payments. |
| 6 | Total demand in a macroeconomy | F | The total value of all final goods and services produced in a macroeconomy in a given year |
| 7 | Government policy instruments | G | The national government of a country or nation state, responsible for planning and decision-making on issues that affect the whole country |
| 8 | Demand-side policies | H | Government investments in long-lived productive assets such as roads, dams, schools, hospitals and other public infrastructure |
| 9 | Supply-side policies | I | Government policy measures used to manage or influence total demand in a macroeconomy |

## Revision summary

*Fill in the missing words and economic terms*

1. The government is a major producer, employer and _ _ _ _ _ _ _ _ in most mixed economies. It also _ _ _ _ _ _ _ _ _ the behaviours of many firms and consumers in different markets to reduce market _ _ _ _ _ _ _ _ and improve market outcomes.

2. Most national governments share similar _ _ _ _ _ _ _ _ _ _ _ _ _ aims for economic growth, for _ _ _ _ employment, for low and stable price _ _ _ _ _ _ _ _ _ and balance of payments stability.

3. Governments will use _ _ _ _ _ _ instruments including public expenditures, taxes, _ _ _ _ _ _ _ _ _ _ _ _ _ and regulations to help them achieve their macroeconomic aims through the impact they have on the actions of producers and consumers.

4. Demand-side policy instruments are used to manage or influence total _ _ _ _ _ _ in a macroeconomy while _ _ _ _ _ - side policy instruments aim to boost its total output and long-run rate of _ _ _ _ _ _ _ growth. Doing so can help to reduce inflationary pressures and _ _ _ _ _ _ _ _ _ _ _ in the economy.

## 4.3.1 Definition of the budget
## 4.3.2 Reasons for government spending

1. Explain the purpose of the budget. [4]

........................................................................................................................

........................................................................................................................

........................................................................................................................

........................................................................................................................

2. Explain the following statement: 'The government is planning for a budget deficit and will need to increase its borrowing to finance it.' [4]

........................................................................................................................

........................................................................................................................

........................................................................................................................

........................................................................................................................

3. Identify and explain **four** reasons for public sector spending in a mixed economy. [8]

........................................................................................................................

........................................................................................................................

........................................................................................................................

........................................................................................................................

........................................................................................................................

........................................................................................................................

........................................................................................................................

........................................................................................................................

**E**

Calculate the budget balance in each of the following countries.

| Country | Public expenditure | Public revenue | Budget balance |
|---------|--------------------|----------------|----------------|
| A | $520 billion | $560 billion | |
| B | $140 billion | $105 billion | |
| C | $35 billion | $35 billion | |

Which country has a budget surplus; budget deficit; balanced budget?

Suggest ways in which a government could reduce its budget deficit.

## 4.3.3 Taxation
## 4.3.4 Principles of taxation

**1.** Define 'the total tax burden' in an economy. [2]

.......................................................................................................................................................

.......................................................................................................................................................


**2.** Explain **two** characteristics of a good tax. [4]

.......................................................................................................................................................

.......................................................................................................................................................

.......................................................................................................................................................

.......................................................................................................................................................


**3.** Explain **two** reasons why a government might impose taxes. [4]

.......................................................................................................................................................

.......................................................................................................................................................

.......................................................................................................................................................

.......................................................................................................................................................


**E**

Use the articles to identify why and how taxes are being used by different governments.

Major hike in taxes expected as government announces boost in healthcare spending

**New plastics tax on the way**
Firms who package their products in unrecyclable plastic will be hit with massive costs under government plans to drive its use 'out of existence'.

The Chinese government has announced a mix of tax cuts and infrastructure spending as it increases efforts to stimulate demand and counteract a weakening economic growth.

Government prepares to cut the lowest rate of income tax to 'reduce inequality and increase the reward to work'.

## 4.3.5 Classification of taxes
## 4.3.6 Impact of taxation

**1.** Explain the difference between a progressive tax and a regressive tax. [4]

..............................................................................................................................

..............................................................................................................................

..............................................................................................................................

..............................................................................................................................

**2.** Using examples, explain the difference between a direct tax and an indirect tax. [4]

..............................................................................................................................

..............................................................................................................................

..............................................................................................................................

..............................................................................................................................

**3.** Explain **three** advantages of direct taxes. [6]

..............................................................................................................................

..............................................................................................................................

..............................................................................................................................

..............................................................................................................................

..............................................................................................................................

..............................................................................................................................

**4.** Explain **three** disadvantages of direct taxes. [6]

..............................................................................................................................

..............................................................................................................................

..............................................................................................................................

..............................................................................................................................

..............................................................................................................................

5. The table below shows the structure of personal income tax in a country.

| Tax-free allowance | Up to $9,999 |
|---|---|
| Income tax rate of 10% | $10,000–$19,999 |
| Income tax rate of 20% | $20,000–$39,999 |
| Income tax rate of 30% | $40,000–$59,999 |
| Income tax rate of 40% | $60,000 and above |

(a) What is the highest marginal rate of tax a person earning $50,000 a year will pay? [1]

..............................................................................................................................................

(b) What average rate of tax will a person earning $50,000 a year pay? Show your calculations. [3]

..............................................................................................................................................

..............................................................................................................................................

..............................................................................................................................................

6. Explain **two** advantages of indirect taxes. [4]

..............................................................................................................................................

..............................................................................................................................................

..............................................................................................................................................

..............................................................................................................................................

7. Explain **two** disadvantages of indirect taxes. [4]

..............................................................................................................................................

..............................................................................................................................................

..............................................................................................................................................

..............................................................................................................................................

**E**

Which of the following taxes is progressive, regressive or proportional?

| Income | TAX A | TAX B | TAX C |
|---|---|---|---|
| | Tax paid | Tax paid | Tax paid |
| $10,000 | $3,000 | $1,000 | 0 |
| $40,000 | $6,000 | $4,000 | $6,000 |
| $100,000 | $10,000 | $10,000 | $15,000 |

## 4.3.7 Definition of fiscal policy
## 4.3.8 Fiscal policy measures
## 4.3.9 Effects of fiscal policy on government macroeconomic aims

**1.** Define *fiscal policy*. [2]

.................................................................................................................................................................

.................................................................................................................................................................

**2.** Explain the difference between an expansionary fiscal policy and a contractionary fiscal policy. [4]

.................................................................................................................................................................

.................................................................................................................................................................

.................................................................................................................................................................

.................................................................................................................................................................

**3.** Analyse how effective fiscal policy instruments may be for managing total demand in an economy. [6]

.................................................................................................................................................................

.................................................................................................................................................................

.................................................................................................................................................................

.................................................................................................................................................................

.................................................................................................................................................................

.................................................................................................................................................................

**E**

Which policy measures highlighted in the following news headlines are expansionary and which ones are contractionary? What impact are they each likely to have on the budget balance?

Government cuts rate of corporation tax

Increase in top rate of income tax designed to reduce inequality

Increase in welfare payments to be paid for by increase in indirect taxes

Government announces boost in infrastructure spending to 'modernise economy and reinvigorate economic growth'

**4.4.1 Definition of monetary policy**
**4.4.2 Monetary policy measures**
**4.4.3 Effects of monetary policy measures on government macroeconomic aims**

1. Define *monetary policy*. [2]

...................................................................................................................................

...................................................................................................................................

2. Explain the difference between an expansionary monetary policy and a contractionary monetary policy. [4]

...................................................................................................................................

...................................................................................................................................

...................................................................................................................................

...................................................................................................................................

3. Analyse how effective monetary policy instruments may be for managing total demand in an economy. [6]

...................................................................................................................................

...................................................................................................................................

...................................................................................................................................

...................................................................................................................................

...................................................................................................................................

**E**

How are monetary policy instruments being used in each case to help achieve different government macroeconomic aims?

The Reserve Bank of India (RBI) has raised key interest rates by a quarter of a percentage point in an attempt to curb double-digit inflation.

Indonesia's central bank cut its benchmark interest rate as falling inflation gives the bank more scope to try to boost economic growth.

**Japanese central bank doubles money supply**

The monetary easing is designed to bring to an end a long spell of deflation which has hindered investment and economic growth in Japan.

1. Identify **four** supply-side policy instruments or measures. [4]

........................................................................................................................................

........................................................................................................................................

........................................................................................................................................

........................................................................................................................................

2. Explain **two** ways a government could use regulations to influence the behaviour of private firms. [4]

........................................................................................................................................

........................................................................................................................................

........................................................................................................................................

........................................................................................................................................

3. Analyse how supply-side policy may be used to influence total supply in an economy. [6]

........................................................................................................................................

........................................................................................................................................

........................................................................................................................................

........................................................................................................................................

........................................................................................................................................

**E**

### Government announces plan to give subsidies to farmers

The government, concerned at the level of malnutrition in the country because many people on low incomes are unable to afford basic food items, has announced that it plans to pay subsidies to farmers.

The subsidies will be used by farmers to reduce their costs of production. The government hopes this will increase farm output and reduce food prices, which it believes will be the most effective way to reduce poverty and malnutrition in the country.

What are likely to be the main benefits and drawbacks of the scheme described in this article?

## Key words

*Match economic terms with their correct definitions*

| | | | |
|---|---|---|---|
| 1 | The budget *O* | A | The percentage of tax payable on each additional $1 or unit of taxable income |
| 2 | Balanced budget | B | The removal or simplification of complex, old or unnecessary legal rules and regulations to reduce their burden on business activity |
| 3 | Budget deficit | C | A tax which takes a lower proportion of income in tax as income rises |
| 4 | Progressive tax | D | Government measures involving changes in the supply of money and/or interest rates in an economy to influence total demand and other macroeconomic conditions |
| 5 | Regressive tax | E | This will occur when a government plans to spend as much as it plans or expects to raise in public revenue in the same year |
| 6 | Proportional tax | F | A direct tax on personal incomes |
| 7 | Direct tax | G | A direct tax on company profits |
| 8 | Indirect tax | H | Government interventions or measures that aim to boost the productive potential of an economy and increase total supply |
| 9 | Income tax | I | A tax which takes a greater proportion of income in tax as income rises |
| 10 | Marginal tax rate | J | A type of tax imposed on and collected from the incomes or wealth of individuals and organizations |
| 11 | Corporation tax | K | A type of tax imposed on good and services. The producers or suppliers of the taxed products are obliged to pay the tax and will therefore pass on much of its burden to consumers by raising the prices of their products |
| 12 | Fiscal policy | L | Government measures that involve the use of taxation and public sector expenditure and which attempt to influence total demand and other macroeconomic conditions |
| 13 | Crowding out | M | A tax which takes the same proportion of income in tax as income rises |
| 14 | Monetary policy | N | This will occur when a government plans to spend more than it plans or expects to raise in public revenue in the same year |
| 15 | Supply-side policies | O | Government plans and estimates for total public sector spending and revenue for the year ahead |
| 16 | Deregulation | P | The displacement of private sector spending by increased public sector spending, financed by increased taxes or public borrowing |

## Revision summary

*Fill in the missing words and economic terms*

1. A government will have a budget deficit if it plans to spend _ _ _ _ than it plans to raise in public revenues in the same year. However, there will be a budget surplus if it plans to spend _ _ _ _ than it expects to raise in public revenues.

2. _ _ _ is by far the most important source of public revenue in most economies.

3. In a _ _ _ _ _ _ _ _ _ _ _ tax system the proportion of income taken in tax rises as income increases. That is, marginal tax rates increase with income. In contrast, with a tax system or tax that is _ _ _ _ _ _ _ _ _ _ _ _, the proportion of income taken in tax falls as income rises.

4. _ _ _ _ _ _ taxes are taken directly from the incomes or wealth of individuals and organizations. That is, the burden of a _ _ _ _ _ _ tax falls on the person or organization responsible for paying it. However, high rates of tax on personal and corporate incomes can _ _ _ _ _ _ incentives for work and enterprise.

5. Taxes imposed on goods and services, such as a sales tax and excise duties, are _ _ _ _ _ _ _ _ _ taxes because their producers or suppliers are responsible for their payment to government. They in turn will raise the prices of their products in order to pass on as much of the tax burden as they can to consumers.

6. A government may cut taxes and increase public expenditure during an economic recession to boost total demand and employment in the economy. However, the use of expansionary _ _ _ _ _ _ policy to increase total demand may result in price inflation if total _ _ _ _ _ _ fails to expand at the same rate.

7. _ _ _ _ _ _ _ _ _ _ _ _ _ _ _ fiscal policy may be required to reduce price inflation. It attempts to reduce total demand in an economy by raising _ _ _ _ _ and cutting public sector spending. However, falling demand may result in higher unemployment and slower or negative economic growth.

8. The main instrument of _ _ _ _ _ _ _ _ policy is the interest rate charged by the central bank for lending money to the banking system in an economy. Raising the interest rate will _ _ _ _ _ _ _ _ the cost of borrowing and _ _ _ _ _ _ the reward to saving. As a result, spending in the economy is likely to fall and should help to reduce inflationary pressures.

9. In contrast, an _ _ _ _ _ _ _ _ _ _ _ _ monetary policy may be followed to boost aggregate demand and employment during an economic recession by cutting interest rates.

10. Increasing total supply in an economy will help to boost employment and incomes while reducing inflationary pressures on market prices. _ _ _ _ _ _ _-_ _ _ _ policies therefore aim to improve the productive potential and total output of an economy by removing barriers to increasing trade, competition and productivity.

## 4.6.1 Measurement of economic growth

1. Define *Gross Domestic Product*. [2]

........................................................................................................................................

........................................................................................................................................

2. Explain **one** of the methods used to calculate the GDP of an economy. [4]

........................................................................................................................................

........................................................................................................................................

........................................................................................................................................

........................................................................................................................................

3. Distinguish between nominal GDP and real GDP. [4]

........................................................................................................................................

........................................................................................................................................

........................................................................................................................................

........................................................................................................................................

4. Explain **two** uses of GDP statistics. [4]

........................................................................................................................................

........................................................................................................................................

........................................................................................................................................

........................................................................................................................................

**E**

In which of the following countries did:

(a) nominal GDP increase the most

(b) real GDP increase the most

(c) real GDP fall

(d) real GDP remain constant?

| Country | % change in nominal GDP over 10 years | % change in CPI over 10 years |
|---------|----------------------------------------|-------------------------------|
| A | 31% | 31% |
| B | 65% | 53% |
| C | 34% | 12% |
| D | 11% | 32% |

## 4.6.2 Definition of economic growth
## 4.6.3 Causes of economic growth

1. Define *economic growth*. [2]

.................................................................................................................................................

.................................................................................................................................................

2. Explain **two** possible causes of economic growth. [4]

.................................................................................................................................................

.................................................................................................................................................

.................................................................................................................................................

.................................................................................................................................................

3. Analyse how an increase in government expenditure can promote economic growth. [6]

.................................................................................................................................................

.................................................................................................................................................

.................................................................................................................................................

.................................................................................................................................................

.................................................................................................................................................

.................................................................................................................................................

**E**

Describe what has happened in the diagram and the possible reasons why.

## 4.6.4 Causes and consequences of recession

**1.** Explain what is meant by the trade, business or economic cycle in a macroeconomy. [4]

.......................................................................................................................................

.......................................................................................................................................

.......................................................................................................................................

.......................................................................................................................................

**2.** Define *recession*. [2]

.......................................................................................................................................

.......................................................................................................................................

**3.** Explain why economists are concerned by the prospect of a recession. [4]

.......................................................................................................................................

.......................................................................................................................................

.......................................................................................................................................

.......................................................................................................................................

**4.** Explain the difference between a 'U-shaped recession' and a 'V-shaped recession'. [4]

.......................................................................................................................................

.......................................................................................................................................

.......................................................................................................................................

.......................................................................................................................................

**E**

The following chart shows the annual percentage change in real GDP in the USA from 2000 to 2015. In which years was the economy in (a) economic recession and (b) recovery?

**Annual change in real GDP (%)**

## 4.6.5 Consequences of economic growth
## 4.6.6 Policies to promote economic growth

1. Explain **two** benefits of an increase in the real GDP of a country. [4]

..................................................................................................................

..................................................................................................................

..................................................................................................................

..................................................................................................................

2. Is economic growth always beneficial? Discuss. [8]

..................................................................................................................

..................................................................................................................

..................................................................................................................

..................................................................................................................

..................................................................................................................

..................................................................................................................

..................................................................................................................

..................................................................................................................

3. Explain **two** policies governments could use to help promote economic growth in their macroeconomies. [4]

..................................................................................................................

..................................................................................................................

..................................................................................................................

..................................................................................................................

**E**

According to the articles, what are some of the problems associated with economic growth?

**How workers can keep up with automation and the demands of the digital economy: train, retrain and retrain again.**

Number of poor people in Africa rising despite faster growth in African economies, finds new report.

Outdoor air pollution has grown by 8% globally in the past five years, with billions of people around the world now exposed to dangerous air, according to new data from more than 3,000 cities compiled by the World Health Organization (WHO).

**By 2050 there will be more waste plastic in our seas than fish, according to a new report.**

## Key words          *Match economic terms with their definitions*

| | | | |
|---|---|---|---|
| 1 | National output E | A | The market value of output less the value of inputs used in the production of that output. It provides a measure of the contribution made by each producer in a national economy and is used in the calculation of GDP |
| 2 | National income | B | A rate of economic growth that can be achieved without causing significant environmental damage and economic problems for future generations |
| 3 | National expenditure | C | A period of very rapid economic expansion during which an economy may 'overheat', i.e. price inflation increases sharply because the aggregate supply of goods and services cannot expand fast enough to meet rising demand |
| 4 | Gross Value Added (GVA) | D | Average income per head or per person. It is a key indicator of the standard of living within an economy |
| 5 | Nominal Gross Domestic Product (GDP) | E | The total market value of all goods and services produced within a national economy in a given period |
| 6 | Real GDP | F | Recurrent fluctuations in the level of economic activity in a national economy between periods of growth and contraction or recession |
| 7 | Economic growth | G | An upturn in the level of economic activity in a national economy following a period of economic recession |
| 8 | Human capital | H | The monetary measure of the market value of all final goods and services produced within a national economy in a given period of time |
| 9 | Economic cycle | I | Nominal or money GDP adjusted for changes in prices. It is therefore a measure of the market value of all final goods and services produced within an economy in a given period of time assuming their prices have remained constant |
| 10 | Economic recession | J | An increase in the real GDP or total output of an economy |
| 11 | Economic recovery | K | The total amount spent on the goods and services produced within a national economy in a given period, equal to the total market value of those goods and services |
| 12 | Economic boom | L | A slowdown in the level of economic activity in a national economy during which total output will often decline, i.e. negative economic growth occurs |
| 13 | Sustainable growth | M | The collective skills, knowledge, experience and abilities of people that contribute to the productive potential of an economy |
| 14 | GDP per capita | N | The total amount of income generated from the production and sale of the total output of goods and services in a national economy in a given period |

## Revision summary

*Fill in the missing words and economic terms*

1. There are three methods which can be used to calculate the Gross Domestic Product (GDP) of an economy. These are known as the income method, the output method and the _ _ _ _ _ _ _ _ _ _ _ method. When GDP has not been adjusted to take into account the effect of inflation, it is known as _ _ _ _ _ _ _ GDP. When it has been adjusted to take into account the effects of inflation, it is known as _ _ _ _ GDP.

2. Economic growth in an economy can be shown in a _ _ _ _ _ _ _ _ _ _ _ curve diagram. When this curve shifts outwards, it means that more can be produced of both goods shown in the diagram.

3. A business or economic cycle can also be known as a _ _ _ _ _ cycle. When economic activity is expanding rapidly, it is known as _ _ _ _ _ _ or expansion. When economic activity is at its peak, it is known as a _ _ _ _. When there is a general slowdown in economic activity, it is known as a recession or a _ _ _ _ _ _ _ _. When there is an upturn in economic activity, it is known as a _ _ _ _ _ _ _ _.

4. Technical _ _ _ _ _ _ _ _ is an important factor in bringing about economic growth. A government could support this by providing tax breaks for firms that undertake research and _ _ _ _ _ _ _ _ _ _ _ or by protecting new inventions from being copied through the issue of _ _ _ _ _ _ _.

5. A recession is defined as _ _ _ _ _ _ _ _ growth in an economy over two successive _ _ _ _ _ _ _ _.

6. A government may attempt to boost total demand during a recession using _ _ _ _ _ _ _ _ _ _ _ _ fiscal and monetary policy measures.

7. However, to achieve _ _ _ _ - _ _ _ economic growth requires an expansion in the productive capability of the economy. A government may need to use _ _ _ _ _ _ - side measures to achieve this. These can involve boosting investments in education, research and development and in modern infrastructure.

## 4.7.1 Definition of employment, unemployment and full employment
## 4.7.2 Changing patterns and level of employment
## 4.7.3 Measurement of unemployment

1. Explain the terms 'full employment' and 'unemployment' and how they can occur at the same time in an economy. [4]

..................................................................................................................................................

..................................................................................................................................................

..................................................................................................................................................

..................................................................................................................................................

2. Describe **two** factors that can affect the labour force participation rate in a country. [4]

..................................................................................................................................................

..................................................................................................................................................

..................................................................................................................................................

..................................................................................................................................................

3. Discuss the main changes that have occurred in the pattern of employment in many economies over the last 50 years. [8]

..................................................................................................................................................

..................................................................................................................................................

..................................................................................................................................................

..................................................................................................................................................

..................................................................................................................................................

..................................................................................................................................................

..................................................................................................................................................

**E**

Research your own economy. Try to find out whether the level of employment is increasing or decreasing in your country. Also, try to find out what have been the main changes in the structure of employment in the country, such as people leaving the primary sector to work in the secondary or the tertiary sector.

## 4.7.4 Causes and types of unemployment
## 4.7.5 Consequences of unemployment

1. Define *unemployment rate.* [2]

.......................................................................................................................................

.......................................................................................................................................

2. Discuss the different possible causes of unemployment. [8]

.......................................................................................................................................

.......................................................................................................................................

.......................................................................................................................................

.......................................................................................................................................

.......................................................................................................................................

.......................................................................................................................................

.......................................................................................................................................

.......................................................................................................................................

3. Discuss if and how a fall in the unemployment rate can benefit a country. [8]

.......................................................................................................................................

.......................................................................................................................................

.......................................................................................................................................

.......................................................................................................................................

.......................................................................................................................................

.......................................................................................................................................

.......................................................................................................................................

.......................................................................................................................................

**E**

> The government has announced that there has been an increase in the level of unemployment in the economy over the past three months. Some of this has been due to weather conditions at this time of the year, especially in relation to employment in the farming and tourism sectors. Some has been due to investment in machinery and equipment, making a number of firms more capital-intensive than they were. A part of the increase is due to a fall in world demand for some of the country's exports. The government has also made it clear that at any time, there will be some people who have left one job and who have not yet started another job.

Read this newspaper article. Identify the different types of unemployment referred to in the article.

## Key words

*Match economic terms with their definitions*

| | | | | |
|---|---|---|---|---|
| 1 | Labour force | *G* | A | The inability of workers to move easily between different occupations due to differences in their skills |
| 2 | Economically active population | | B | A type of employment contract that normally requires the employee to work more than 35 hours per week, often spread over 5 days each week |
| 3 | Labour force participation rate | | C | Temporary unemployment as people change jobs |
| 4 | Full-time employment | | D | Unemployment associated with employees losing jobs they would prefer to keep, for example, due to closure of the firms they work for |
| 5 | Part-time employment | | E | Unemployment caused by falling aggregate demand during an economic downturn or recession |
| 6 | Unemployment rate | | F | Unemployment associated with falling demand for different goods or services at certain times of the year |
| 7 | Frictional unemployment | | G | The working population of a country: people already in employment and those actively seeking employment |
| 8 | Seasonal unemployment | | H | Unemployment caused by the substitution of labour in production processes by advanced capital equipment |
| 9 | Cyclical unemployment | | I | The percentage of a working population that is registered as being without paid employment |
| 10 | Multiplier effect | | J | The labour force or working population of a country: that part of a population that is willing and able to work to undertake productive activities |
| 11 | Structural unemployment | | K | Unemployment associated with people deciding not to work |
| 12 | Regional unemployment | | L | A type of employment contract that normally requires the employee to work fewer hours per week than a full-time employee |
| 13 | Technological unemployment | | M | The percentage of the working age population that are either in work or actively seeking employment |
| 14 | Voluntary unemployment | | N | Unemployment caused by a decline in once major industries |
| 15 | Involuntary unemployment | | O | The inability of workers to easily move location to find work, often due to differences in housing costs and family commitments |
| 16 | Occupational immobility of labour | | P | A term used to describe how small initial changes in consumer, public or investment spending can result in much larger changes in income, output and employment in an economy |
| 17 | Geographic immobility of labour | | Q | A form of structural unemployment that is heavily concentrated in particular areas of a country |

1. When a person loses their job as a result of changes in the different sectors of an economy, it is known as _ _ _ _ _ _ _ _ _ _ unemployment. Sometimes, this can be particularly bad in certain areas of a country, when it is known as _ _ _ _ _ _ _ _ unemployment. Some people are more likely to be unemployed at certain times of the year than at other times and this is known as _ _ _ _ _ _ _ _ unemployment.

2. Some people are unemployed because the economy is going through a difficult stage and fewer people are buying products. This is known as either _ _ _ _ _ _ _ _ _ _ _ _ _ or _ _ _ _ _ _ _ _ unemployment.

3. Other people may become unemployed as a result of a move from labour-intensive production to capital-intensive production and this is known as _ _ _ _ _ _ _ _ _ _ _ _ _ unemployment. Some people may actually be between jobs when the number of people is being calculated and this is known as _ _ _ _ _ _ _ _ _ _ unemployment.

4. The labour force of a country refers to the number of people of _ _ _ _ _ _ _ age who are in work and the number of people who are _ _ _ _ _ _ _ _ seeking work.

5. An increase in unemployment can have disastrous consequences for an economy. The fall in demand for goods and services can lead to further job losses. This is known as a _ _ _ _ _ _ _ _ _ _ _ _ _ _ _ _ _ effect.

6. People may decide not to work for a variety of reasons and this is known as _ _ _ _ _ _ _ _ _ unemployment. However, many workers are unemployed through no fault of their own and this is known as _ _ _ _ _ _ _ _ _ _ _ unemployment.

7. In some countries, some unemployment could exist as a result of a government intervening in labour markets through the introduction of _ _ _ _ _ _ _ wage legislation.

8. Immobility of labour can be a problem in many countries. When workers are unwilling to change jobs by moving to different types of work, this is known as _ _ _ _ _ _ _ _ _ _ _ _ _ immobility of labour. When workers are unwilling to change jobs by moving to different areas of a country, this is known as _ _ _ _ _ _ _ _ _ _ _ _ immobility of labour.

9. Expansionary _ _ _ _ _ _ - side policies may be used by a government to reduce _ _ _ _ _ _ _ _ _ unemployment during a recession. But measures to retrain workers with out-of-date skills and to support new industries will be required to reduce _ _ _ _ _ _ _ _ _ _ unemployment resulting from industrial decline.

## 4.8.1 Definition of inflation
## 4.8.2 Measurement of inflation

**1.** What is meant by an increase in the rate of inflation in an economy? [2]

..................................................................................................................................

..................................................................................................................................

**2.** Explain the difference between 'inflation' and 'hyperinflation'. [4]

..................................................................................................................................

..................................................................................................................................

..................................................................................................................................

..................................................................................................................................

**3.** Explain how a consumer prices index (CPI) is calculated. [4]

..................................................................................................................................

..................................................................................................................................

..................................................................................................................................

..................................................................................................................................

**4.** Describe **two** ways a consumer prices index may be used in an economy. [4]

..................................................................................................................................

..................................................................................................................................

..................................................................................................................................

..................................................................................................................................

**E**

The chart shows the annual rate of price inflation in a country between 2008 and 2016. In which year was the (a) general price level rising at its fastest rate, (b) general price level rising at its slowest rate, and (c) general price level at its highest?

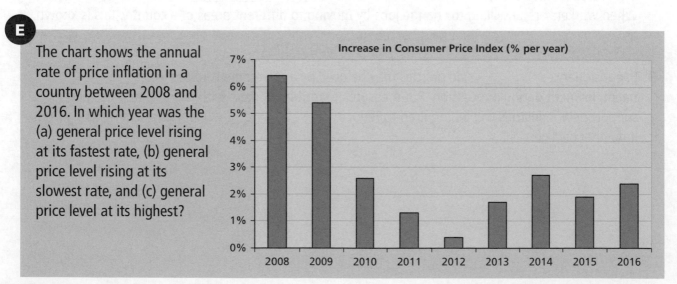

Increase in Consumer Price Index (% per year)

## 4.8.3 Causes of inflation

1. Explain the following statement: 'Inflation is caused by too much money chasing too few goods'. [4]

..................................................................................................................................................

..................................................................................................................................................

..................................................................................................................................................

..................................................................................................................................................

2. Explain the meaning and causes of a demand-pull inflation. [6]

..................................................................................................................................................

..................................................................................................................................................

..................................................................................................................................................

..................................................................................................................................................

..................................................................................................................................................

..................................................................................................................................................

3. Explain the meaning and causes of a cost-push inflation. [6]

..................................................................................................................................................

..................................................................................................................................................

..................................................................................................................................................

..................................................................................................................................................

..................................................................................................................................................

..................................................................................................................................................

**E**

Look at the news headlines and articles below. What cause or type of inflation does each one describe?

**CPI in lowest rise for 17 years**

Australia's inflation rate has fallen to its lowest level for 17 years. Intense competition among supermarkets is one factor. The other factor has been the falling cost of many imported goods.

**Increase in fuel prices pushes up UK inflation rate to 0.6%**

**Indonesian inflation on the rise**

The increase in the monthly inflation rate in July to 0.7 percent from 0.6 percent in June was caused mainly by an increase in spending by the end of Ramadan (the Islamic fasting month) and Idul Fitri, according to the Minister for the Economy.

## 4.8.4 Consequences of inflation
## 4.8.5 Policies to control inflation

1. Explain how price inflation affects the value of money. [4]

..................................................................................................................................................

..................................................................................................................................................

..................................................................................................................................................

..................................................................................................................................................

2. Analyse the reasons why maintaining low and stable inflation is an important goal for many governments and central banks. [6]

..................................................................................................................................................

..................................................................................................................................................

..................................................................................................................................................

..................................................................................................................................................

..................................................................................................................................................

3. Analyse the use and effectiveness of different policy measures that may be used by goverments to control inflation in their macroeconomies. [6]

..................................................................................................................................................

..................................................................................................................................................

..................................................................................................................................................

..................................................................................................................................................

..................................................................................................................................................

**E**

### Who gains and who loses with inflation?

Inflation is generally regarded as something that is essentially negative. This is because an increase in the general level of prices in an economy reduces the real value, i.e. the purchasing power, of money.

However, it must also be remembered that inflation can have positive consequences for some people. For example, a person who has borrowed money will make that debt smaller in real terms, so while savers lose as a result of inflation, borrowers gain.

Who is likely to benefit, and who is likely to suffer, as a result of inflation in an economy?

## 4.8.6 Deflation

1. Explain the difference between deflation and disinflation in an economy. [4]

..................................................................................................................................

..................................................................................................................................

..................................................................................................................................

..................................................................................................................................

2. Explain **two** possible causes of deflation. [4]

..................................................................................................................................

..................................................................................................................................

..................................................................................................................................

..................................................................................................................................

3. Discuss whether falling prices in an economy are beneficial or not. [8]

..................................................................................................................................

..................................................................................................................................

..................................................................................................................................

..................................................................................................................................

..................................................................................................................................

..................................................................................................................................

..................................................................................................................................

**E**

Look at the following table. In which year was there deflation?

| Year | CPI |
|------|-----|
| 2013 | 100 |
| 2014 | 108 |
| 2015 | 102 |
| 2016 | 106 |

## Key words

*Match economic terms with their definitions*

| | | | |
|---|---|---|---|
| 1 | Inflation  **M** | **A** | An increase in the general level of prices in an economy due to a fall in the exchange rate and/or increases in prices of imported products |
| 2 | Hyperinflation | **B** | Inflation caused by total demand in an economy exceeding and rising at a faster rate than total supply |
| 3 | Consumer prices index | **C** | The income of an individual or household after taking into consideration the effects of inflation on its purchasing power |
| 4 | Base year | **D** | Rampant or runaway inflation in which prices rise so quickly that money becomes almost worthless |
| 5 | Indexation | **E** | A prolonged period of deflation, usually over many years, in which prices continue to fall resulting in many serious economic problems |
| 6 | Stagflation | **F** | The first year in a price index. In this year the weighted average price level is normally set to 100 |
| 7 | Demand-pull inflation | **G** | A measure of changes in the weighted average price level of a basket of consumer goods and services purchased by a 'typical' household |
| 8 | Cost-push inflation | **H** | Increasing certain payments, such as welfare payments or public pensions, at the same rate as inflation so that their real value or purchasing power is maintained |
| 9 | Wage-price spiral | **I** | An economic situation in which both the inflation rate and unemployment rate in an economy are both high or rise together |
| 10 | Imported inflation | **J** | A fall in the general level of prices in an economy |
| 11 | Real income | **K** | A fall in the inflation rate in an economy |
| 12 | Nominal income | **L** | A situation in which rising prices cause workers to demand higher nominal wages, which in turn results in rising cost-push inflation and further demands for higher nominal wages and so on |
| 13 | Deflation | **M** | A sustained increase in the general level of prices in an economy |
| 14 | Disinflation | **N** | Inflation caused by an increase in production costs |
| 15 | Malign deflation | **O** | The cash or monetary income of an individual or household |

## Revision summary

*Fill in the missing words and economic terms*

1. Changes in the general level of prices in an economy over a period of time can be measured through changes in a consumer _ _ _ _ _ _  _ _ _ _ _. The changes in prices are measured in relation to the average level of prices in a _ _ _ _ year which is given the index value of 100.

2. Changes in the prices of a selection of goods and services purchased by a typical household, known as a _ _ _ _ _ _ of products, are recorded and each of these products is given a _ _ _ _ _ _ _ _ _ to reflect the relative importance of expenditure on these products.

3. When there is a general and sustained increase in the general level of prices in an economy over a period of time, it is known as _ _ _ _ _ _ _ _ _. When the rate of increase in the general price level is high, damaging confidence in the currency, it is known as _ _ _ _ _ _ _ _ _ _ _ _ _ _ _.

4. When prices rise, but at a slower rate than before, it is known as _ _ _ _ _ _ _ _ _ _ _ _. When there is a general decrease in the general level of prices in an economy, it is known as _ _ _ _ _ _ _ _ _.

5. In many economies, certain payments are linked to the country's inflation rate. This process is known as _ _ _ _ _ _ _ _ _ _.

6. When spending in an economy is greater than the ability of that economy to supply what is required, and the general level of prices rise, this is known as _ _ _ _ _ _  _ _ _ _ inflation. When inflation is caused by increases in wages and other payments for factors of production, above any increase in the productivity of the factors, this is known as _ _ _ _  _ _ _ _ inflation.

7. Price inflation erodes the purchasing power or real value of _ _ _ _ _. Living standards for many people, especially those with low or fixed incomes, will fall.

8. The _ _ _ _ value of savings will also fall if the rate of price inflation is _ _ _ _ than the rate of interest.

9. Many governments have an inflation _ _ _ _ _ _. They use their policy instruments to keep it at a low and stable level. This is because a high or rising inflation creates economic uncertainty and hardship, and imposes additional costs on firms.

10. A government may tighten or _ _ _ _ _ _ _ its fiscal and monetary policies to reduce a _ _ _ _ _ _ _ _ _ _ inflation. Inflationary pressures may also be reduced by supply-side measures to expand total output and to encourage more competition between firms.

11. A sustained fall in the average level of prices in an economy may also be damaging as consumers delay their spending, stocks accumulate and firms are forced to cut back production and employment in response. As a result, household incomes and consumer demand continue to fall. These are features of a _ _ _ _ _ _ deflation.

It is important to be able to calculate the rate of inflation in a country and the first question focuses on how this figure can be calculated from data on the percentage of expenditure on different categories, the weighting of each expenditure category and the increase in price of the different categories.

It is also important to distinguish between the rate of growth of nominal GDP and real GDP. If the rate of increase of nominal GDP is exactly equal to a country's inflation rate, then there has been no real growth; all of the growth can be explained by the increase in the value of what has been produced as a result of price increases. There has been no actual economic growth. The second question is concerned with this distinction between nominal and real growth.

It is not only through data that economic growth in a country can be demonstrated. It can also be shown through a shift of a production possibility curve. The third question is concerned with how economic growth can be shown on a production possibility curve. It needs to be stressed that a movement from within a production possibility curve to a point on a production possibility curve does not show economic growth.

Although it is possible to draw the long-term growth rate of an economy as a straight line, it actually goes through a series of stages or fluctuations. This is known as an economic or business or trade cycle. These stages can be described as growth, boom, recession, slump and recovery. The fourth question is concerned with how these different stages of the economic cycle can be shown in a diagram.

1. Calculate the rate of inflation in a country, using the information provided. [2]

| Expenditure category | Percentage of expenditure | Weighting | Increase in price since base year |
|---|---|---|---|
| Food | 50 | 5 | 20% |
| Clothing | 20 | 2 | 10% |
| Transport | 20 | 2 | 10% |
| Other products | 10 | 1 | 20% |
| Total | 100 | 10 | |

.........................................................................................................................................................

.........................................................................................................................................................

2. Calculate the real GDP growth rate of a country, using the information provided. [2]

| Average annual rate of increase of nominal GDP | 4.75% |
|---|---|
| Average annual rate of inflation | 2.15% |

.........................................................................................................................................................

.........................................................................................................................................................

3. Look at the diagram below. Indicate where the following stages can be shown on the economic cycle: growth, boom, recession, slump and recovery. [5]

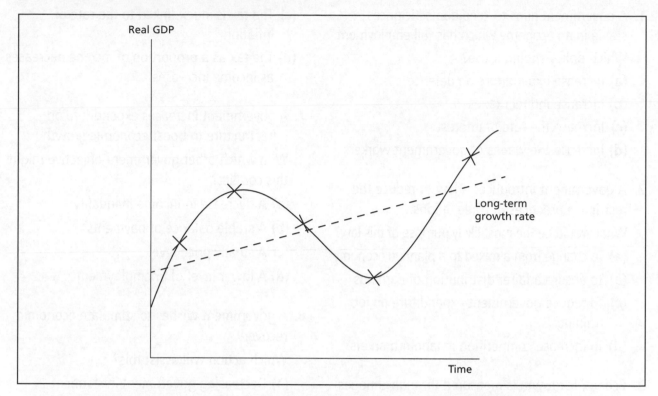

4.

| Country | Average annual rate of economic growth in the last five years |
|---------|---------------------------------------------------------------|
| Brazil | 3.1% |
| Chile | 4.0% |
| Cuba | 5.8% |
| Egypt | 3.2% |
| Ethiopia | 10.9% |
| Libya | −0.5% |
| Malaysia | 4.3% |
| Nigeria | 6.7% |
| Qatar | 14.1% |
| Slovenia | 1.4% |

(a) Which country experienced the fastest rate of economic growth? [1]

..............................................................................................................................................

(b) Which country experienced the slowest rate of economic growth? [1]

..............................................................................................................................................

(c) Which country experienced a shrinking economy? [1]

..............................................................................................................................................

## Multiple choice questions (Paper 1)

*Tick or circle the correct answers*

1. A government aims to keep domestic prices stable in an economy which has full employment.

   Which policy should it use?

   (a) Increase expenditure on defence

   (b) Increase indirect taxes

   (c) Increase the rate of interest

   (d) Increase the wages of government workers

2. A government introduces a law to reduce the restrictive practices of trade unions.

   What would be the most likely purpose of this law?

   (a) To change from a mixed to a planned economy

   (a) To ensure a fairer distribution of earnings

   (c) To reduce government expenditure on job training

   (d) To increase competition in labour markets

3. Economic growth is measured through changes in the:

   (a) Balance of payments

   (b) Distribution of income

   (c) Gross Domestic Product

   (d) Level of prices

4. Which is an example of monetary policy?

   (a) A decrease in interest rates

   (b) A decrease in public expenditure

   (c) An increase in taxation

   (d) The privatization of an industry

5. Which is a supply-side policy?

   (a) Improving education and training

   (b) Reducing direct taxation

   (c) Increasing the money supply

   (d) Raising interest rates

6. A tax is regressive when:

   (a) Some goods have a lower rate of tax than others

   (b) The tax is levied on incomes rather than goods and services

   (c) The tax is index-linked to the rate of inflation

   (d) The tax as a proportion of income decreases as income increases

7. A government increases expenditure on infrastructure to boost economic growth.

   With which other government objective might this conflict?

   (a) A decrease in income inequality

   (b) A stable balance of payments

   (c) A steady price level

   (d) A lower level of unemployment

8. A government wishes to stimulate economic recovery.

   Which action will assist this?

   (a) Decreasing government investment

   (b) Increasing indirect taxation

   (c) Decreasing direct taxation

   (d) Increasing interest rates

9. Which is an example of fiscal policy?

   (a) An increase in the money supply

   (b) Moving from a flexible to a fixed exchange rate system

   (c) Leaving interest rates unchanged

   (d) A reduction in taxation

10. The table shows a government's receipts from taxation.

| | $m |
|---|---|
| tobacco duties | 10 |
| company profits tax | 100 |
| import tariffs | 75 |
| income tax | 400 |
| inheritance tax | 10 |
| Value Added Tax | 200 |

What is the total amount of revenue raised by indirect taxes?

(a) $95m          (c) $295m

(b) $200m         (d) $510m

Questions 11–13 are based on the following data.

| Country | Consumer Prices Index (CPI) Base year | CPI End of year 1 | CPI End of year 2 |
|---------|---------------------------------------|-------------------|-------------------|
| A | 100 | 105 | 112 |
| B | 100 | 110 | 121 |
| C | 100 | 102 | 103 |
| D | 100 | 101 | 97 |

11. Which country experienced an increase in inflation?

12. Which country experienced a period of disinflation?

13. Which country experienced a period of deflation?

14. In 2015, the weight applied to food was reduced in the calculation of the consumer prices index in the UK. What does this change indicate?

    (a) The average price of food had increased in 2015

    (b) Spending on food by consumers as a proportion of their total expenditure had fallen

    (c) The quality of food had increased

    (d) The government reduced the number of shops it collected food price data from

15. Which of the following is most likely to contribute to a demand-pull inflation?

    (a) A decrease in income tax

    (b) A decrease in the exchange rate

    (c) An increase in the costs of raw materials

    (d) An increase in interest charges

16. Who will be made worse off during a period of deflation?

    (a) People with fixed incomes

    (b) Debtors (borrowers)

    (c) Lenders (creditors)

    (d) Savers

17. Between 2008 and 2010, many national economies experienced a deep economic recession. What type of unemployment is most likely to rise during an economic recession?

    (a) Structural

    (b) Frictional

    (c) Cyclical

    (d) Voluntary

18. How is economic growth measured?

    (a) By an increase in aggregate demand

    (b) By an increase in output

    (c) By an increase in profits

    (d) By an increase in wages

19. Which one of the following countries experienced the most growth in its real GDP over the 10-year period?

| Country | 10-year average annual growth in nominal GDP (%) | 10-year annual average inflation rate (%) |
|---------|--------------------------------------------------|-------------------------------------------|
| A | 3.5 | 2.0 |
| B | 5.0 | 2.9 |
| C | 7.1 | 12.6 |
| D | 10.2 | 9.3 |

20. Which one of the following changes identifies an economic recession?

    (a) A fall in the Consumer Prices Index

    (b) A fall in cyclical unemployment

    (c) A fall in the real value of money

    (d) A fall in total output

1.

# The government is facing an increase in both the inflation rate and the unemployment rate!

The government is concerned that the economy is facing an increase in both inflation and unemployment at the same time, a situation known as stagflation. Output in the country has grown by 8.7% in the past year. Much of this, however, has been due to the increase in prices, with inflation running at 7.8% over the past year. The government is worried about the possible consequences of a high rate of inflation and is concerned that if the rate of inflation continues to rise significantly, it could lead to a situation of hyperinflation.

The increase in unemployment has been largely of two kinds. Firstly, frictional unemployment leads to people taking much longer between leaving one job and obtaining another, partly because of the relatively high level of transfer payments paid to the unemployed and partly because of the lack of information about job vacancies in different parts of the country. Secondly, there is seasonal unemployment, especially in the agriculture and tourism sectors of the economy. The government is also concerned about the consequences of a high rate of unemployment, especially if the country experiences a recession.

a) Calculate the 'real' rate of growth of output in the country over the past year. [2]

b) Define *hyperinflation*. [2]

c) Discuss why the government is concerned about the consequences of a high rate of inflation. [6]

d) Distinguish between the causes of frictional unemployment and of seasonal unemployment. [4]

e) Discuss why the government is concerned about the consequences of a high rate of unemployment. [6]

f) Define *recession*. [2]

g) Discuss whether a low inflation rate is always beneficial in an economy. [8]

## Structured questions (Paper 2, Section B)

2. a) Define *inflation*. [2]

   b) Explain why an increase in aggregate demand in an economy could lead to inflation. [4]

   c) Analyse the potential usefulness of government measures to influence the patterns and levels of employment in an economy. [6]

   d) Discuss whether a government should always be concerned about the consequences of deflation. [8]

3. a) Define *Gross Domestic Product* (GDP). [2]

   b) Explain why tax revenues will fall during an economic recession. [4]

   c) Analyse how an increase in the rate of interest could increase unemployment in an economy.

   d) Discuss whether the consequences of economic growth are always positive. [8]

4. a) Define *economic growth*. [2]

   b) Explain why a government would want to encourage the consumption of merit goods. [4]

   c) Analyse the use of fiscal policy measures to control the rate of inflation. [6]

   d) Discuss whether there will always be a conflict between government economic aims. [8]

## 5.1.1 Differences in economic development between countries

1. Explain what is meant by economic development. [4]

   ....................................................................................................................................................
   ....................................................................................................................................................
   ....................................................................................................................................................
   ....................................................................................................................................................

2. Describe **two** characteristics of a developing economy. [4]

   ....................................................................................................................................................
   ....................................................................................................................................................
   ....................................................................................................................................................
   ....................................................................................................................................................

3. Describe **three** reasons for the relatively low economic development of some countries. [6]

   ....................................................................................................................................................
   ....................................................................................................................................................
   ....................................................................................................................................................
   ....................................................................................................................................................
   ....................................................................................................................................................
   ....................................................................................................................................................

Discuss how the relative importance of different productive sectors in a developing country is likely to change over time as its economy develops.

## 5.2.1 Indicators of living standards
## 5.2.2 Comparing living standards and income distribution

**1.** Define *GDP per capita*. [2]

..........................................................................................................................................................

..........................................................................................................................................................

**2.** GDP per capita is one of three measures of living standards and economic development combined into a single composite indicator called the Human Development Index (HDI). What other **two** measures are also used in the HDI? [4]

..........................................................................................................................................................

..........................................................................................................................................................

..........................................................................................................................................................

..........................................................................................................................................................

**3.** Discuss whether an increase in a country's GDP will always reduce poverty in that country. [8]

..........................................................................................................................................................

..........................................................................................................................................................

..........................................................................................................................................................

..........................................................................................................................................................

..........................................................................................................................................................

..........................................................................................................................................................

..........................................................................................................................................................

**E** The table below lists a number of human and economic development indicators. Suggest which ones are likely to score relatively 'high' or relatively 'low' in a developed economy and one of the least developed economies in the world.

| Development indicator | Developed economy | Least developed economy |
|---|---|---|
| GDP per capita ($) | | |
| Population living on less than $2 per day | | |
| Life expectancy from birth (years) | | |
| Adult literacy rate (%) | | |
| Children completing primary education (%) | | |
| Population without access to safe water supplies (%) | | |
| Prevalence of underweight children under 5 years (%) | | |
| Fertility rate (total births per female 15–44 years) | | |
| Hospital beds (per 1,000 people) | | |
| Access to electricity (% of population) | | |
| Secure internet servers (per 1 million people) | | |

## 5.3.1 Definition of absolute and relative poverty
## 5.3.2 The causes of poverty

**1.** Define *absolute poverty*. [2]

..................................................................................................................................................

..................................................................................................................................................

**2.** Define *relative poverty*. [2]

..................................................................................................................................................

..................................................................................................................................................

**3.** Discuss whether GDP per head (or per capita) is the best way to compare living standards in different countries. [8]

..................................................................................................................................................

..................................................................................................................................................

..................................................................................................................................................

..................................................................................................................................................

..................................................................................................................................................

..................................................................................................................................................

..................................................................................................................................................

**E**

### Government concerned by the increase in poverty in the country!

The government has expressed its concern about the increase in the extent of poverty in the country over the past five years. It has stated that there has been an increase in the number of people who have been unable to afford basic necessities and an increase in the number of people having to live on less than $1 a day.

Read this newspaper article and consider whether the poverty described is absolute or relative.

## Revision summary

*Fill in the missing words and economic terms*

1. A developed economy has a relatively _ _ _ _ level of economic development. A less-developed or _ _ _ _ _ _ _ _ _ _ economy has a relatively _ _ _ level of economic development.

2. _ _ _ _ _ _ _ _ _ _ _ _, or average income per person, is a commonly used measure of the level of economic development and living standards in a country. However, it is narrow measure of living standards and is easily distorted if the _ _ _ _ _ _ distribution is very unequal in a country.

3. A developing economy is usually characterized by relatively _ _ _ GDP per head, whereas a developed economy is characterized by relatively _ _ _ _ GDP per head.

4. A developing country is usually characterized by an overdependence on _ _ _ _ _ _ _ _ _ _ _ and other primary industries to provide jobs and incomes, a lack of _ _ _ _ _ _ _ and low levels of _ _ _ _ _ _ _ _ _ in infrastructure, education and healthcare.

5. Other measures of the level of human and economic development are the adult _ _ _ _ _ _ _ _ rate, life _ _ _ _ _ _ _ _ _ _ from birth, _ _ _ _ _ _ _ _ _ of different consumer goods and the proportion of the population with access to safe water supplies. All these measures will tend to be much _ _ _ _ _ in a developing country when compared to a developed country.

6. The extent of poverty in a country can be measured in two ways. The extent of _ _ _ _ _ _ _ _ poverty is usually measured by the number of people living below a certain income threshold who are unable to afford basic necessities, such as food, water, education, healthcare and shelter. In contrast, _ _ _ _ _ _ _ poverty is usually measured by how much a person's or household's income falls below the average income per person in the economy. This means they will have fewer resources than others in the same society.

7. A government may use _ _ _ _ _ _ _ _ _ _ _ _ taxation to help reduce relative poverty in an economy. Revenues raised from taxes may also be used to reduce unemployment and to provide affordable housing, income support and welfare services to poorer households.

8. The governments of many of the least developed economies in the world often lack the resources needed to reduce poverty and to improve _ _ _ _ _ and _ _ _ _ _ _ _ _ development in their countries. They may require help from other countries and international organizations in the form of _ _ _ _ _ _ _ _ or direct foreign aid.

9. Overseas aid can take many forms including the provision of food, technical assistance and financial help including loans, grants and the full or partial cancellation of external _ _ _ _ .

## 5.4.1 The factors that affect population growth
## 5.4.2 Reasons for different rates of population growth in different countries

1. Define *birth rate*. [2]

   .........................................................................................................................................

   .........................................................................................................................................

2. Define *death rate*. [2]

   .........................................................................................................................................

   .........................................................................................................................................

3. Define *net migration*. [2]

   .........................................................................................................................................

   .........................................................................................................................................

4. Describe what is meant by a 'natural increase in the population of a country'. [4]

   .........................................................................................................................................

   .........................................................................................................................................

   .........................................................................................................................................

   .........................................................................................................................................

5. Discuss why the rate of population growth in one country may be different to that of another country. [6]

   .........................................................................................................................................

   .........................................................................................................................................

   .........................................................................................................................................

   .........................................................................................................................................

   .........................................................................................................................................

   .........................................................................................................................................

**E**

Research your own economy. Try to find out what the population of your country is. Consider whether the size of the population is declining, staying about the same or rising. Think about the possible reasons for any changes in population size and the effects it may be having on the economy of your country.

## 5.4.3 The effects of changes in the size and structure of population on different countries

1. Describe the changes that are most likely to occur as a country becomes more developed in:

   (a) the occupational structure and

   (b) the geographical distribution of its population. [4]

........................................................................................................................

........................................................................................................................

........................................................................................................................

........................................................................................................................

2. Analyse the problems and consequences of population change for developing countries. [6]

........................................................................................................................

........................................................................................................................

........................................................................................................................

........................................................................................................................

........................................................................................................................

........................................................................................................................

3. State what is meant by an ageing population and explain why it is regarded as a problem. [6]

........................................................................................................................

........................................................................................................................

........................................................................................................................

........................................................................................................................

........................................................................................................................

........................................................................................................................

**E**

| Country | % of population under 15 | % of population over 60 | Average male life expectancy | % employed in agriculture | % of urban population |
|---|---|---|---|---|---|
| Finland | 16.4% | 26.3% | 78.1 years | 3% | 84.2% |
| Vietnam | 22.7% | 9.6% | 72.2 years | 18% | 33.6% |

Outline the main differences in the structure of the populations of Finland and Vietnam.

## Key words

*Match economic terms with their definitions*

| | | | |
|---|---|---|---|
| 1 | Overpopulation | A | The difference between a country's birth rate and death rate |
| 2 | Dependent population | B | A graph showing the age–sex distribution of a given population |
| 3 | Dependency ratio | C | A population that is the perfect size for a country to enable it to use its available resources to maximize output per head |
| 4 | Optimum population | D | The dependent population as a proportion of the working population. It measures how many people on average each person in the labour force must support in the population through their productive activity |
| 5 | Natural rate of increase in population | E | The average number of children born to women of childbearing age |
| 6 | Fertility rate | F | The difference between the number of people leaving a country to live overseas and the number of people arriving to live in that country in the same period |
| 7 | Birth rate | G | That part of a population who are not economically active and therefore rely on others to produce the goods and services they consume |
| 8 | Death rate | H | How people are spread out over a given area, i.e. where they live |
| 9 | Net migration | I | When the population of an area or country greatly exceeds the amount of available food, water, space and other available resources needed |
| 10 | Age distribution | J | A measure of the average number of people per square kilometre or mile of land space |
| 11 | Ageing population | K | An excess of males or females in a population |
| 12 | Population pyramid | L | The number of live births per 1,000 people in a population each year |
| 13 | Sex distribution | M | Term used to describe the increasing average age of a population within a country due to rising life expectancy and/or a declining birth rate |
| 14 | Gender imbalance | N | The number of deaths per 1,000 people in a population per year |
| 15 | Geographic distribution | O | The percentage of the working population of a country in each industrial sector |
| 16 | Population density | P | The percentage of the total population, or the population of each sex, at each age level |
| 17 | Occupational distribution | Q | The relative proportions of males and females in a population |

1. The world population is expected to grow to 9.8 billion by 2050 due to high _ _ _ _ _ rates and _ _ _ _ _ _ _ death rates, especially in many _ _ _ _ _ _ _ _ _ _ countries. Population growth increases pressure on scarce resources, especially on water supplies and land for housing, food production and industry.

2. A country or region is considered _ _ _ _ _ _ _ _ _ _ _ _ _ if it has too few resources to adequately support its population.

3. The _ _ _ _ _ _ _ _ population in an economy supports the _ _ _ _ _ _ _ _ _ population. Dependency ratios are rising in many countries. This is the result of high _ _ _ _ _ rates in many developing countries and low _ _ _ _ rates in many developed countries. As a result there is a growing number of older people in many _ _ _ _ _ _ _ _ _ countries.

4. A natural increase in a population occurs when the _ _ _ _ _ rate in a country exceeds its _ _ _ _ _ rate.

5. Birth rates remain high in many _ _ _ _ _ _ _ _ _ _ _ countries. In contrast, birth rates have fallen significantly over time in most _ _ _ _ _ _ _ _ _ _ countries as living standards and _ _ _ _ _ _ participation in their labour forces have increased.

6. Death rates also remain high in many of the least developed countries. This is due to a lack of healthcare and often because of famines and wars. However, vaccination programmes and improved access to medicines are helping to reduce death rates including infant mortality rates. Combined with high birth rates this has _ _ _ _ _ _ _ _ _ population growth in many of these countries.

7. The population of a country can also grow due to net _ _ _ _ _ _ _ _ _ _ _ _ _ _. There has been an increase in the number of people migrating from less developed economies to more developed economies in search of higher living standards and incomes. This is depleting the skilled labour force in many developing countries.

8. The _ _ _ _ _ _ _ _ _ _distribution of a population shows where people live. Most people, almost 90% of the world population, live in _ _ _ _ _ _ _ _ _ _ _ countries. This places significant pressure on scarce resources in these countries.

9. Over half the world's population now lives in urban areas. The movement of people from _ _ _ _ _ areas to urban areas is called _ _ _ _ _ _ _ _ _ _ _ _ . This is occurring rapidly in many developing countries as they become more _ _ _ _ _ _ _ _ _ _ _ _ _ _ _. It has increased the production of goods and services and raised living standards but it has also increased pressure on their scarce resources and problems of congestion and pollution.

It is important to be able to calculate the change of population in a country and the first question focuses on how this figure can be calculated from data on the number of live births in a year, the number of deaths in a year (these two figures enable the natural change in population to be calculated), the number of immigrants in a year and the number of emigrants in a year (these two figures enable the net migration to be calculated).

It is also important to be able to calculate the annual population growth of a country from data provided. The second question is concerned with this calculation.

The population structure of countries can be contrasted through diagrams. In particular, a population pyramid can be used to display information about the age distribution and the gender distribution of a country. The third question is concerned with a population pyramid of a developing country and the fourth question is concerned with a population pyramid of a developed country.

1. Calculate the change in population of this country, using the information provided. [2]

| Number of live births in a year | 2,423,864 |
|---|---|
| Number of deaths in a year | 1,896,452 |
| Number of immigrants in a year | 665,890 |
| Number of emigrants in a year | 431,892 |

....................................................................................................................

....................................................................................................................

2. Calculate the annual population growth of a country, using the information provided. [2]

| Population at the beginning of the year | 50 million |
|---|---|
| Population at the end of the year | 55 million |

....................................................................................................................

....................................................................................................................

3. The first diagram shows a population pyramid that is typical of a developing country. In the second box, draw the population pyramid for a developed country. [4]

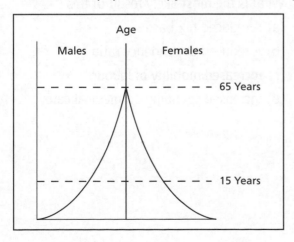
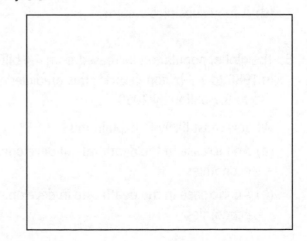

## Multiple choice questions (Paper 1)

1. Which of the following is most likely to be found in a developed economy and not in a developing economy?

   (a) A small leisure and entertainment sector

   (b) A small average family size

   (c) A small number of old people

   (d) A small number of professional people

2. What is Gross Domestic Product (GDP) divided by to calculate GDP per head?

   (a) The total population

   (b) The working population

   (c) The dependent population

   (d) The adult population

3. What is most likely to be an indicator that an economy is developed rather than a developing economy?

   (a) A large tertiary sector

   (b) A high birth rate

   (c) A lack of capital-intensive production

   (d) A low level of adult literacy

4. An effective way of reducing relative poverty in a country is:

   (a) A progressive tax system

   (b) A proportional tax system

   (c) A regressive tax system

   (d) A food subsidies system

5. The global population increased from 4.4 billion in 1980 to 7.3 billion in 2015. It is predicted to rise to 9.7 billion by 2050.

   What is most likely to explain this?

   (a) An increase in the death rate in developed economies

   (b) An increase in the death rate in developing economies

   (c) An increase in the birth rate in developing economies

   (d) An increase in migration from developing to developed economies

6. Most developing economies have relatively more poor people than developed economies.

   What is the reason for this?

   (a) Developing economies have much higher fertility rates

   (b) Migrants from developing economies cannot work in developed economies

   (c) The natural rate of increase in population is lower in developing economies

   (d) There is an ageing population in many developing economies

7. What combination of changes in the birth rate and death rate is most likely to increase the dependency ratio in a country?

   |   | Birth rate | Death rate |
   |---|------------|------------|
   | A | Increase   | Increase   |
   | B | Increase   | Decrease   |
   | C | Decrease   | Increase   |
   | D | Decrease   | Decrease   |

8. The average age of the population is rising in many developed countries.

   What is the most likely result of this?

   (a) A reduced tax base

   (b) A reduced dependency ratio

   (c) Increased mobility of labour

   (d) Increased spending on medical care

1.

## The government aims to try to reduce the extent of poverty in the country

A country has many of the characteristics of a developing economy and is concerned about the extent of absolute poverty, especially in the rural areas.

The country's government has decided to take a number of policy initiatives in an attempt to reduce the extent of this poverty. Subsidies will be given to a number of producers, especially in the agriculture industry, as a way of keeping down the prices of essential food items. Also, the government has decided to increase the benefits that are given to poorer people. The government has also decided to increase the minimum wage that is paid to workers.

One problem that the country is facing is a rapid increase in population. Many couples have decided to have more children, increasing the birth rate, and the healthcare provision in the country has improved in the last 20 years, decreasing the birth rate. There has also been an increase of net migration into the country. The government is concerned that the size of the country's population is now above its optimum size.

There is some occupational mobility of labour, as workers have moved from the primary sector to the secondary and tertiary sectors, but this mobility has not been as great as had been hoped. The government has decided to try to make it easier for workers to move from one sector of the economy to another as it is thought that this will reduce the rate of unemployment and take some people out of poverty.

One feature of the movement of labour that has taken place so far is that as workers have moved from the rural to the urban areas of the country, this has created a number of problems in the urban areas.

a) Define a *developing country*. [2]

b) Describe the main characteristics of a developing economy. [4]

c) Define *absolute poverty*. [2]

d) Discuss how likely the government's policy initiatives to reduce poverty are to be effective. [6]

e) Define *net migration*. [2]

f) Explain why the government is concerned that the size of the country's population is above its optimum size. [4]

g) Describe how the government could try to make it easier for workers to move from one sector of the economy to another. [4]

h) Discuss the possible problems that could occur in urban areas as more people move there. [6]

2. a) Define *birth rate*. [2]

   b) Explain why people may migrate from one country to another. [4]

   c) Analyse why many countries are experiencing an ageing population. [6]

   d) Discuss whether the consequences of an ageing population are always negative. [8]

3. a) Define *relative poverty*. [2]

   b) Explain what is meant by economic development. [4]

   c) Analyse why standards of living may differ within a country. [6]

   d) Discuss whether an increase in a country's standard of living will always lead to an increase in its quality of life. [8]

## 6.1.1 Definition of globalization
## 6.1.2 Specialization at a national level
## 6.1.3 Advantages and disadvantages of specialization at a national level

1. Using examples, explain what is meant by regional or national specialization. [4]

...........................................................................................................................................

...........................................................................................................................................

...........................................................................................................................................

...........................................................................................................................................

2. Explain how specialization and international trade can benefit a country. [6]

...........................................................................................................................................

...........................................................................................................................................

...........................................................................................................................................

...........................................................................................................................................

...........................................................................................................................................

...........................................................................................................................................

3. Define *overspecialization*. [2]

...........................................................................................................................................

...........................................................................................................................................

4. Explain **two** reasons why overspecialization can create problems for an economy. [4]

...........................................................................................................................................

...........................................................................................................................................

...........................................................................................................................................

...........................................................................................................................................

**E**

Saudi Arabia, Iran, Iraq, Russia and Venezuela have vast natural reserves of crude oil that allow them to specialize in its production. In contrast, Germany, Japan and the USA are among the largest producers and exporters of vehicles in the world. Investigate other examples of specialization.

## 6.2.1 The role of multinational companies (MNCs)

1. What is a *multinational company*? [2]

.......................................................................................................................................

.......................................................................................................................................

2. Analyse why a government might try to persuade a multinational to locate in its country. [6]

.......................................................................................................................................

.......................................................................................................................................

.......................................................................................................................................

.......................................................................................................................................

.......................................................................................................................................

.......................................................................................................................................

3. Explain **two** potential problems the location of a foreign multinational might create in an economy. [4]

.......................................................................................................................................

.......................................................................................................................................

.......................................................................................................................................

.......................................................................................................................................

**E**

What advantages and disadvantages does the article describe concerning the location of foreign-owned multinationals in Indonesia?

### Korean palm oil firm accused of illegal forest burning in Indonesia

The Korindo conglomerate has been accused of using fire to clear land illegally in the Papua region of Indonesia, destroying rainforest and releasing toxic smoke, contributing to the country's annual haze.

Korindo is one of a number of large international corporations active in the Indonesian palm oil industry, which employs around 3.7 million people in the country.

Indonesia is the world's leading producer of palm oil, much of which is exported, earning the country around $20bn each year. However, the clearing of forests to increase palm oil production has been heavily criticised over time for destroying the natural habitats of many species, including tigers, elephants and orangutans. It is also alleged that working conditions in the industry are very poor.

## 6.2.2 The benefits of free trade

1. Define *free trade*. [2]

   ...................................................................................................................................................

   ...................................................................................................................................................

2. Explain **two** reasons why free trade may be beneficial to an economy. [4]

   ...................................................................................................................................................

   ...................................................................................................................................................

   ...................................................................................................................................................

   ...................................................................................................................................................

3. Analyse the potential disadvantages of increasing free and open trade to a large developed economy and a small developing economy. [6]

   ...................................................................................................................................................

   ...................................................................................................................................................

   ...................................................................................................................................................

   ...................................................................................................................................................

   ...................................................................................................................................................

   ...................................................................................................................................................

**E**

What do the following articles suggest are some of the potential gains from free trade?

**Increased exports of clean and abundant US natural gas could support 'between 220,000 and 452,000 additional American jobs and add up to $73 billion to the US economy by 2040', a new study concludes.**

The Bahrain Economic Development Board (EDB) announced a record year for inward investment in 2017, having attracted 71 new foreign companies to Bahrain with investments amounting to $733 million. This is expected to generate more than 2,800 local jobs over the next three years.

**Tariffs mean less choice and higher costs for consumers**

For example, according to a new report by the US Trade commission, more than 75 percent of clothes imported to the US are subject to tariffs of between 16 and 19 percent. These tariffs cost each family nearly $300 in additional costs each year – or around $2.4 billion in total.

### 6.2.3 Methods of protection
### 6.2.4 Reasons for protection
### 6.2.5 Consequences of protection

1. Describe how a tariff could reduce imports. [4]

..............................................................................................................................

..............................................................................................................................

..............................................................................................................................

..............................................................................................................................

2. Explain **two** reasons why a government may protect domestic industries in its economy from overseas competition. [4]

..............................................................................................................................

..............................................................................................................................

..............................................................................................................................

..............................................................................................................................

3. Discuss the reasons why some economists prefer free trade to trade agreements. [8]

..............................................................................................................................

..............................................................................................................................

..............................................................................................................................

..............................................................................................................................

..............................................................................................................................

..............................................................................................................................

..............................................................................................................................

**E**

A number of countries have formed regional trading blocs. One example is the Caribbean Community (CARICOM). Members within a trading bloc agree to reduce or eliminate barriers to trade between each other while protecting themselves from imports from non-members. Find other examples of regional trading blocs and investigate the difference between free trade areas and customs unions.

## Key words

*Match economic terms with their correct definitions*

| | | |
|---|---|---|
| 1. Globalization **Q** | **A** | A mature industry that continues to be important to an economy but which is in decline in terms of its contribution to output, employment and trade |
| 2. Open economy | **B** | A form of predatory pricing that involves producers in one country 'flooding' other countries with their product at a price that is well below its global market price. This is so it can increase its exports at the expense of sales of firms in those other countries |
| 3. International specialization | **C** | The process of reducing or removing barriers to trade between different countries |
| 4. International trade | **D** | A national economy that engages freely in trade with other countries |
| 5. Overspecialization | **E** | A limit on the amount or volume of an imported good that is allowed into a country |
| 6. Multinational company (MNC) | **F** | A new industry in its early stages with future growth potential but as yet without sufficient scale to compete with larger established overseas competitors |
| 7. Protectionism | **G** | A stated policy of a government to defend domestic industries and jobs from international competition |
| 8. Trade barriers | **H** | Government measures, actions or requirements designed to restrict and/or increase the cost of imports |
| 9. Tariff | **I** | An indirect tax imposed on the price of an imported good to reduce domestic demand for that product |
| 10. Quota | **J** | This occurs when countries focus on the production of a limited range of goods and services they are individually best able to produce with their scarce natural and human-made resources. Their mass production allows each country to produce a surplus, which can then be traded internationally |
| 11. Embargo | **K** | A ban on the importation of a product |
| 12. Non-tariff barriers | **L** | When an economy focuses its production on too narrow a range of products leaving it vulnerable to falling global demand for one or more of its products and heavily dependent on one or more other countries to obtain the goods and services it needs |
| 13. Infant (or sunrise) industry | **M** | The movement and exchange of goods, services, ideas, money and labour across international borders |
| 14. Sunset industry | **N** | Trading agreements between two or more countries to promote and increase free trade in goods and services between each other |
| 15. Dumping | **O** | Measures used by a country to restrict imports other than through the imposition of tariffs. They include quotas, embargos, subsidies paid to domestic producers of competing products, excessive licensing regulations and standards |
| 16. Trade liberalization | **P** | A company with premises and productive operations located in more than one country |
| 17. Trade integration | **Q** | Increasing economic, social, technological and cultural interactions and interdependencies between different countries |

1. Economies tend to concentrate their production on those goods and services they are individually best able to produce with their scarce resources. International _ _ _ _ _ _ _ _ _ _ _ _ _ _ allows each economy to produce a greater volume of goods and services more efficiently.

2. By developing and exploiting their own scarce resources, each country can produce a _ _ _ _ _ _ _ and exchange it for other resources. This allows firms and consumers to benefit from the biggest and cheapest sources of labour, capital, natural materials and technologies from anywhere in the world.

3. Through _ _ _ _ _ _ _ _ _ _ _ _ _ _ _ _ _ _ _ each country can obtain a wider variety of goods and services than it would be able to produce with its own resources.

4. Increased international specialization and trade has increased global output, competition and consumer choice, allowing more human needs and _ _ _ _ _ to be satisfied. Expanding international _ _ _ _ _ _ _ have also created new business opportunities in many countries.

5. However, growing international trade and economic interdependence between countries can also cause problems e.g. it is increasing the rate at which natural resources are being _ _ _ _ _ _ _ _ _.

6. The free movement of capital across international borders has also made it easier for _ _ _ _ _ _ _ _ _ _ _ _ _ corporations to shift their production from _ _ _ _ _ _ _ _ _ economies to _ _ _ _ _ _ _ _ _ _ economies where labour is usually much cheaper and there are fewer regulations.

7. Some governments introduce _ _ _ _ _ _ _ _ _ _ _ _ _ _ to protect infant, sunset and strategically important industries in their economies from the impact international competition can have on their sales, output and employment. Measures may include imposing _ _ _ _ _ _ _ on the prices of goods imported from low-cost producers located in other countries and _ _ _ _ _ _ on quantities that can be imported.

8. For example, _ _ _ _ _ _ _ industries with significant growth potential may initially need to be protected from larger, foreign competitors to allow them the time and chance to grow and become more globally competitive.

9. Similarly, protection from international competition can help to slow the rate of decline in a _ _ _ _ _ _ industry allowing time for new industries to grow to provide alternative employment opportunities in the economy.

10. Trade protection can also be used to prevent unfair competition from _ _ _ _ _ _ _ _, when one country floods the market in another with cheap, subsidized products to force its domestic producers out of business.

11. Trade barriers can therefore help prevent _ _ _ _ _ _ _ _ _ _ _ _ _ _ _ _ _ _ _ _ in an economy by maintaining a wider range of industries that may otherwise have been forced to close by foreign competitors.

12. However, trade barriers may also be used by some countries to protect inefficient domestic firms at the expense of more _ _ _ _ _ _ _ _ _ producers located in other countries. The removal of trade restrictions can therefore force inefficient firms to improve their productivity or close. This will help to _ _ _ _ _ _ _ _ consumer choice, increase specialization and boost economic growth.

## 6.3.1 Definition of a foreign exchange rate
## 6.3.2 Determination of foreign exchange rates in the global foreign exchange market

1. What is a foreign exchange rate? [2]

   ..................................................................................................................................

   ..................................................................................................................................

2. On 21 June 2018, 1 US dollar could be exchanged for 1.33 Canadian dollars on the global foreign exchange market. How many US dollars would 10 Canadian dollars have bought that same day? [2]

   ..................................................................................................................................

   ..................................................................................................................................

3. Draw and label a diagram to show the equilibrium exchange rate for the US dollar (USD) against the Canadian dollar (CAD) on the global foreign exchange market on 21 June 2018. [4]

4. Analyse the reasons why countries exchange their national currencies. [6]

   ..................................................................................................................................

   ..................................................................................................................................

   ..................................................................................................................................

   ..................................................................................................................................

   ..................................................................................................................................

   ..................................................................................................................................

**E**

Suggest **three** reasons why the owner of a small business trading on the internet may need to buy foreign currencies.

## 6.3.3 Causes of foreign exchange rate fluctuations

1. Yesterday, 1 US dollar could be exchanged for 1.2 euros. One week earlier, the US dollar to euro exchange rate was $1 = 1.3 euros.
   (a) Describe what happened to the value of the US dollar against the euro. [2]

   .................................................................................................................................................

   .................................................................................................................................................

   (b) Explain **two** reasons that may have caused this change in the value of the US dollar against the euro. [4]

   .................................................................................................................................................

   .................................................................................................................................................

   .................................................................................................................................................

   .................................................................................................................................................

2.

   > **Value of Kenyan Shilling falls against US dollar as demand for imports rises sharply in Kenya**

   (a) Using information from the news headline above, draw a diagram to show a depreciation in the value of the Kenyan shilling (Ksh) against the US dollar (USD) on the global foreign exchange market from 100 Ksh = 1 USD to 100 Ksh = 0.8 USD.

   (b) Explain why an increase in demand for imports will have this effect, other things unchanged. [4]

   ..............................................................................

   ..............................................................................

   ..............................................................................

   ..............................................................................

**E**

The newspaper headlines below describe some changing economic conditions affecting the Indian economy. What effect could each one have on the external value of the Indian rupee?

> **Indian central bank raises interest rates**

> **Indian inflation rate falls**

> **Indian trade deficit worsens**

> **Slowdown in US economy threatens recovery in India**

## 6.3.4 Consequences of foreign exchange rate fluctuations

1. Explain why exchange rates fluctuate. [4]

..............................................................................................................................................

..............................................................................................................................................

..............................................................................................................................................

..............................................................................................................................................

2. Spain imports flat screen televisions from South Korea, priced at 500,000 won (KRW) each. Last week, 1 euro exchanged for 1,000 won. Yesterday, the won depreciated to 1,200 won = 1 euro. Use this information to explain what effect this will have on the price of imported televisions in Spain. [4]

..............................................................................................................................................

..............................................................................................................................................

..............................................................................................................................................

..............................................................................................................................................

3. Analyse how the trade deficit of a country may be affected by a depreciation in the value of its currency on the foreign exchange market. [6]

..............................................................................................................................................

..............................................................................................................................................

..............................................................................................................................................

..............................................................................................................................................

..............................................................................................................................................

**E**

Use your knowledge of economics to explain the following newspaper headline.

**Fall in UK pound benefits UK manufacturers as export orders rise but analysts say dearer imports may force them to raise their prices soon**

## 6.3.5 Floating and fixed exchange rates

1. Explain the difference between a floating exchange rate and a fixed exchange rate. [4]

..............................................................................................................................................

..............................................................................................................................................

..............................................................................................................................................

..............................................................................................................................................

2. Explain **two** reasons why a country may operate a fixed exchange rate system. [4]

..............................................................................................................................................

..............................................................................................................................................

..............................................................................................................................................

..............................................................................................................................................

3. Analyse the reasons why a country with a fixed exchange rate may devalue its currency. [6]

..............................................................................................................................................

..............................................................................................................................................

..............................................................................................................................................

..............................................................................................................................................

..............................................................................................................................................

..............................................................................................................................................

**E**

What does the article suggest are the disadvantages of fixed exchange rate systems?

**World News: October 2017**

The National Bank of Ethiopia last week devalued the Ethiopian currency, the birr, by 15% against the US dollar. The exchange rate was reduced from USD 1 = ETB 23.40 to USD 1 = ETB 26.91.

The birr's external value has always been strictly managed but rising demand for imports has increased downward pressure on the value of the birr and drained the nation's foreign currency reserves. It is hoped that a cheaper birr will improve Ethiopia's export competitiveness.

## 6.4.1 Structure of the current account of the balance of payments

1. Using examples, explain how exports and imports are recorded in the current account of the balance of payments of a country. [4]

........................................................................................................

........................................................................................................

........................................................................................................

........................................................................................................

2. Using the information in the table, calculate what has happened to the balance on the current account of the balance of payments over time. [4]

| Balances ($bn) | Year 1 | Year 5 |
|---|---|---|
| Trade in goods | −115 | −127 |
| Trade in services | 81 | 95 |
| Primary income | −16 | −12 |
| Secondary income (net current transfers) | −10 | 1 |

........................................................................

........................................................................

........................................................................

........................................................................

3. Explain any **two** of the four sections of the current account. [4]

........................................................................................................

........................................................................................................

........................................................................................................

........................................................................................................

4. Explain what is meant by 'a deficit on the current account of the balance of payments'. [4]

........................................................................................................

........................................................................................................

........................................................................................................

........................................................................................................

**E**

Why do you think your country trades with other countries? What are its main exports and imports? What has happened to the trade balance of your country over time and why? If exports from your country became more expensive, what impact could this have on your country and in countries importing products from your country?

Explain how it is possible for a country to have a trade deficit but a surplus on its balance of payments current account.

**6.4.2 Causes of a current account deficit and surplus**
**6.4.3 Consequences of current account deficits and surpluses**
**6.4.4 Policies to achieve balance of payments stability**

1. Explain **two** consequences of a trade deficit for an economy. [4]

   .................................................................................................................................................

   .................................................................................................................................................

   .................................................................................................................................................

   .................................................................................................................................................

2. Briefly describe **four** actions a government could take to try to reduce a trade deficit. [4]

   .................................................................................................................................................

   .................................................................................................................................................

   .................................................................................................................................................

   .................................................................................................................................................

3. Explain **two** possible causes of a surplus in the current account of the balance of payments. [4]

   .................................................................................................................................................

   .................................................................................................................................................

   .................................................................................................................................................

   .................................................................................................................................................

4. Describe **two** problems that may be caused by a large and persistent trade surplus. [4]

   .................................................................................................................................................

   .................................................................................................................................................

   .................................................................................................................................................

   .................................................................................................................................................

**E**

Explain why, if one country has a large trade surplus, one or more of its trading partners must have a trade deficit with the country.

## Key words

*Match economic terms with their definitions*

| | |
|---|---|
| 1. Foreign exchange rate  **M** | **A** A flow of money out of a country in exchange for a good or service supplied by a producer located in another country |
| 2. Depreciation | **B** This occurs when the value of imports to a country exceeds the value of its exports over the same period |
| 3. Appreciation | **C** An exchange rate determined by market demand and supply conditions on the global foreign exchange (forex) market |
| 4. Devaluation | **D** A net measure of financial transactions between a country and the rest of the world involving the exchange of goods, services, incomes and current transfers in a given period |
| 5. Floating exchange rate | **E** A fall in the external value of a currency due to changes in demand and/or supply conditions on the forex market |
| 6. Fixed exchange rate | **F** An official exchange rate set and maintained by the government or central bank of a country |
| 7. Export | **G** A flow of money received by a country from the sale of a good or service to a resident of another country |
| 8. Import | **H** The value of visible exports from a country less the value of its visible imports over the same period |
| 9. Visible trade | **I** A record of all financial flows between a country and the rest of the world over a given period of time |
| 10. Invisible trade | **J** A measure of the difference between flows of money into and out of a country in a given period for the payment of primary income (wages, salaries, interest, profits and dividends) |
| 11. Balance of trade in goods | **K** A rise in the external value of a currency resulting from changes in demand and/or supply conditions on the forex market |
| 12. Balance of trade in services | **L** A reduction in a fixed exchange rate determined by the government or central bank of the country |
| 13. Trade deficit | **M** The external value of a national currency in terms of another currency. It is the equilibrium price at which it can be exchanged for another currency on the forex market |
| 14. Trade surplus | **N** Trade in services |
| 15. Unfavourable trade balance | **O** A country has this if it records a trade deficit |
| 16. Balance of payments | **P** The difference between payments received by a country from residents of other countries for exports of services and payments made in the same period by residents of that country for services by other countries |
| 17. Current account of the balance of payments | **Q** A net measure of secondary income flows between a country and other countries for which no goods or services are exchanged. They include transfers of money for gifts, donations, international aid and pensions |
| 18. Balance on income | **R** This occurs when the value of exports from a country exceeds the value of its imports over the same period |
| 19. Net current transfers | **S** Trade in goods: the exchange of physical products (consumer goods and capital goods) with other countries |

## Revision summary

*Fill in the missing words and economic terms*

1. Payments for imports, exports and other international transactions require the exchange of national currencies on the _ _ _ _ _ _ _ _ _ _ _ _ _ _ _ _ (forex) market. In a _ _ _ _ _ _ _ _ exchange rate system, the external value is determined by changes in demand and supply conditions.

2. Many factors can affect the demand for a currency and its supply. For example, an _ _ _ _ _ _ _ _ _ _ _ in interest rates or speculation that a currency will rise in value can increase global demand for the currency. In contrast, a _ _ _ _ _ _ _ _ _ _ in interest rates and rising export prices due to inflation can make a currency less attractive, causing demand for the currency to fall.

3. If a country spends more on _ _ _ _ _ _ _ than it earns from the sale of _ _ _ _ _ _ _, it will have to supply more of its currency to the forex market in order to buy the other currencies to pay for imports.

4. A currency will rise, or _ _ _ _ _ _ _ _ _ _ _, in value against one or more other currencies if there is an _ _ _ _ _ _ _ _ in demand for that currency or if there is a _ _ _ _ in its supply.

5. A currency will fall, or _ _ _ _ _ _ _ _ _ _ _, in value against one or more other currencies if there is a _ _ _ _ in demand or if there is an _ _ _ _ _ _ _ _ in its supply on the forex market.

6. International transactions in goods, services, incomes and transfers undertaken by a country are recorded in the current account of its _ _ _ _ _ _ _ _ _ _ _ _ _ _ _ _ _ _.

7. If a resident of the United States receives dividends from shares he holds in an Indian company, this will be recorded as a _ _ _ _ _ _ to the primary income balance in the US current account. If the same resident then makes a donation to a charity in India, this will be recorded as a _ _ _ _ _ to net current _ _ _ _ _ _ _ _ _ (or secondary income balance) in the US current account.

8. By far the largest transactions recorded in the current account are revenues received from the sale of _ _ _ _ _ _ _ and payments for _ _ _ _ _ _ _ _. A country will have a trade deficit if the value of its _ _ _ _ _ _ _ exceeds the value of its _ _ _ _ _ _ _ in the same period.

9. A decrease in the exchange rate can help a country to reduce its trade deficit because it will _ _ _ _ _ _ the price that residents of other countries must pay for its exports and will _ _ _ _ _ _ _ _ the cost of imported products.

10. A government may attempt to reduce a large and persistent trade deficit by introducing trade restrictions or by _ _ _ _ _ _ _ interest rates and _ _ _ _ _ _ _ _ _ _ _ _ fiscal policy to reduce consumer demand for imports. If the government maintains a fixed exchange rate, it could _ _ _ _ _ _ _ the currency to make exports from its country cheaper in other countries.

11. An increase in the exchange rate can help a country to reduce a trade surplus because it will _ _ _ _ _ _ _ _ the price that residents of other countries must pay for its exports and will _ _ _ _ _ _ the cost of imported products. However, an appreciation in the exchange rate could also place many jobs and incomes at risk in the country if it is heavily reliant on exports.

Examination questions on international aspects of economics will often require you to:

- calculate the current account of the balance of payments from trade data
- draw demand and supply diagrams to demonstrate the impact changing market conditions can have on the exchange rate of a currency.

1.

| Credits to current account, 2016 | $bn |
|---|---|
| Exports of goods | 150 |
| Exports of services | 90 |
| Primary income received | 51 |
| Secondary income received | 8 |

| Debits to current account, 2016 | $ bn |
|---|---|
| Imports of goods | 225 |
| Imports of services | 64 |
| Primary income paid overseas | 85 |
| Secondary income paid overseas | 20 |

From the table, calculate:

a) the balance of trade in goods

b) the balance of trade in services

c) the primary income balance *(balance on income)*

d) the secondary income balance *(net current transfers)*

e) the balance on the current account = $(a + b + c + d)$.

a) .........................................................................................................

b) .........................................................................................................

c) .........................................................................................................

d) .........................................................................................................

e) .........................................................................................................

2. The two diagrams below show the foreign exchange market for US dollars. It shows the exchange rate of $1 in terms of Swedish krona (kr). Currently $1 can be exchanged for 10 kr. In diagram (a) show the impact of an increase in demand for US dollars. In diagram (b) show the impact of an increase in the supply of US dollars. Don't forget to use labels.

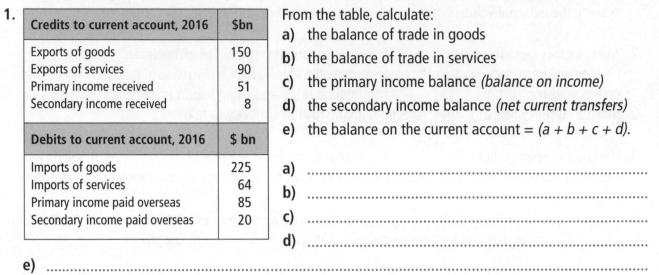

3. Complete the table below which lists some changing economic conditions that could affect the external value of the US dollar. The first one has been completed for you.

| Changing economic conditions | Most likely impact on demand for US dollars? | Most likely impact on supply of US dollars? | Most likely impact on US exchange rate? |
|---|---|---|---|
| An increase in the US trade deficit | - | *Increase* | *Decrease* |
| An increase in the US inflation rate | | | |
| An increase in US interest rates | | | |
| Speculation that the value of the US dollar will fall | | | |

## Multiple choice questions (Paper 1)

1. What is argued to be an important benefit of global free trade?

   (a) It reduces a country's reliance on other countries

   (b) It increases protection for domestic producers against competition from firms overseas

   (c) It reduces the transport costs involved in trading

   (d) It increases the opportunity for domestic producers to specialize

2. A government argues it has to increase its trade protection policies. What might this involve?

   (a) Increased taxes on external costs

   (b) Eliminating waste in the use of resources

   (c) Increased self-sufficiency and barriers to trade

   (d) Price controls on monopoly industries

3. Why might a government increase trade protection?

   (a) To reduce the price of imported goods

   (b) To increase demand for goods produced by domestic industries

   (c) To increase the efficiency of domestic industries

   (d) To increase the prices of goods produced by domestic industries

4. What might explain a fall in the volume of goods imported into a country?

   (a) An appreciation in the exchange rate

   (b) A reduction in tariffs on imported goods

   (c) An increase in income tax rates in the country

   (d) A reduction in interest rates in the country

5. A truck priced for export at $20,000 by a US manufacturer is exchanged for 80,000 Qatari rials on import to Qatar. What will be the imported price of the truck following a depreciation in the value of the US dollar to $1 = 3 rials?

   (a) 10,000 rials      (c) 40,000 rials

   (b) 20,000 rials      (d) 60,000 rials

6. In addition to trade in goods and services, which of the following two items will be included in the current account of the balance of payments of a country?

   (a) Direct and indirect tax revenues

   (b) Primary incomes and current transfers

   (c) Government spending and international loans

   (d) Foreign reserves and international investments

7. Below are the recommended retail prices of a DVD in four different countries.

   United Kingdom £12.99 (UK pounds sterling)

   Germany €18.00 (Euros)

   Bahamas $19.80 (Bahamian dollars)

   Brazil R$77.00 (Brazilean reals)

   What further information is required to make a proper comparison of the different prices?

   (a) Exchange rates      (c) Inflation rates

   (b) Direct taxes        (d) Transport costs

8. The table shows how the trade flows of one country have changed over time.

   | Year | Exports ($m) | Imports ($m) |
   |------|--------------|--------------|
   | 2010 | 140          | 170          |
   | 2015 | 120          | 260          |

   Which statement covering the period 2010 to 2015 is correct?

   (a) The balance of trade improved

   (b) The exchange rate appreciated

   (c) The current account improved

   (d) The trade deficit increased

9. The United Arab Emirates is a major trading partner of India. What will happen to the prices of Indian exports and imports if the Indian rupee depreciates in value against the UAE dirham?

   |   | Prices of Indian exports to the UAE | Prices of Indian imports from the UAE |
   |---|-------------------------------------|---------------------------------------|
   | A | Increase                            | Increase                              |
   | B | Decrease                            | Decrease                              |
   | C | Increase                            | Decrease                              |
   | D | Decrease                            | Increase                              |

1.

# The cap comes off the Swiss Franc

In 2015, the Government of Switzerland ended its cap on the Swiss Franc exchange rate with the euro. The cap had been used to keep the value of the Franc low relative to the euro with the aim of boosting Swiss exports at the cost of making Eurozone exports less attractive.

The Swiss National Bank said that market conditions would now determine the exchange rate and immediately following the decision the value of the Swiss Franc soared in value against the euro by over 30 per cent. The euro went from buying 1.20 Francs to buying just 0.8052, but it later recovered to buy 1.04.

Switzerland has had a surplus on the current account of its balance of payments in recent years and economists believe that the appreciation of its currency should help to reduce the size of this surplus.

While Switzerland still exports large amounts of traditional products like chocolate and watches, today more than half of Swiss exports are in mechanical and electrical engineering and chemicals. The top destinations for its export are Hong Kong, Germany, the United States, India and France. Hong Kong and India have large trade deficits with Switzerland.

a) What evidence is there in the extract that Switzerland has moved from a fixed to a floating exchange rate for its currency? [2]

b) What determines the value of a currency in a floating exchange rate system? [3]

c) Explain the possible effects on the Swiss economy of a rise in the value of its exchange rate. [6]

d) What evidence is there in the extract of specialization in the Swiss economy? [3]

e) Explain the advantages of specialization in a national economy. [4]

f) Explain why a trade surplus in Switzerland over many years could be problematic for some of its trading partners, such as India and Hong Kong. [4]

g) Discuss whether a floating exchange rate system is always to be preferred to a fixed one. [8]

2. The government of a country may try to reduce a deficit on the current account of the balance of payments through changes in the external value of its national currency and the introduction of trade protection measures.

a) Define *trade protection*. [2]

b) Explain **two** methods of trade protection that a government could use. [4]

c) Analyse why a depreciation in the external value of the national currency may lead to a reduction in the country's current account deficit. [6]

d) Discuss whether a government should protect its industries from foreign competition. [8]

3. At the end of March 2015 the deficit on the current account of the balance of payments of the United States was just over $118 billion. The US Government is looking at ways to boost exports.

a) Define *trade deficit*. [2]

b) Explain the structure of the current account of a country's balance of payments. [4]

c) Analyse **three** possible causes of a current account deficit. [6]

d) Discuss whether a current account surplus should be regarded as desirable. [8]

# 1.1 The nature of the economic problem

## 1.1.1 Finite resources and unlimited wants

1. The two articles highlight the problem of scarcity of resources including natural resources and labour.

2. Human wants exceed the resources available to produce goods and services to satisfy those wants.

3. It illustrates scarcity of resources. The shortage of parts means the factory cannot continue production of motor vehicles. As a result, some people's wants for cars will not be satisfied.

4. Unlike basic human needs for food, water and shelter, human wants are for goods and services that are not necessary to sustain life. Human wants for products such as cars, designer clothes, computers, holidays and entertainment, far exceed our needs for products that will enable us to survive.

**E** Because our wants are without limit and will therefore always exceed the amount of resources available to produce goods and service we want. This will remain true even if resources increase over time, for example, due to a growing population that will eventually increase the supply of labour but which will also increase human needs and wants. However, many natural resources can never be replaced as they are used up.

## 1.1.2  Economic and free goods

1. Air is a free good because it is unlimited in supply.

2. Cars are economic goods because they are limited in supply. This is because scarce resources must be used to produce them. The purchase and use of a car by a consumer will therefore reduce the quantity of cars available to other consumers.

3. Free goods and economic goods are similar in that they both satisfy human needs or wants. The key difference is that economic goods are limited in supply, but free goods are not.

4. A new idea posted on the internet is available for everyone to use. There are no limits to its use. It is a free good. An example is the sharing of new recipes on social media applications.

**E**

|  | Free good | Economic good |
|---|---|---|
| Pebbles on the beach | X |  |
| Computers |  | X |
| Air | X |  |
| Factories |  | X |

# 1.2 The factors of production

## 1.2.1 Definitions of the factors of production and their rewards

1. Many people supply their labour to firms to help produce goods and services in return for wages or salaries. However, not all workers have the skills, knowledge or desire to risk running a business. These skills and attributes are called 'enterprise'. They are possessed and supplied by entrepreneurs. If they are successful they will earn a profit from their productive activities.

2. People can choose to supply their labour to firms in return for wages. Labour is the physical and mental effort of workers used up in the production of goods and services. In contrast, land refers to natural products used to produce other goods and services, including water used to wash hair in a hair salon, plants and animals that provide food and minerals such as iron and oil.

3. Capital refers to human-made resources made specifically for use in the production of other goods and services. It includes machinery, tools, vehicles and work premises such as factories, offices and shops. They are not produced to satisfy an immediate consumer want. They are wanted only because they can help to make or supply other products.

**E** Some examples:

| Clothing | Milk | Teaching | Road construction |
|---|---|---|---|
| Designer | Farmer | Teacher | Engineer |
| Machinist | Veterinarian | College office | Truck driver |
| Cotton | Grass | staff | Oil (in |
| Natural dyes | Animal feed | Canteen food | tarmac) |
| Sewing | Milking | and water | Limestone (in |
| machine | machine | Computers | cement) |
| Scissors | Milk urn | College | Excavator |
|  |  | building | Drills |

## 1.2.2 The mobility of the factors of production

1. Factor mobility refers to the ease with which resources or factors of production can be moved from one productive activity to another without incurring significant costs or a loss of output.

2. A lorry is a factor of production because it is an item of capital equipment used in the production of other goods. It is a mobile factor of production because it can be easily moved or reallocated between different productive uses and locations.

3.  a) Geographic immobility occurs when workers are reluctant to move to jobs in different locations because of family ties or because moving home can be expensive.

    b) Occupational immobility means that workers cannot change jobs very easily because they have very specific skills.

4.  An area of farmland may be used to grow different crops or to graze farm animals. It may even be possible to build houses or factories on the land instead or to convert it to parkland. In these ways the farmland may be considered a relatively mobile factor of production because it has different productive uses. However, an area of land is a geographically immobile factor of production because its location is fixed: it cannot be moved or reallocated to a different productive use in another location.

**E** Firms can provide training for workers so that they are able to move to new jobs more easily. However, training might be expensive if the new jobs are highly skilled. Firms can offer to pay relocation allowances for workers to move to new locations, but this might be expensive. Firms can invest in capital equipment that will be able to carry out several different jobs. However, this will increase the cost of the equipment that, in the end, may never be required to carry out the different jobs.

## 1.2.3 Quantity and quality of the factors of production

1.  Wood is an example of a renewable resource because it is possible to plant and grow more trees over time to replace those that have been cut down. In contrast, coal is an example of a non-renewable natural resource. It took millions of years to form, is finite in supply and cannot be replaced once it has all been used up.

2.  Farmers could improve the quality of their farmland by (select two from the following): using fertilisers and better land management to improve soil conditions; planting crops that are more resistant to drought and insect infestations; using organic and more humane farming methods that can improve the quality of crops, meat and milk produced.

3.  Training and education can improve workforce skills that will increase the amount, range and quality of goods and services people can produce.

4.  Select two from the following: an increase in rents may persuade more land owners to release their land into productive uses; new equipment and techniques can improve the amount able to be extracted from land; planting and growing more trees and plants; recycling and re-using used vegetable oils and engine oils, and metal and wooden parts in durable consumer and capital goods that we no longer use or want.

**E** Modern technologies have been applied widely to improve factor quantity and quality. For example, in the case of land, they have enabled us to use the sun, wind and other renewable resources to produce energy. This represents improved factor quantity for land. Improvements in the factor quality of land have come from new technologies that improve the resilience of plants to drought and insect infestations. In the case of capital, internet banking has improved access to financial capital, increasing the quantity available. Advances in technology have improved the speed and accuracy of modern machinery and equipment. This represents improved factor quality for capital. Social media on the internet has made it easier for unemployed workers to find jobs, improving the quantity and mobility of labour. Working with modern equipment, such as computers, allows workers to produce more goods and services, improving the quality of labour.

## Key words

| 1 K | 2 H | 3 Q | 4 P | 5 F | 6 C | 7 N | 8 O | 9 L | 10 E | 11 R |
|-----|-----|-----|-----|-----|-----|-----|-----|-----|------|------|
| 12 J | 13 A | 14 B | 15 M | 16 S | 17 D | 18 G | 19 I | | | |

## Revision summary

| 1. scarcity; unlimited | 2. limited | 3. factors of production | 4. firms; profit |
|---|---|---|---|
| 5. enterprise | 6. land | 7. labour | 8. capital; capital |
| 9. quality; satisfied | 10. mobility | 11. immobile | 12. geographically; occupationally |

## 1.3 Opportunity cost
### 1.3.1 Definition of opportunity cost
### 1.3.2 The influence of opportunity cost on decision making

1.  The benefit that could have been enjoyed from the next best alternative use of scarce resources will be sacrificed each time a decision is made regarding their use.

2.  As resources are scarce we must choose which goods and services to produce with them and which needs and wants they will satisfy. This is because it is impossible to satisfy all human needs and wants. The opportunity to produce other products and to satisfy other wants with those resources is sacrificed. The benefit given up is the cost of making a choice.

3.  All organizations have limited resources and must therefore choose how best to use them. For example, firms that aim to make a profit should allocate their scarce resources to their most profitable use. In contrast, not-for-profit organizations should allocate their resources to uses that best achieve their goals in the most cost effective way.

**E** Like all other governments and organizations, the Australian government does not have limitless resoures. Therefore, if it increases the amount it spends more on defence then it must cut its spending on other things such as education, roads or the wages of government employees. Or it may be able to increase taxes or borrow more money which will need to repaid at a later date. However, increasing taxes now or in the future will reduce the amount of money Australian people and businesses have to spend on the goods and services they want.

Similarly, if more soybeans are to be grown in South America then either the production of other crops must be cut or the amount of land available for agriculture must increase. Because land is scarce this will require clearing more areas of natural vegetation.

## 1.4 Production possibility curve (PPC) diagrams

### 1.4.1 Definition of PPC

### 1.4.2 Points under, on and beyond a PPC

### 1.4.3 Movements along a PPC

1.
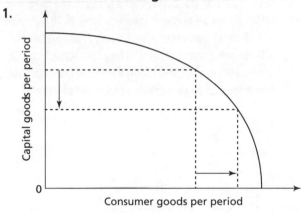

2. A firm or an economy can produce any combination of outputs of two products with its limited resources along its production possibility curve. For example, it could choose to produce at point X or Y in the diagram below. However, more resources will be needed to increase the output of product A leaving fewer resources available to make the other product B. The reduction in output of product B is the opportunity cost of the decision to increase output of A.

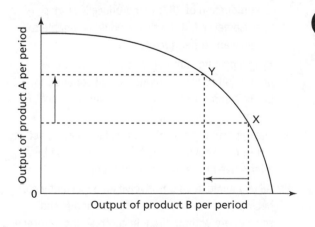

**E** Production possibility curve for a firm producing handbags and shoes

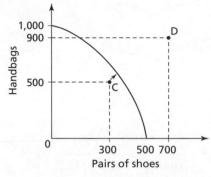

The firm is currently producing at point C. This is below its PPC and therefore represents an inefficient allocation of its resources. The firm could increase its total output if it makes better use of its existing resources. For example, it could produce more output each period at any point along its PPC.

However, the firm currently cannot produce 900 handbags and 700 pairs of shoes each period. This is point D in the diagram and is above its PPC. The firm does not have enough resources at present to attain this level of output.

### 1.4.4 Shifts in a PPC

1. A has expanded its productive capacity; B has experienced negative economic growth.

2. Select two from the list: more natural resources are discovered; the supply of labour increases; the stock of capital equipment is increased; new technologies create new and more advanced materials, equipment and production processes; education and training increases skills; improvements in healthcare reduce days lost at work due to illness and accidents; investment in modern business infrastructure including road and telecommunication.

3. Select two from the following: non-renewable resources are depleted; the supply of labour and/or enterprise falls; capital equipment wears out and is not replaced; workforce and enterprise skills decline; the economy has an aging and decaying infrastructure.

**E** An increase in labour and enterprise

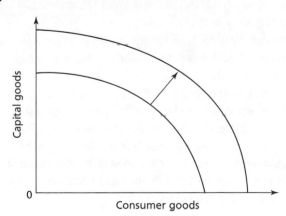

**A decrease in labour and enterprise**

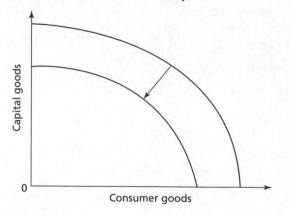

## Key words

| 1 E | 2 C | 3 F | 4 E | 5 A | 6 B |
|-----|-----|-----|-----|-----|-----|

## Revision summary

| 1. wants | 2. opportunity cost | 3. opportunity cost | 4. production possibility |
|----------|---------------------|---------------------|---------------------------|
| 5. outwards | 6. inwards | | |

## Working with data and diagrams

1.
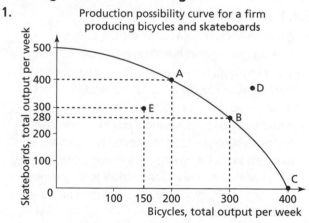
Production possibility curve for a firm producing bicycles and skateboards

2. The opportunity cost of reallocating resources in the firm to increase its output of bicycles from 200 to 300 each week is the lost output of 120 skateboards each week.

3. If the firm used all its resources to produce bicycles, then no skateboards could be produced. The opportunity cost of producing 400 bicycles each week is therefore 500 skateboards foregone.

4. The firm does not have enough resources to produce at point D each week. It will need more labour, natural resources and capital equipment to do so.

5. Production at point E is inefficient. The firm could produce more skateboards and bicycles each week if it made full and better use of all its factors of production. For example, some workers may lack the skills they need to complete the tasks they have been given. Production may be slow and quality poor. Some capital equipment may be broken and in need of repair.

## Multiple choice questions

| 1 D | 2 B | 3 B | 4 C | 5 B |
|-----|-----|-----|-----|-----|
| 6 C | 7 C | 8 D | | |

## Structured questions

1. a) The loss of 767, 747 and 777 aircraft. This is because some of the resources once used to produce them at Boeing are now being used instead to increase output of 737 and 787 models.

   b) The extract refers to labour, capital and enterprise. Labour includes the engineers and machinists at Boeing's US factories. Advanced machinery, industrial robots and the factory buildings in which Boeing makes its aircraft are all examples of capital. The business know-how of the Chief Executive in charge of Boeing and responsible for taking major decisions about aircraft production and the future of the company is an example of enterprise.

   c) The production possibility curve (PPC) in the diagram below shows all possible combinations of 787 aircraft and all other aircraft models Boeing could make with its current resources and level of technology. All combinations of output along the curve are attainable if Boeing uses all its available resources efficiently.

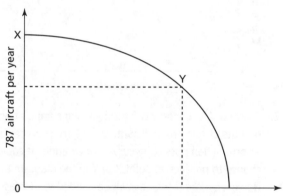

The diagram shows that Boeing could choose to allocate all its labour, capital and other resources to the production of 787s and produce X of these each year. However, if it did this it would be unable to produce any other aircraft.

By reallocating some of its resources to the production of other aircraft it could continue to produce some 787s as well as all other models, for example, at point Y on its PPC.

2. a) The opportunity cost of a particular decision, activity or use of resources is the benefit of the next best alternative or option that is given up.

   All economic decisions involve an opportunity cost because human wants for different goods and services are without limit. In contrast, the natural and other resources required to make them are limited in supply, so if they are used to make one type of product they cannot be used to produce others. This means every economy must choose which goods and services to produce with their limited resources and, therefore, which human wants they will satisfy and which ones they will not.

c) The diagram below shows a production possibility curve for an economy producing consumer goods and capital goods. It can produce any combination of outputs along the curve with its limited resources if they are fully employed and used efficiently. The curve shows that more consumer goods could be produced but only if resources are diverted away from the production of capital goods. The resulting reduction in capital goods will be the opportunity cost of this decision.

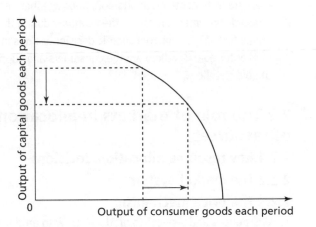

d) Governments have to determine how best to spend the revenue they raise from taxes. For example, the more they spend on healthcare the less they have to spend on schools or law enforcement. If a government wants to spend more it will have to raise taxes but that will involve an opportunity cost for taxpayers. They will have less to spend or save. Raising taxes payable by businesses may also result in some closing down or relocating overseas to countries with lower taxes. As a result, jobs and output will be lost.

However, opportunity cost matters to all people and organizations because productive resources are scarce compared to their needs and wants. This means they will all have to make choices about how best to use the limited resources they have available.

For example, private firms must decide what to produce. For example, a vehicle manufacturer may decide to produce more coaches but this will reduce the resources it has available to produce cars. If cars are more profitable to make and sell, then it would not be a good decision.

Similarly, consumers have limited incomes. They must decide what to spend their money on. Spending more on holidays may give them more satisfaction but will

leave them with less income to spend on food and other necessities.

Workers will also have to decide what job they will do and how many hours they will work each week. A job nearer to home may involve less travel time but may pay less in wages than one further away. Further, choosing to work more hours each week means giving up more leisure time.

3. a) The central problem in economics is the scarcity of resources needed to make goods and services to satisfy human needs and wants. It is impossible to satisfy them all because they are without limit.

b) Land refers to all natural resources used up in the production of other goods and services, including wood, minerals and farmland.

Labour is the physical and human effort supplied to firms by workers and includes engineers, machine operators, sales assistants and teachers.

Capital includes productive resources such as computers, machines, vehicles and tools produced by some firms to be used by other firms to produce other goods and services.

Production using land, labour and capital is organized by entrepreneurs. They are people who are willing to take the risks and decisions necessary to set up and run businesses. This is called enterprise.

c) In the diagram below, a firm is using its factors of production to produce hats and shoes. The firm can produce any combination of these two products along its production possibility curve if it uses all its resources efficiently.

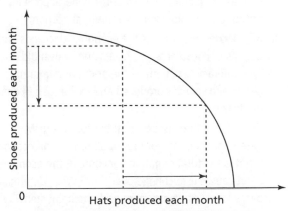

However, to produce more hats the firm will need use more of its limited resources. Fewer resources will be available to produce shoes. The consequence will be a reduction in the amount of shoes produced each period. Alternatively, the opportunity cost of reallocating resources from hat production to shoe production will be a reduction in the volume of hats produced.

d) A decision to build more roads will result in fewer productive resources being available to produce other goods and services. For example, land available for farming may be reduced by the decision to build more roads. Land and capital used in road construction could have been used to build more houses instead. The government that paid for the new roads to be built could have used tax revenue to spend more on healthcare or education instead.

However, roads can provide significant benefits to many people and firms in an economy. For example, their construction will provide work and incomes. Roads can also improve access and journey times to different areas of a country and to other countries. This can help to improve trade. It may also allow people to relocate further away from their places of work to areas where houses are cheaper. If these benefits exceed the benefits of providing other goods and services instead, then building more roads will be good for an economy.

Roads can also provide an alternative means of travel that may be cheaper than rail or air travel. However, increased car travel and traffic congestion can increase pollution and reduce air quality. These in turn can cause health problems for people who live near roads.

## 2.1 Microeconomics and macroeconomics
### 2.1.1 Microeconomics
### 2.1.2 Macroeconomics

1. Microeconomics studies how prices and quantities are determined in individual markets while macroeconomics studies the factors that affect the general price level, total output and employment in a national economy.

2. Microeconomics studies the economic decisions and actions of consumers, producers and households and how they interact to determine the prices and quantities of goods and services produced and exchanged in different markets.

3. Choose any three issues from the following: What determines the total output of all firms in an economy? What is the total or national income of the economy and what causes it to change over time? What determines the overall level of employment and unemployment? What causes inflation in the general level of prices and what impact does it have? How can governments influence total consumer spending, the rate of price inflation, the level of employment and the total output of all firms in the economy? What impacts can changes in taxes and government spending have on an economy? What are the reasons for differences in living standards between countries? What affects population growth and how is it affecting different economies? Why do different countries engage in international trade with each other and what impact can it have on their macroeconomies?

**E** The Czech central bank has raised interest rates because it is worried about the impact low unemployment may have on wage and price inflation in the economy. This is a macroeconomic issues. The government and central bank are the decision makers.

Porsche, a vehicle producer, is concerned about the fall in consumer demand for diesel cars. This is a microeconomic issue affecting the market for cars. The decision makers in this case are consumers and Porsche itself.

The gold jewellery case study mentions both micro and macroeconomic issues. A new tax has been imposed on all goods and services in the Indian macroeconomy. The decision to introduce the tax was taken by the Indian government. The tax will have increased the market price(s) of gold jewellery causing consumer demand for these items to contract. In addition, poor weather also reduced consumer demand in the economy during the Diwali festival. The microeconomic decision makers in market for gold jewellery are the consumers and suppliers of gold jewellery.

## 2.2 The role of markets in allocation of resources
### 2.2.1 Key resource allocation decisions
### 2.2.2 The market system
### 2.2.3 The price mechanism

1. What goods and services to produce? How to produce them? Who to produce them for?

2. The price of a product and the quantity exchanged each period will be stable in any market in a state of equilibrium. This is because the amount consumers are willing and able to buy each period at the market price is exactly equal to the amount producers of that product are willing and able to supply. However, if the quantity supplied differs from the quantity consumers are willing and able to buy, the market will be in a state of disequilibrium. Price and quantities will need to change to restore equilibrium.

3. The role of the price mechanism in a market economy is to determine how scare resources are allocated to different productive uses and how the goods and services they produce are distributed among different consumers. Changes in market prices provide signals to producers about what consumers want to buy and what they are willing to pay. An increase in the price of a product is a signal that consumers want more of that product and are willing to pay more to get it. As a result, firms producing the product will earn more profits and will allocate more resources to its production. Because resources are scarce, they will be reallocated from the production of products for which consumer demand, prices and profits are falling.

**E** Growth in demand for plant-based (vegan) food: producers are likely to increase production of vegan foods and reduce the production of meat- and dairy-based foods. This will require a reallocation of resources from non-vegan food production to vegan food production.

UK manufacturers feel the pinch as raw material costs rise: an increase in production costs will reduce profitability. As a result, UK manufacturers are likely to cut output unless they can find other ways to reduce their costs without cutting production.

Sales and profitability of hard-disk drives declining: producers are likely to cut back production and may instead increase output of solid-state drives.

## Key words

| 1 E | 2 G | 3 J | 4 C | 5 B |
|-----|-----|-----|-----|------|
| 6 H | 7 D | 8 A | 9 F | 10 I |

## Revision Summary

| 1 resource allocation; economic system | 2 market | 3 price; market; profit |
|----------------------------------------|----------|-------------------------|
| 4 micro | 5 macro; mixed | |

## 2.3 Demand

### 2.3.1 Definition of demand

### 2.3.2 Price and demand

### 2.3.3 Individual and market demand

1.  Demand is the desire a consumer has to buy and use a product to satisfy a need or want.

2.  People may want or demand certain products but unless they have enough money to buy them their demand will not be effective. An effective demand is therefore one that is backed by the ability to pay.

3.  **(a)** The price per unit; **(b)** The quantity of the product demanded or supplied per period, that is, each day, week, month or year.

4.  A downward sloping demand curve shows how consumer demand for a product will expand as the price of that product falls. This is because consumers will be able to afford to buy more of a product and satisfy more of their wants the lower the price they must pay. The same will apply to the vast majority of products consumers demand.

5.  Consumers will 'move along' their demand curve in response to a change in the price of the product they are willing and able to buy. That is, they will demand more of the product as its price falls and will contract their demand for it as its price rises. In contrast, a shift in a demand curve shows that consumers now demand more or less of the product than they did before regardless of its price.

### 2.3.4 Conditions of demand

1.  Complementary products are in joint demand. This means, the demand for one product depends on the demand for another. For example, people demand petrol because they also demand motor vehicles to drive. In contrast, products are substitutes if they can satisfy the same demand. For example, a consumers demand for a hot drink may be satisfied by either tea or coffee.

2.  Demand for normal goods will increase as disposable incomes rise because consumers want to buy more of them and can now afford to do so. However, demand for inferior goods will fall as disposable incomes rise because consumers are now able to buy more expensive and better quality products instead. For example, a consumer may decide to travel by taxi instead of by bus as his or her income rises.

3.  **(a)** Choose three from the following: an increase in consumers' incomes, for example due to rising employment; a reduction in taxes on incomes; a rise in the price of substitutes; a fall in the price of complements; consumers' tastes or fashions changing to favour the product; increased advertising of the product; an increase in the population; other factors, for example, a hot summer can boost demand for cold drinks and summer clothes. **(b)** Choose three from the following: a fall in consumers' incomes, for example due to rising unemployment; an increase in taxes on incomes; a fall in the price of substitutes; a rise in the price of complements; consumers' tastes or fashions changing in favour of other products; product advertising being cut back or banned; a fall in the population; other factors, for example, a ban on smoking in public places may reduce demand for cigarettes.

**E** If a rise in the price of A causes a fall in demand for B then A and B must be complements. If a rise in the price of A results in an increase in demand for C then A and C are substitutes.

## 2.4 Supply

### 2.4.1 Definition of supply

### 2.4.2 Price and supply

### 2.4.3 Individual and market supply

1.  Supply refers to the willingness of producers to provide a good or service for sale to consumers at a given price.

2.  Assume that ten different firms produce and sell the same product. The total amount they are willing and able to supply to consumers each week or period at each possible price is therefore the market supply of that product. The market supply curve for a given product is therefore the sum of all the individual supply curves of those firms willing and able to supply that product to consumers.

3.  **(a)** The price per unit; **(b)** The quantity of the product demanded or supplied per period, that is, each day, week, month or year.

4. An upward supply curve shows by how much producers of a product will expand the amount they are willing and able to supply as the price of that product increases. This is because as the price of a product rises, the more profit producers may be able to earn from its sale.

5. Producers will 'move along' their supply curves in response to a change in the price of the product. They will expand supply as its price increases and will contract their supply as price falls. In contrast, if price is unchanged but producers reduce or increase the amount they supply compared to the previous period, then this will cause a shift in their supply curves.

### 2.4.4 Conditions of supply

1. If product A is more profitable to produce than before and product B is less profitable, then producers are likely to want to increase the amount of A they are willing to supply to consumers and reduce the quantity of B they will supply. Additional resources will be required to increase production of A but fewer resources will be needed to produce B. Resources no longer required to make and sell product B can therefore be reallocated to the production of A.

2. **(a)** Choose three from the following: a fall in the profitability of other products; a fall in the cost of factors of production, for example, due to a reduction in wage costs or raw material prices; an increase in the availability of resources, for example, due to an expanding labour supply or the discovery or new mineral deposits; technical progress and improvements in production processes and machinery; an increase in business optimism and expectations of profit; an increase in government subsidies; a reduction in taxes on profits; other factors, such as the impact of good weather conditions on the supply of agricultural produce. **(b)** Choose three from the following: an increase in the profitability of other products; an increase in the cost of factors of production, for example, due to higher wages and raw material prices; a fall in the availability of resources, for example, due to a fall in the supply of labour or depletion of non-renewable natural resources; a fall in business optimism and lower profit expectations; a cut in government subsidies; an increase in taxes on profits; other factors, such as the impact of wars and natural disasters.

**E** 'Government announces a big cut in subsidies for solar panels': this will reduce the profits of suppliers of solar panels who are likely to reduce their supply in response.

'Japanese car manufacturers struggle to continue production as earthquake hits part suppliers': the reduction in the supply of car parts will, in turn, reduce the supply of cars.

'Warm spring is welcome news for strawberry growers': the good weather will increase the output and supply of strawberries.

'Falling oil prices hits manufacturing costs': as costs rise, the profitability of many products will fall. In response many manufacturers may cut output and the quantities of good they are willing to supply to consumers.

'Minimum wage rise (in China) … could impact tech costs worldwide': the global supply of hi-tech consumer products could fall leading to an increase in prices because of the impact of rising wage costs on the profitability of Chinese manufacturing plants.

## 2.5 Price determination
### 2.5.1 Market equilibrium
### 2.5.2 Market disequilibrium

1. The market will be in equilibrium at a market price of $500 per tonne. At this price the market demand for refined sugar is exactly equal to the amount producers are willing to supply.

2. At a market price of $300 per tonne there will be an excess demand of 10 million tonnes per month.

3. At a market price of $800 per tonne there will be an excess supply of 15 million tonnes per month.

4. At an equilibrium market price there will be no excess demand or excess supply: the amount of the product consumers are willing and able to buy each period will be exactly equal to the amount producers are willing to supply. In contrast, at a disequilibrium market price, market demand will not be equal to market supply. If there is an excess supply, price will have to fall for consumers to buy up the excess. If there is an excess demand, price will have to rise to encourage producers to expand supply.

**E**

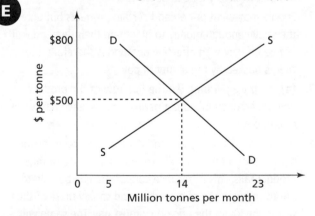

## 2.6 Price changes
### 2.6.1 Causes of price changes
### 2.6.2 Consequences of price changes

1. **(a)** Market <u>demand</u> has <u>increased</u>. The equilibrium price has <u>increased</u>. The quantity traded has <u>increased</u>; **(b)** Market <u>supply</u> has <u>decreased</u>. The equilibrium price has <u>increased</u>. The quantity traded has <u>decreased</u>.

2.

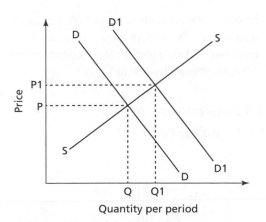

Quantity per period

Advertising can create or increase a consumer want for a product. This will shift the market demand curve for the product to the right (from DD to D1D1). As a result, the equilibrium market price will rise from P to P1 and the quantity supplied and traded will expand from Q to Q1.

**E** 'Avocado prices set to rise …' because market demand has increased as the market supply has fallen.

'Slump in China auto sales …': falling demand for Chinese cars has resulted in falling market prices.

'Iron ores prices fall…' because the global market supply of iron ore has increased.

'Retailers are expected to raise prices…' because retail market supplies are likely to be fall following the increase in wage costs which will reduce retail profits.

## Key words

| 1 I | 2 C | 3 L | 4 J | 5 K |
|-----|-----|-----|-----|------|
| 6 G | 7 B | 8 F | 9 D | 10 N |
| 11 H | 12 E | 13 A | 14 M | |

## Revision summary

| 1. effective; downward; contract | 2. disposable; substitute | 3. right |
|-----|-----|-----|
| 4. upward | 5. fall | 6. right; left |
| 7. equilibrium | 8. disequilibrium; increase | 9. increase; reduce |

## 2.7 Price elasticity of demand (PED)
### 2.7.1 Definition of PED
### 2.7.2 Calculation of PED

1. Price elasticity of demand measures how consumer demand for a product responds to small changes in its price. For example, if a small percentage change in price causes a larger percentage change in the quantity demanded, then demand for that product is said to be price elastic. If instead there is very little response in demand it is said to be price inelastic.

2. Price elasticities of demand will differ depending on how essential products are, how many substitutes they have, how much people spend on them and how often. For example, products such as electricity and bread are essential items for many consumers and have few alternatives. An increase in their prices may have very little impact on demand for them. In contrast, cakes are non-essential and a rise in their price may result in a big contraction in demand for them as consumers are able to buy biscuits, sweets or other close substitutes instead. It can sometimes take a long time to shop around for alternative products, so the longer the period of time consumers have to make their buying decisions, the more price elastic their demand tends to be. For example, a car is an expensive luxury item that a consumer may only buy once every few years. An increase in the price of one particular type of car by 10% will therefore have a big impact on the amount a consumer will have to pay so it will be worth spending time considering alternatives. In contrast, milk is a low cost item which the average consumer will buy several times each week. If the price of milk in a nearby shop increases by 10% the impact on the amount a consumer must pay will be relatively small and it will not be worth spending a lot of time looking for cheaper alternatives.

3. Price elasticity of demand = % change in quantity demanded / % change in price,
where the % change in quantity demanded = (40kg/200kg) × 100 = 20%
and the % change in price = ($0.50/$5.00) × 100 = 10%.
Therefore, PED = 20%/10% = 2, so demand for tomatoes is price elastic.

4. (a) is correct.

## 2.7.3 PED and total spending on a product and revenue
## 2.7.4 Significance of PED

1. a) PED = % change in quantity demanded / % change in price.
   % change in quantity demanded = 100/1,000 × 100/1 = 10%
   % change in price = $0.10/$5.00 × 100/1= 2%
   PED = 10%/2% = 5. Demand is elastic because the percentage change in quantity demanded is greater than the percentage change in price.

   b) total revenue = price × sales
   total revenue before change = $5 × 1,000 = $5,000
   total revenue after change = $5.10 × 900 = $ 4,590

   c) Because demand is elastic, total spending by consumers on the product has fallen following the price increase. As a result, revenues from sales fell from $5,000 to $4,590 per week. The decision to raise price was therefore not a good one.

**2.**

| Change in product price | Change in quantity demanded each period | Is demand price elastic or inelastic? | Will total revenue each period increase or decrease? |
|---|---|---|---|
| Increase by 2% | Decrease by 4% | *Price elastic* | *Revenue will fall* |
| Increase by 2% | Decrease by 1% | *Price inelastic* | *Increase* |
| Decrease by 5% | Increase by 10% | *Price elastic* | *Increase* |
| Decrease by 5% | Increase by 3% | *Price inelastic* | *Decrease* |
| Increase by 1% | Unchanged | *Price inelastic* | *Increase* |

**E** revenues; elastic; reduce; time; raise or increase.

# 2.8 Price elasticity of supply (PES)
## 2.8.1 Definition of PES
## 2.8.2 Calculation of PES

1. Price elasticity of supply is a measure of the responsiveness of supply to a small change in the price of a product. For example, if a small reduction in price causes a proportionately larger contraction in the quantity supplied then the supply of that product is said to be price elastic. If instead there is very little contraction in supply it is said to be price inelastic.

2. The more time producers have to increase their output of a product and the more resources available to do so, the more price elastic its supply will be. For example, the supply of many vegetables is fixed and price inelastic in the short run but producers will be able to plant and grow more in future seasons if they can obtain more land. In contrast, producers of smart phones may be able to significantly expand production in a matter of weeks by using their existing machinery and other resources more intensively.

3. Price elasticity of supply = % change in quantity supplied / % change in price,
   where the % change in quantity supplied = (200/1,000) × 100 = 20%
   and the % change in price = ($25/$250) × 100 = 20%.
   Therefore, PES = 20%/20% = 1, i.e. unitary price elasticity.

4. Price elasticity of supply = % change in quantity supplied / % change in price,
   where the % change in quantity supplied = (400/1000) × 100 = 40%
   and the % change in price = ($25/$250) × 100 = 20%.
   Therefore, PES = 40%/20% = 2, so supply is more price elastic after twelve months.

5. Supply is forecast to become more price elastic over time because the manufacturer will be able to install new plant and machinery to raise production from 1,000 bicycles each week to 1,400.

## 2.8.3 Determinants of PES
## 2.8.4 Significance of PES

1.

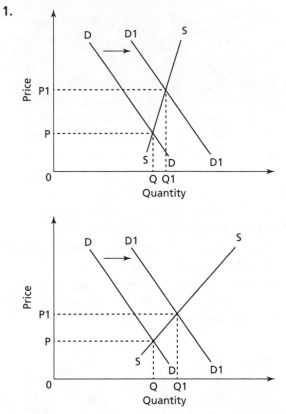

Supply to the market in the first diagram is price inelastic. The supply curve is very steep. This means the increase in demand from DD to D1D1 will have much greater impact on market price (the increase from P to P1) than on the quantity supplied and exchanged (the increase from Q to Q1).

In contrast, the expansion in supply in response to the increase in demand is much greater in the second diagram than in the first. Supply is price elastic. The increase in demand therefore has a proportionately greater impact on quantity than it does on market price.

2. Most firms will want to expand their supply as quickly as possible to take full advantage of any increase in demand and the prices of their products. Increased demand means more customers and more sales and higher prices means more profit. A firm may increase the price elasticity of its supply by holding more of its products in stock so it can release them quickly when there is an increase in demand, and by expanding its productive capacity and increasing the mobility of its resources.

Natural rubber: price inelastic because it takes a long time to grow more rubber trees.

Synthetic rubber: relatively price elastic, because output can be increased relatively easily assuming there is sufficient oil and spare capacity in existing production facilities to do so. Production can also be cut or stopped relatively quickly if rubber prices were to fall.

Cars: relatively price elastic, assuming there is sufficient spare capacity in existing producing facilities to increase production following an increase in price. Production can also be cut reasonably quickly if prices were to fall.

Cruise ships: these can take many years to build so supply will be highly price inelastic.

## Key words

| 1 E | 2 A | 3 D |
|-----|-----|-----|
| 4 B | 5 C |     |

### Revision summary

| 1 elasticity; revenue | 2 elastic | 3 inelastic |
|-----------------------|-----------|-------------|
| 4 more | 5 inelastic; elastic | |

# 2.9 Market economic system

## 2.9.1 Definition of market economic system

## 2.9.2 Advantages and disadvantages of the market economic system

1. The allocation of scarce resources in a market economic system is determined by changes in consumer demand for different products and the profit motives of producers. Prices act as signals to producers indicating when and how resources should be reallocated. The price and profitability of a product will rise if there is excess demand for it. In response, producers will expand supply of the product by reallocating resources to its production from less profitable activities. For example, falling consumer demand for a product will create an excess supply causing the market price and profitability of the product to fall. In response, producers will reallocate resources out of this market.

2. Two advantages of a market economic system are (explain two from the following): it produces a wide variety of goods and services to satisfy consumers' wants; firms will respond quickly to changes in consumer wants and spending patterns; the profit motive of private firms encourages them to develop new products and more efficient methods of production; there are very few, if any, taxes and regulations.

3. Two disadvantages of a market economic system are (explain two from the following): some worthwhile goods and services will not be produced if it is not profitable to do so; firms will only supply products to consumers who are able to pay the most for them; there may be unemployment because resources will only be employed if it is profitable to do so; harmful goods may be produced if it is profitable to do so; firms seeking to maximize their profits may disregard the impact of their production decisions on the welfare of people, animals and the environment.

The two articles reveal how private firms in a market economy will allocate resources to the production of products which are in demand and profitable.

# 2.10 Market failure

## 2.10.1 Definition of market failure

## 2.10.2–3 Causes and consequences of market failure

1. Market failures reduce economic welfare. They occur when markets result in undesirable outcomes or wasteful or harmful activities.

2. Consumers may over-consume products that may be dangerous or harmful to other people and the natural environment. This is because they often overlook the harmful effects their consumption can have. Private firms will continue to supply dangerous or harmful products if consumers are willing to pay for them and it is profitable to do so. In contrast, the consumption of some goods and services, for example, education and healthcare, can benefit the economy and all of society but might may be under-consumed by people if they had to pay for these services in full. Individual consumers will undervalue the wider benefits of their education and health.

3. Markets may fail to produce desirable outcomes in the following ways (select two of the following): private firms will not provide public goods such as street-lighting, national parks or national defence because it will be impossible for them to charge individual consumers according to how much they benefit from these services – it is therefore impossible for them to make a profit; merit goods such as education and healthcare will be underprovided because fewer people will consume them if a market price is charged for them; private firms and consumers will not take account of the harmful effects their actions can have on other people, organizations and the environment; some people may suffer long periods of unemployment and hardship because resources will only be employed if it is profitable to do so; private firms may produce dangerous and harmful goods if consumers want them and it is profitable to do so; some large, powerful firms may restrict competition and consumer choice in order to charge high prices and maximize their profits.

'Thousands protest against lack of affordable housing': private firms will produce goods for consumers with the greatest ability to pay for them.

'Tesco is fined £300,000…' : private firms may mislead consumers to boost their sales and profits.

'Factory workers in Bangladesh…' : private firms may exploit workers in order to minimize their costs and maximize their profits.

'The largest Coca-Cola plant in India...' : private firms may ignore the harmful effects of their activities on other firms, communities and the environment.

## 2.11 Mixed economic system

### 2.11.1 Definition of the mixed economic system

### 2.11.2 Government intervention to address market failure

1. The actions of consumers and producers determine the allocation of resources in a market economy. This also occurs in a mixed economy. However, some resource allocation decisions will also be made or regulated by a government in a mixed economy.

2. By increasing prices, indirect taxes can reduce consumer demand for products that result in negative externalities such as pollution. As sales of these products fall, producers are likely to cut back their production. Alternatively, laws and regulations can be introduced by governments to ban or control productive activities that create significant external costs. For example, anti-pollution laws can stop firms contaminating land and water supplies with untreated waste. In contrast, subsidies may be paid to firms to encourage them to produce more goods and services that have major external benefits.

3. The social cost of car use is likely to exceed its social benefit. This is because car use causes congestion and noise and air pollution. These impose external costs on other people and organizations. Increasing taxes on vehicles and petrol may help to reduce demand for cars and reduce some of these external costs. Additionally, if more people can be encouraged to travel by buses or trains instead of by car, then the social costs of car use may be reduced further. Subsidizing bus and rail services will reduce the private costs of their provision. In response, suppliers will expand the services they offer and fares should reduce. This in turn should encourage some people to use bus and rail services for travel instead of their cars and reduce external costs.

4. A government may set a legal minimum price in a market to raise the price of a demerit good, such as cigarettes or alcohol, in an attempt to reduce their consumption and their external costs. Similarly, governments may force private firms to charge higher prices for products that cause excessive pollution, waste or other external costs. Demand for these products should contract as their prices are raised. A government may also set a minimum wage to prevent powerful employers from paying some groups of workers very low wages.

5. The maximum price in the first market (diagram A) will have no effect because it has been set well above the equilibrium market price. In contrast, the Pmax has been set below the market price in the second market (B). At this price quantity supplied will be less than the quantity demanded by consumers. There will be excess demand. The available supply may have to rationed. It may also encourage illegal trading and smuggling.

6. The price elasticity of demand for cigarettes is below 1 and therefore price inelastic. Therefore the imposition of a 20% tax on the price of a packet of cigarettes will (a) result in a contraction in demand by 12% (or less than 20%) and (b) increase total spending on cigarettes. Government tax revenue will increase as a result of the tax.

7. (a) diagram (ii); (b) diagram (i).

8. It will be desirable for a government to be a producer of goods and services that will benefit society and the economy if private firms are unwilling to provide them because it is not profitable to do so or they will only provide them at prices many people cannot afford. A government can fund the provision of such goods and services from taxes and other revenues and it can choose to provide them to people on low incomes for free or at subsidized  prices they are able to afford.

For example, services regarded as essential or beneficial to public and economic welfare are provided by the public sector in many countries because it is considered desirable for everyone to have access to them regardless of their ability to pay. Examples of publicly provided services include water and sanitation, electricity and education.

Similarly, a government will need to provide public goods such as national defence. Private firms will not provide public goods because it is impossible for them to charge consumers directly for their use. This is because public goods benefit every person equally regardless of whether they have paid for them or not.

The public sector provision of goods and services will also provide jobs and incomes for people who may otherwise have been unemployed because it was not profitable for private firms to employ them.

**E** 'High taxes forcing companies to relocate overseas': high taxes on businesses will reduce their profits and therefore the reward for enterprise. As a result there will be fewer businesses and less employment.

'The cost of complying with employment laws and other regulations...': regulations can increase the costs and lower the profits of running businesses. As a result, they may be fewer businesses and jobs.

'Subsidies paid to farmers has resulted in an excess supply of corn...': subsidies distort price signals. There have encouraged farmers to reallocate resources to the production of corn from other crops. As a result, the supply of corn has outstripped demand causing corn prices and farm revenues to collapse.

## Key words

| 1 M | 2 H | 3 O | 4 E | 5 A | 6 K | 7 P | 8 N | 9 C |
|-----|-----|-----|-----|-----|-----|-----|-----|-----|
| 10 B | 11 G | 12 R | 13 F | 14 J | 15 | 16 Q | 17 L | 18 D |

## Revision summary

| 1 prices; demerit | 2 failures; market | 3 mixed; under; regulations |
|---|---|---|
| 4 below; excess | 5 over; above; supply | 6 maximum; below |
| 7 taxes; private; increase | 8 increase; reduce | 9 costs |

### Working with data and diagrams

1.

| Movement | Explanation |
|---|---|
| a to b | The shift in the market demand curve from DD to D1D1 (a decrease in demand) |
| a to c | The movement along the market supply curve (a contraction in supply) |
| P to P1 | The fall in the equilibrium market price |
| Q to Q1 | The fall in the equilibrium quantity traded |

2. quantity demanded; price

3. a) PED = 8%/5% = 1.6 (i.e. price elastic)

   b) Demand for the window cleaner's services is price elastic because (choose one of the following) consumers will probably be able to switch to one of many competing suppliers of the same service; many consumers may choose to clean their own windows instead; consumers may choose to have their windows cleaned less often; it is a non-essential product.

   c) By increasing the price he charges for his services, the window cleaner will lose revenue. This is because the demand for his services is price elastic.

4.

| Movement | Explanation |
|---|---|
| a to b | The shift in the market supply curve from SS to S1S1 (a decrease in supply) |
| a to c | The movement along the market demand curve (a contraction in demand) |
| P to P1 | The increase in the equilibrium market price |
| Q to Q1 | The fall in the equilibrium quantity traded |

5. quantity supplied; price

6. a)
$$\text{PES (year 1)} = \frac{(2,000/10,000) \times 100}{(50/200) \times 100} = \frac{20\%}{25\%} = 0.8$$

$$\text{PES (year 2)} = \frac{(3,000/10,000) \times 100}{(50/200) \times 100} = \frac{30\%}{25\%} = 1.2$$

   b) In year 1 supply is relatively price inelastic. In year 2 it is relatively price elastic.

   c) The price elasticities above show that the supply of corn is expected to become more price elastic over time. This is because it will take time and require more land and seeds to plant and grow more corn.

## Multiple choice questions

| 1C | 2A | 3B | 4C | 5C |
|-----|-----|-----|-----|-----|
| 6C | 7A | 8D | 9D | 10B |
| 11A | 12D | 13B | 14C | 15C |
| 16B | 17D | 18D | 19A | 20C |

### Structured questions

1. a) The allocation of scarce resources in a market economic system is determined by the price mechanism. Changes in prices gives signals to producers indicating when and how resources should be reallocated. The price and profitability of a product will rise if consumer demand for it increases. In response, producers will allocate additional resources to its production to expand its supply.

   b) The extract states that the economic system in Cuba 'now operates more like a market economic system'. It explains that Cuba's economy is dominated by government-run enterprises but in recent years growth in private sector enterprise and employment has been encouraged. In 1981, the private sector employed just 8% of Cuban workers but is now around 28% and still growing.

   c) Two factors are (choose two of the following): the government may have wanted to reduce the size and cost of the public sector in order to reduce taxes in the economy; private sector provision of goods and services may be more efficient than public sector provision because private firms have to compete with each other to make a profit; private sector firms may offer consumers more choice and better value than public sector firms and may be able to respond more quickly to changes in consumer demand; to provide new business and employment opportunities for workers made unemployed as a result of the closure of the sugar mills and reduction in public sector employment; to improve the allocation of resources in the economy so that more goods and services can be produced and more needs and wants satisfied with its available resources.

   d)

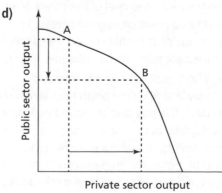

   Because resources are scarce, Cuba must choose what goods and services to produce, how to produce them and who to produce them for. In the past, these decisions have been made by the government of

Cuba, but more recently it has decided to allow the private sector to own and control a larger share of resources. The opportunity cost of more goods and services being produced by the private sector is a loss of public sector output. This, for example, can be represented by the move from A to B along the production possibility curve in the diagram above.

e)

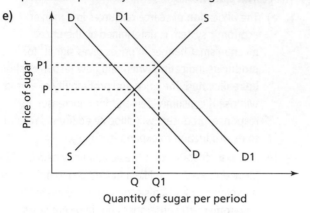

Quantity of sugar per period

The global demand for sugar is likely to have increased (represented by the movement in the demand curve from DD to D1D1) resulting in a higher market price (P1) and larger quantity traded (Q1).

f) The social benefit of healthcare exceeds its private benefit because it has external benefits. For example, a person treated for an infectious disease will not be able to pass on the disease to other people. The same person will also be able to return to productive work more quickly.

g) Other economies may benefit from using more of their resources to increase the provision of healthcare if it is underprovided and the reallocated resources are used efficiently. This is because reallocating resources to healthcare provision will reduce the resources available to provide other goods or services. For example, it may not be sensible to cut education to provide more public healthcare if the social benefit of education is far greater than the social benefit of additional healthcare. Some economies, for example, may already have a good level of healthcare. More public healthcare provision may not necessarily increase the quality of healthcare and may simply be used to treat more minor health problems.

However, where healthcare is poor, increased provision may help to reduce death rates and increase life expectancy. This may help to expand the labour force and the total output the economy can produce. A healthier work force is also a more productive one. Output will be higher and production costs lower if, for example, sickness absences from employment are reduced. Expanding healthcare can also provide more job opportunities for healthcare workers and revenue opportunities for firms producing medical equipment and drugs. However, if the main benefit of increased

provison in an economy is that more people are able to survive longer into retirement and old age then the labour force may not expand. Instead, a government may have to spend more on pensions and the provision of long-term care for elderly people.

2. a) In a market economy there is no or very little government ownership or control of resources. Resources are allocated by private sector firms to their more profitable uses based on consumer demand for different goods and services.

b) The price elasticity of demand for a product measures the responsiveness of consumer demand to a small change in the price of that product. For example, if a 1% increase in price results in a contraction in quantity demanded by more than 1%, then demand is said to be price elastic. However, if demand is insensitive to price or price inelastic, for example because the product is an essential item, then demand will contract by less than 1% following a 1% increase in the product price.

c) An increase in the average income of consumers will increase their demand for a normal good but may reduce their demand for an inferior good. The diagram below shows the impact of an increase in demand for a normal good. The market demand curve shifts to the right from DD to D1D1. As a result, the equilibrium market price increases from P to P1 and as the price rises supply expands from Q to Q1 to satisfy the increased level of demand.

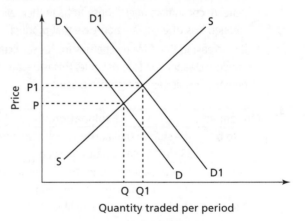

Quantity traded per period

d) All businesses selling products will benefit from knowing how consumer demand for their products will respond to changes in their prices. This is because changes in demand will affect their sales revenues and therefore the amount of profit they can make. For example, if a business knows that demand for its product is highly price elastic, then even a small increase in its price will reduce its revenue. In contrast, cutting its price will cause a much larger proportionate increase in demand and its revenue but only if it is able to expand its supply by the same amount. If the supply of its product is price inelastic, then it will not be able to increase its sale and revenues.

If a business knows that demand for its product is price elastic, it can indicate that it has many competitors. In contrast, if demand for its product is price inelastic, it may indicate that the business has few competitors and, therefore, significant market power. If so, it will be able to increase its revenues by raising its prices.

However, price elasticity of demand is difficult to measure and many other factors affect demand other than price. For example, a firm may believe demand for its product is inelastic and raises its price in order to increase its revenues. However, if average consumer incomes are falling in the economy due to rising unemployment, then demand for its product may fall. Or a new competitor may have recently entered the market offering consumers a better quality product and at a lower price. All businesses must therefore have knowledge about how changes in other market conditions over time can affect demand for their products and their revenues.

3. a) The social cost of an economic activity is its total cost to society. It includes both private costs, such as the cost of materials and wages, and external costs such as pollution.

b) Owning and running a car can be expensive. Car users will need to pay for petrol, insurance, maintenance and repairs and also possibly road tolls and parking tickets. These financial costs are their private costs. However, their car use can impose much greater external costs on many other people and organizations. These costs may be difficult to value but will include air and noise pollution, reduced journey times due to traffic congestion and the loss of lives or injuries due to accidents. Harmful engine emissions can also cause health problems and are contributing to global warming.

c) The market supply curve for petrol will shift upwards by the amount of the tax imposed on top of each possible price per litre. As a result, the equilibrium market price of petrol will increase (from P to P1 in the diagram) and demand will contract (from Q to Q1). However, because demand for petrol is price inelastic the contraction in demand may be relatively small.

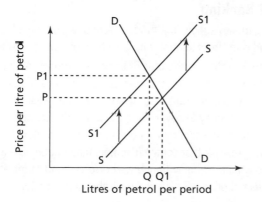
Litres of petrol per period

d) Private sector firms will provide bus, rail and other public transportation services only if they are profitable. Any services, routes or times that are not profitable will not be supplied. Any consumers who would want to use such services will have to travel by private car, taxi or other methods of transport. Even on services that are profitable, fares may be higher than many people on low incomes could afford to pay. As a result, car usage will be greater and, therefore, pollution and traffic congestion higher than they would have been had more people been able to travel by public transport. Private firms providing bus and rail services will not take account of these external costs when they are working out what fares they will charge in order to maximize their profits.

In contrast, a government may choose to run more public transport services even if they do not make a profit. Running more services than the private sector is willing to provide will increase employment opportunities. This may be an important government objective if unemployment in the economy is high.

A government may also keep fares low so they are affordable to people on low incomes. This can help to reduce car use and the external costs it creates. However, if public sector services are not required to make a profit, they may not be run efficiently: costs will be higher and service quality lower. Taxes will therefore have to be raised to pay for them. As a result, disposable incomes will be lower, reducing the amount consumers have to spend on other goods and services.

Because private sector firms have a profit motive they may be better at controlling the costs of transport services than public sector transport providers. Fewer resources will be wasted. If so, rather than the public sector providing public transport services it may be cheaper and more efficient for a government to subsidize private firms to provide those services that would otherwise be unprofitable.

4. a) A mixed economy is an economic system in which resource allocation decisions are taken by a private sector and a public sector owned and controlled by a government.

b) If fresh fruit and vegetables are normal goods, demand for them will increase as the disposable incomes of consumers rise; a rise in the price of canned and frozen fruit and vegetables may increase the demand for fresh produce; changes in consumers' tastes and desires for healthier lifestyles; advertising may increase consumer wants for fresh fruit and vegetables; a growing population will increase demand for all types of foods over time; a fall in the price of meats may reduce demand for fruit and vegetables.

c) If the objective of the government is to reduce the consumption of cigarettes, then it will want to know if demand for the product is elastic or inelastic. If demand is price elastic, an increase in price due to the imposition of an indirect tax of say 10%, will contract demand for cigarettes by more than 10%. For example, if the price elasticity of demand is 2, then the quantity of cigarettes consumed will contract by 20%. However, if the price elasticity of demand is less than 1, demand will contract by less than 10%. That is, the tax will fail to achieve a significant reduction in the consumption of cigarettes. However, the government will receive additional tax revenues that it may then be able to spend on advertising campaigns to persuade people to stop smoking.

d) Prices provide important signals to producers in both mixed and market economies about the products consumers want and how profitable they are to make and sell. Producers will use this information to decide how to allocate their scarce resources. However, in a totally free market economy, prices are determined by the actions of producers and consumers who will only be concerned with their own private costs and benefits. For example, by striving to make as much profit as possible, private firms may ignore the negative impacts their productive activities can have on other people, firms and the environment. These external costs will not be reflected in the prices they will charge consumers or in their profits. As a result, private firms may overproduce goods that are harmful. Similarly, private firms may fail to allocate sufficient resources to the production of merit goods such as education and healthcare, despite their significant social benefits. That is, merit goods will be underprovided and under-consumed in a market economy. Private firms will also fail to provide public goods such as street lighting and national defence because it is impossible to charge consumers prices that reflect how much they have individually used or benefited from these services. However, in a mixed economy a government can use tax revenues to pay for the provision of public goods and merit goods. A government can also 'adjust' the market prices of goods or services using indirect taxes to reduce the consumption of harmful or uneconomic goods and, through subsidies, encourage producers to supply more products that are socially beneficial.

Prices are therefore important for resource allocation in both types of economic system. However, governments in mixed economies can intervene in markets to correct any product prices that fail to reflect their full social costs or benefits. However, sometimes indirect taxes are used just to raise revenue and subsidies may be used to protect old, inefficient industries from more efficient overseas competitors. Taxes and subsidies used in these ways will distort price signals and the allocation of resources.

# 3.1 Money and banking

## 3.1.1 Money

1. A money is any item or commodity that is widely accepted as a medium of exchange or means of payment for other goods and services.

2. Any two of the following functions: money must be generally accepted as a medium of exchange in return for all other goods and services; money provides a unit of account used to measure and compare the values of different goods and services; money should provide a good store of value which allows people to save it and spend it later; money provides a means of deferred payment, allowing people to buy goods and services on credit.

3. Any three of the following characteristics: a good money should be generally acceptable so that it can be used to buy goods and services from different people or firms; it should be relatively strong, durable and hard-wearing so it does not perish or wear out quickly; it should be portable and easy to carry around; it should be divisible into different values so that it can be used to pay for expensive and inexpensive items and to receive change; it should be limited in supply or scarce so that it has value.

4. If there was no method of exchanging goods and services, people would have to be self-sufficient. However, as economies have developed, there has been increasing specialization on the basis of division of labour. This has led to an increase in production, but specialization can only work if people are able to trade to obtain the goods and services they need and want but do not produce for themselves.

**E** The main limitation of barter is that it is reliant on a double coincidence of wants. This means that exchange can only take place when two people each want the good the other person has. Money is much more flexible and allows people to buy whatever they wish, as long as they have enough money to finance a transaction.

## 3.1.2 Banking

1. The money supply in a modern economy consists of notes and coins in circulation and the value of bank deposits.

2. Interest rates are the cost of borrowing money. An interest rate will normally be charged as a percentage of the total value of a loan. Banks charge customers interest rates to borrow money to cover the costs of administering loans and to yield a profit. An interest rate will also help to cover the risk that some customers may not be able to repay all the money they have borrowed and to offset the effect of price inflation reducing the value of a loan.

3. Any two of the following: commercial banks enable people and businesses to save money safely by providing a variety of different savings accounts; they provide current accounts which can be used by the account holders to make and receive payments; they can lend money to people and businesses in a variety of ways, such as through a loan, an overdraft or a mortgage; some commercial banks may also sell insurance policies, operate pension funds, provide financial advice and sell foreign currencies.

4. Any two of the following: a central bank will supervise the conduct of the banking system in a country through a number of rules and regulations; it has a key role in operating the government's monetary policy (for example, by setting the interest rate in the economy); it can act as a lender of last resort by lending to banks that run short of money; as well as being the banker's bank, it also acts as the government's bank and the government will hold an account at the central bank to make and receive payments; it is responsible for managing the national debt of a country and holding its gold and foreign currency reserves used to make international payments and to stabilize the value of the national currency on the global foreign exchange market; a central bank will also usually have the exclusive right in a country to issue new notes and coins and replace old and worn out ones in that country.

**E** A central bank deals directly with the commercial banks and with the government, but it does not usually deal with members of the public. For example, if a person wanted to open a savings account or arrange a loan, they would have to deal with a commercial bank, not a central bank.

## Key words

| 1 L | 2 G | 3 C | 4 J | 5 H | 6 K | 7 A |
|-----|-----|-----|-----|-----|-----|-----|
| 8 N | 9 O | 10 B | 11 E | 12 I | 13 D | 14 F |

## Revision summary

| | |
|---|---|
| 1. Money; barter | 5. notes; coins; deposits |
| 2. unit of account | 6. save; borrow |
| 3. divisible; scarce | 7. commercial |
| 4. barter | 8. central |

# 3.2 Households
## 3.2.1(i) The influences on spending

1. Consumption or spending decisions are strongly influenced by a person's income, but a person is not able to spend all of their money because some of their income will have been taken away before they received it. For example, people will have to pay various taxes and charges out of their income, such as income tax and national insurance. The amount that is left, after all these deductions have been made, is known as disposable income.

2. Richer people are generally able to spend more than poorer people because their income is higher and so there is more money to spend. However, although they may spend more in absolute terms, it is likely that they will spend a smaller proportion of their income compared to poorer people who are likely to spend a very high proportion of their income.

3. People may have a number of different motives for spending money. The main one is to purchase goods and services to satisfy needs and wants: some of this spending will be on necessities to satisfy needs, such as food; some of this spending will be on non-essential items to satisfy wants, such as a television. The price of goods and services is also a factor that will influence spending decisions, as people will usually be more likely to buy products at a lower price than at a higher price.

## 3.2.2(ii) The influences on saving

1. People who earn approximately the same income can vary a great deal in terms of the proportion that they save. One major factor is the spending commitments that a person has, i.e. how much is there left to save. It may also depend on whether a person is saving for a particular reason, such as saving for a deposit to put on a property. The age of a person may also be a factor; for example, older people may save a higher proportion of their income as they get nearer to retirement. The rate of interest is an important influence on savings and some people may be more inclined to save if the interest rate rises significantly above the rate of inflation.

2. Poorer people are usually able to save less than richer people because much of their income will be required to pay for essential items, such as food, clothing and shelter. Richer people will be in a better position to save some of their income because there is a greater likelihood that some of the income will be unspent even after essential and non-essential items have been paid for.

3. Interest rates are a major influence on savings decisions. If a person wishes to save, he or she will be more tempted to do so if the rate of return on their savings, i.e. the interest they will receive, is relatively high. This is especially the case if the rate of interest on a savings account is above the rate of inflation in an economy: if the interest rate was less than the inflation rate, the money would be worth less because inflation reduces or erodes the purchasing power of a given sum of money. Savers therefore want a real return on their savings, i.e. they want to receive a rate of interest that is above the rate of inflation.

However, interest rates are not the only factor that influences savings decisions. The income that a person receives is an important factor, especially the income that is left after all essential expenditure has been made. The existence of secure financial institutions, with appropriate savings schemes, is also an important factor. Another influence is the purpose of the saving, i.e. the more important the savings goal, the more likely it is that a person will save.

 Poorer people may find it very difficult to save money. Their income will be relatively low and much of this income will be needed to meet their needs for essential items, such as food, shelter and basic clothing. There is usually very little, if any, money that is 'spare' at the end of a week or month that poorer people could save.

### 3.2.3 (iii) The influences on borrowing

1. People may have different motives for borrowing money. A major reason is where a person's expenditure is greater than their income and this deficit has to be made up by borrowing. It may also depend on whether people need to finance the purchase of an item, such as a property, where funds can be borrowed through a mortgage, which is usually paid off over a period of 25 years. People may also be more inclined to borrow money if they expect their income to increase substantially in the near future. Some people who are thinking of borrowing will also be tempted by relatively low rates of interest on borrowing products.

2. Poorer people, on the whole, are more likely to borrow than richer people because most, if not all, of their income will have been used to pay for essential items. The savings ratio of poorer people will be much lower than for richer people and so they will need to borrow money if they need something that their income does not allow them to afford. Richer people, because they are able to save some of their income, are less likely to need to borrow.

3. High levels of borrowing could become a serious economic problem in an economy. It is not a problem as long as the borrower is able to repay both the amount of money that has been borrowed and the interest payments associated with the borrowing product. It is a problem when the borrower is unable to meet the repayments on a loan. If they have borrowed money to buy a property, through a mortgage, and they find that they cannot meet the repayments, it may be that the mortgage provider repossesses the property. People who are unable to pay their personal debts can be declared insolvent or bankrupt. If a person has bought something through what is known as hire purchase, such as a car, and they fall behind with their repayments, the car could be taken from them. The financial crisis of 2007–2008 was, to a large extent, caused by problems in the sub-prime loans sector, with people having to default on loans taken out to buy a property.

 The ability to spend and save rises with income. An older, skilled worker may earn more than a younger, unskilled worker because they have more experience and their skills may be in greater demand. As a result, the market wage a skilled worker can earn may be much higher than the rate earned by someone who is unskilled.

However, patterns of spending and savings can vary significantly between people with very similar incomes because people have different tastes or preferences. To explain likely differences in spending, saving and borrowing patterns between an older, skilled worker and a younger, unskilled worker we should therefore consider these factors.

For example, people may become more health conscious as they get older, and may increase their spending on healthcare products and exercising. Older workers may also be more likely to have families than younger people and will tend to spend money on goods and services their children will need and want, such as clothes, toys and schooling. They may also set up savings schemes for their children's future and also for themselves, such as a pension for when they retire from work. In contrast, a younger person may spend most, if not all, of their income on rented accommodation, fashionable clothes, music, travel and enjoying their leisure time.

Older workers with higher incomes, more secure jobs and who are also home owners may also be able to borrow more money from banks to enable them to buy luxury items such as overseas holidays, a new car and furnishings for their homes. Older workers may therefore spend more on loan repayments. In contrast, loan repayments may be at greater risk from younger people who have only recently started in work, earn relatively low incomes and have no property to offer as collateral or security against the loans. Consequently, banks may be less inclined to offer loans to younger, unskilled workers.

### Key words

| 1 L | 2 C | 3 F | 4 A | 5 N | 6 G | 7 H |
|-----|-----|-----|-----|-----|-----|-----|
| 8 M | 9 D | 10 K | 11 E | 12 B | 13 I | 14 O |

### Revision summary

| | |
|---|---|
| 1. disposable | 6. wants |
| 2. utility | 7. saving; more; less |
| 3. experience; utility | 8. consumption; less; cost |
| 4. inflation | 9. more |
| 5. low; needs | 10. wealth; collateral |

## 3.3 Workers

### 3.3.1 Factors affecting an individual's choice of occupation

1. Any two from the following: some people may be prepared to work for a low wage because they are unwilling to relocate or travel to areas where there are higher paid jobs; they may be unskilled and unable to command higher wages; because the job rewards them in other non-financial ways (for example, by allowing them to work

flexible hours); because it provides a pension, free private healthcare and gym membership or has better promotion prospects and is more secure than other, higher paid jobs.

2. Employees supply their labour to firms in return for payments known as wages. These payments can be made in a number of ways (select and explain two). For example, a person may be paid a fixed annual salary and in this situation they will receive 12 equal monthly payments. Alternatively, a person may be paid a fixed weekly wage for working a certain number of hours each week, known as a time rate, although an overtime rate will be paid for additional hours worked. Sometimes a person will be paid per unit of output produced and this is known as piece rate. Some workers may receive payment in relation to their productivity and this is known as a performance-related payment.

3. Non-wage factors refer to those influences on an individual's choice of occupation, other than those related to pay. These could include the hours of work, holiday entitlement, prospects of promotion, better working conditions, such as in relation to health and safety, flexible working arrangements, job security, work satisfaction, training opportunities, entitlement to a good pension, opportunities for promotion, convenience of travel, and fringe benefits, such as subsidized housing or the payment of school fees.

**E** Non-wage factors are likely to be more important than wage factors in influencing a person to apply for such a job. The salary is only $10,000 p.a., but the advertisement does stress a number of important non-wage factors: an opportunity to work in a lively and expanding bookshop; flexible hours of work; generous holiday entitlement; good promotion prospects and job security; extensive training opportunities; good working conditions; interesting and varied work.

## 3.3.2 Wage determination

1. An equilibrium or market wage rate is the rate of remuneration each worker will receive, per period of time or per unit of output, in a given labour market. At the market wage rate the supply of labour will be exactly equal to the demand for labour from firms.

2. a), b):

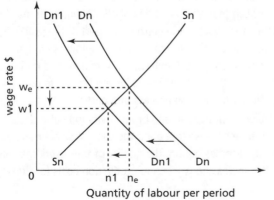

3. Two factors that may have caused the fall in demand for petrochemical engineers are (explain two from the following): a fall in demand for petrochemicals; a fall in the market price and profitability of petrochemicals; a fall in the productivity of petrochemical engineers; a fall in the price and/or increase in the productivity of capital equipment able to perform some of the functions or tasks of petrochemical engineers; an increase in non-wage employment costs, such as an increase in employment or payroll taxes or an increase in statutory pension contributions.

4. A training scheme could help an individual to earn a higher wage over time because training is likely to make an employee better at what they do. If the training scheme involves an employee learning new skills and gaining more qualifications, they are likely to become more productive and, as such, become more valuable to a firm. It is likely, therefore, that the employee will receive a higher wage.

**E** 'UK manufacturing businesses are facing a shortage of factory workers as the number of EU workers in the UK falls': decrease in labour supply is likely to increase market wage rates across a number of labour market.

'Economists fear falling productivity will prevent rise in living standards': demand for labour likely to fall resulting in falling market wage rates.

'US unemployment falls to lowest level for 18 years': US labour demand is high and firms may be finding it difficult to recruit new workers. These market conditions will tend to force up market wage rates.

'Demand for organic food and drink products soars': producers/suppliers of organic food and drink are likely to increase output in response and increase their demand for labour. This will push up market wage rates within the sector.

## 3.3.3 Reasons for differences in earnings

1. Wage differentials are differences in the market wage rates received by workers with different skills in the same industry, or between workers with similar skills in different industries or localities.

2. Two factors that explain occupational wage differentials are (choose two): differences in labour supply and demand conditions in different occupational labour markets. For example, market wage rates will be relatively high in those occupational labour markets in which there is a high demand for labour with the occupational skills and experience firms require and a relative shortage of workers with those skills. In contrast, where the supply of labour exceeds demand, wage rates will be relatively low; Some jobs are dirty, dangerous or require working at night and during other unsociable hours. Wage rates in these jobs must therefore be relatively high to compensate for these negative features in order to attract

a supply of labour; People will not study or train for long periods to acquire the specialized skills and knowledge they need to become surgeons, airline pilots or lawyers, for example, unless these occupations offer much higher wages than those that do not require specialized skills and qualifications; Some people may work for lower wages than they could earn in other occupations or areas simply because they do not know about the availability of better-paid jobs elsewhere. Lack of information about job availability can restrict the supply of labour to those jobs and can therefore help explain some differences in earnings between different jobs in different areas.

3.  An individual's earnings are likely to increase over time as they gain higher qualifications, learn new skills and go on training courses. They will also gain in experience and have a better understanding of a job. The individual is likely to be promoted during their working life. In many types of work, there will be more opportunities to earn additional income through overtime and bonuses.

4.  Male workers, on average, tend to earn more than female workers in many countries for a number of reasons. Male workers are generally more likely to be in a trade union than female workers and trade unions, especially those with strong collective bargaining power, can be influential in securing higher wages for their members. It is more likely that male workers will be in full-time employment, whereas many female workers will be in part-time employment, so it may simply be the case that higher wages are a reflection of longer working hours. It is also more likely that females will take a break from work, for example to bring up children, and in some jobs it may be difficult for them to start again at the same position in a firm as they were previously. However, in those countries which have strong equal pay legislation, it may be that the gap between males and female earnings is getting smaller.

5.  Skilled workers are likely to be paid more than unskilled workers for a variety of reasons. Skilled workers are likely to be more efficient and more productive than unskilled workers and this could explain the difference. There are also likely to be fewer skilled workers, and yet there will be a greater demand for them, contributing to the fact that their wages will be higher than those of unskilled workers.

6.  In many countries, workers in the public sector earn more than those in the private sector. The difference is sometimes described as the public sector premium. This is the case in the UK and the USA.

7.  In many countries, average earnings in the agricultural sector tend to be rather low. This is often because such work is relatively unskilled and so some workers migrate from the rural areas in search of higher earnings in the urban areas. Earnings in the manufacturing sector are likely to be higher than in the agricultural sector because, in many cases, a higher level of skill is required, especially where the job involves working with capital equipment. It

is the services or tertiary sector that has seen the biggest increase in employment in recent years in many countries and so there is an increase in the level of demand for such workers. Where there is also a shortage of appropriately skilled and qualified workers, the average level of earnings is likely to be quite high.

8.  A minimum wage needs to be set above an equilibrium wage in a labour market because this will make sure that the wage is higher than it would otherwise be. There would be no point imposing a minimum wage below the equilibrium wage in a labour market because it would have no effect on market conditions or the wage rate offered by employers.

## Key words

| 1 P | 2 N | 3 D | 4 J | 5 B | 6 O | 7 K | 8 C | 9 F | 10 H |
|-----|-----|-----|-----|-----|-----|-----|-----|-----|------|
| 11 R | 12 A | 13 G | 14 E | 15 S | 16 M | 17 I | 18 L | 19 Q | |

## Revision summary

| | |
|---|---|
| 1. derived | 6. differentials |
| 2. wages; non-wage | 7. more |
| 3. rate; piece; salary | 8. discrimination |
| 4. market; supply | 9. minimum |
| 5. contract; expand (or extend) | 10. higher |

## 3.3.4 Division of labour and specialization

1.  The division of labour involves dividing up a production process into a series of sequential tasks. Each task is then assigned to a different employee or group of employees to perform so they are able to specialize and improve their efficiency.

2.  The division of labour can benefit firms and their employees in a number of ways. Because it allows workers to specialize in particular tasks, it increases the speed, quality and cost of production, especially if it enables more of the production process to be automated. Time is saved and best use is made of each employee's abilities. Not only should this increase motivation but should also allow employees to maximize earnings linked to their productivity.

    However, overspecialization of labour reduces labour mobility within firms and between firms. Firms will find it difficult to use workers flexibly. For example, it may be difficult to move workers from one part of the production process to another to stand-in for employees who are off sick or on leave. Similarly, workers may find it difficult to change their jobs if their skills are limited to one particular production process in a particular firm.

    Employee motivation and productivity may also decline over time because repeating the same task over and over again becomes boring. The quality of their work may also suffer, increasing waste and production costs for firms.

3. There are a number of benefits of specialization for the individual. A worker will concentrate on a particular task and this will lead to an increase in skill in the performance of that task. Specialization can lead to a worker taking pride in what has been produced. It is also likely that division of labour can lead to a worker securing higher earnings as a result of the increase in quality and production.

4. There are a number of possible disadvantages of specialization for the individual. It is possible that the specific skill is no longer required, or that the demand for people with particular skills falls, and this could lead to the unemployment of such workers. Specialization tends to involve repetitive work and this could lead to boredom, demotivation and possibly a sense of alienation from what a worker is doing. It is possible that this could lead to a greater likelihood of accidents because of a lack of attention to what a worker is doing.

**E** Firms could try to overcome some of the problems associated with the division of labour in production and overspecialization of their workers in the following ways: making jobs more interesting by increasing variety of tasks; training workers to increase their range of skills so they can be used more flexibly; reducing levels of automation so that workers perform more of the production tasks themselves.

# 3.4 Trade unions

## 3.4.1 Definition of a trade union

## 3.4.2 The role of trade unions in the economy

1. A worker might decide to join a trade union for a number of possible reasons. He or she may think that they would not be able to have much power in negotiations with employers by themselves and so would stand a better chance of gaining higher pay and better working conditions if they were represented by a trade union with thousands, and even millions, of members. If the negotiations broke down, a trade union could threaten to call out its members on an official strike. This would be likely to have a major impact, whereas if just one worker withdrew their labour, it would not be likely to have much effect.

2. The bargaining strength of a trade union in negotiations with employers over improved wages may be greater if the union represents all the workers in the industry. The threat of an all-out strike or other industrial actions that will halt production and cause firms to lose sales and revenues may persuade employers to agree to union wage demands. However, if very few workers are union members then industrial action by those workers who do belong to a union may be much less disruptive.

   Employers, including the government, will also be keen to avoid industrial actions by unions that may disrupt the provision of essential services, such as such as electricity, public transport, healthcare and education. These products are socially and economically beneficial and have very few close substitutes. Many firms and consumers may be badly affected if the supply of these services is disrupted.

   Workers who take strike action will lose their incomes for the duration of the strike. As a result, support for strike action may be very low and, if so, a union may have little bargaining strength in wage negotiations with employers. However, a trade union that is financially strong will be able to support the incomes of its members during strike action to compensate them for their loss of earnings. As a result, the union is more likely to gain the support of its members for long periods of strike action if necessary to secure the wage increases it is seeking from employers.

3. Trade unions can play a positive role in an economy. Employers may prefer to negotiate with unions rather than deal with small groups of workers separately, and union representatives can sometimes be directly involved in the decision-making of firms. Also, unions can provide training and help to improve productivity, especially when this is linked to increases in pay. They can also bring certain issues to the attention of the employers, making them aware of possible grievances at an early stage.

   On the other hand, trade unions may demand significant wage increases for their members and this will lead to an increase in the costs of production for firms. This could have a negative effect on profits and could lead to firms making some workers redundant, leading to an increase in the rate of unemployment in the economy. Trade unions may resort to industrial action, such as strikes, to achieve their objectives and this could be extremely disruptive to levels of production in an economy.

   It can therefore be seen that trade unions can play both a positive and a negative role in an economy.

## Key words

| 1 C | 2 G | 3 E | 4 F | 5 H |
|-----|-----|-----|-----|-----|
| 6 B | 7 I | 8 A | 9 D |     |

## Revision summary

| 1. wages | 4. collective bargaining |
|----------|--------------------------|
| 2. industrial | 5. overtime; strike |
| 3. non-manual | |

# 3.5 Firms

## 3.5.1 Classification of firms

1. Industries in the primary sector produce or extract natural materials, such as oil, minerals, wood and fruits and vegetables. They include the farming, mining, fishing and timber/logging industries.

   Industries in the secondary sector of an economy process natural and other materials to produce other finished and semi-finished products. They include all manufacturing industries, such as food processing, car manufacturing and carpet weaving as well as the construction industry that produces buildings, roads, ports and railway infrastructure.

Industries in the tertiary sector provide personal and business services, including banking, transportation, telecommunications, healthcare, education and retailing.

2. A government may take over the ownership and control of private sector enterprises through a process called nationalization. Some entire industries are nationalized because they are considered too important to the economy to be owned privately and at risk of being closed down if they are not profitable. For example, they may be major employers or providers of essential services, such as power and water supplies, or they may be vital to national security, such as defence equipment manufacturers and nuclear energy generators. Nationalization can protect these industries from closure and also stop many jobs from being lost. It can also stop large powerful firms from abusing their market power by cutting services and raising prices to earn excess profits.

3. The transfer of a state-owned enterprise to the private sector is called privatization. This may occur through the sale of shares in the state-owned enterprise to private investors in order to raise revenue to help fund public expenditures. As a private company it may also be run more efficiently and supply a better quality product and customer service because it will have an incentive to maximize its profit and may also face competition from other suppliers. Privatization will also reduce the size of the public sector in an economy.

**E**

| Industry | Sector |
|---|---|
| Retailing | *Tertiary* |
| Oil extraction | *Primary* |
| Ship building | *Secondary* |
| Farming | *Primary* |
| Construction | *Secondary* |
| Advertising | *Tertiary* |
| Textiles | *Secondary* |
| Fishing | *Primary* |
| Coal mining | *Primary* |
| Insurance | *Tertiary* |
| Car production | *Secondary* |
| Food processing | *Secondary* |

## 3.5.1 Classification of firms
## 3.5.2 Small firms

1. Two methods of measuring the size of firms are (choose two from the following): the number of workers it employs; firms with less than 50 employees are often considered small. However, some firms are highly capital intensive and may not employ large numbers of workers. The market share of the firm; that is, the percentage of the total market value of sales each period that the firm is responsible for. However, a small local firm may have a very large percentage of a local market but the value of the market sales may be relatively low compared to a large firm that has only a small share of very large and valuable national or international market.

The amount of capital employed in a firm; for example, in machinery and production equipment, factory space and stocks of materials and semi-finished goods.

How a firm is organized can also be used as a measure of its size. This is because large firms are often divided into different departments or divisions, each one specializing in a particular function such as marketing, finance, human resources, production, sales and distribution. In a small firm all of these functions will be carried out by one or a small number of employees.

2. The international trading company employs only 40 full-time workers and has a global market share of just 3%. By these measures alone the firm might be considered small. However, the global market is clearly very large if a 3% share results in sales of $1.5 billion each year. The company is also clearly highly capital intensive and therefore does not need to employ large numbers of employees to generate revenues. The company is clearly a large firm on these measures.

3. Most firms in an economy are small and remain small. This is because most serve small local markets. The size of their markets therefore prevents them from growing. To increase their sales they may have to enter other markets at home and overseas. However, many small firms lack the capital they will need to expand, often because banks will not lend them money because of their high risk of business failure.

Other reasons most firms remain small, despite the advantages of growth and large scale production, is that many small business owners do not want to grow. This is because a larger firm may be more difficult to control and more stressful to run. They may also lack the skills needed to manage a much larger enterprise.

Small firms have also benefited significantly from improvements in technology over time. This has allowed them to enjoy some of the cost advantages previously only available to much larger firms. New advanced computers are now small and affordable enough to be employed by many small businesses allowing them to communicate with suppliers and consumers all over the world and to produce their own accounts and to access online help quickly and easily.

## 3.5.3–4 Mergers and the causes and forms of the growth of firms

1. External growth in the size of a firm involves the acquisition of or merger with one or more other firms. In contrast, internal growth in firm size involves expanding the scale of production through the employment of additional capital, labour and other factors of production.

2. Two reasons why two firms producing the same or similar products in the same industry may merge into a single organization are (choose two from the following): such horizontal integration will create a much larger firm which may be able to benefit from economies of large-scale production; the two firms will no longer have to compete with each other; it will reduce competition; the combined firm will have a much larger combined market share which may increase its ability to compete more effectively with rival producers; the combined firm may be able to raise more capital to fund further expansion; if the two firms produce different but similar products then it will reduce the impact of a fall in demand on the combined business for any one of its products; one of the firms may export its products overseas and this will allow the combined firm to increase the range and volume of products it exports.

3. Two reasons why two firms in different industries may choose to merge into a single organization might include (choose two from the following): the combined firm will have a wider product range and this can reduce market risks; vertical backwards integration (for example, between a manufacturer and a supplier of the materials or components it needs will allow the manufacturer to control more of its costs and also to reduce the risk of it running out of supplies); vertical forwards integration (for example, between a manufacturer and a retail chain will give the manufacturer direct and possibly exclusive access to the final consumers of its products). It can also help to reduce competition if it stops the retail chain from stocking and selling the products of rival producers; in both examples, integration allows the manufacturer to absorb the profits of the other firm.

**E**

| Description | Type of merger? |
|---|---|
| A clothes manufacturer takes over a chain of clothing shops | Vertical forwards |
| An investment company takes over a solar energy supplier | Conglomerate |
| A restaurant chain merges with a food wholesaler | Vertical backwards |
| Two internet service providers merge | Horizontal |

## 3.5.5 Economies and diseconomies of scale

1.

| Cost advantages | Type of economy of scale? |
|---|---|
| Large firms can afford to employ their own specialist staff and equipment | Technical economies |
| Bank are willing to lend more money to large firms and often at lower interest rates because they are less likely to fail than smaller firms and have assets they can offer as security | Financial economies |
| Suppliers will often offer price discounts for bulk purchases of items | Purchasing economies |
| Large firms can spread the high fixed costs of distribution and advertising over a much larger output | Marketing economies |

2. Risk-bearing economies.

3. Firms within an industry can benefit from external economies of scale if the industry is large or increasing in size. For example, if the industry is large and employs many skilled workers, then each firm will have access to a large pool of labour they can recruit from their competitors. Firms in other industrial sectors may also develop to supply the industry with the specialized services it needs; for example, specialized transport, equipment and training. Instead of each firm within the industry having to develop and provide their own they can use the services of these 'ancillary firms' and benefit from their economies of scale.

Firms in the same industry may also be able to benefit from marketing their products jointly. They may also benefit from shared infrastructure, especially if they locate together in the same area. For example, the growth of an industry may persuade firms in other industries to invest in new rail or road freight facilities nearby to transport their goods.

4. Two diseconomies of scale a firm could experience as it continues to expand its scale of production are (choose two): Management diseconomies because controlling and coordinating production in a large firm can be difficult especially if it produces and sells a wide variety of products in many different locations. A large firm can have many thousands of employees and many different layers of management and this can cause communication problems and disagreements; Labour diseconomies, for example due to labour shortages or disputes. Very large firms may experience labour shortages and may have to increase wages to attract the workers they need. Labour disputes may also become more common and frequent

in large firms, especially those employing highly capital-intensive mass production methods. As a result jobs may be uninteresting for many workers who may feel that their skills are being undervalued; Some very large firms may need vast quantities of materials, components or power for production. As a result they may run into supply constraints that hold up production. To overcome these problems they may have to pay much more to obtain the vast quantities they need for new and additional suppliers; Regulatory risks may also be greater for very large firms, notably those that attain dominant market positions in an economy. The government may introduce laws and regulations that control the prices charged by large firms and the quality of the services they provide. The need to understand and comply with regulations will increase running costs in the affected firms.

## Key words

| 1 J | 2 L | 3 D | 4 K | 5 O | 6 I | 7 A | 8 E | 9 Q | 10 P |
|-----|-----|-----|-----|-----|-----|-----|-----|-----|------|
| 11 F | 12 N | 13 G | 14 C | 15 M | 16 S | 17 R | 18 H | 19 B | |

## Revision summary

| | |
|---|---|
| 1. primary; secondary; tertiary | 7. technical |
| 2. public | 8. average |
| 3. internal; external | 9. external |
| 4. horizontal; increasing | 10. diseconomies; increase |
| 5. backward; forward | 11. capital |
| 6. economies (of) scale | |

# 3.6 Firms and production

## 3.6.1 Production and productivity

1. Production refers to output; that is, how many units of a product are produced in one or more firms per week, month or year using a combination of resources. How efficient resources are at producing outputs concerns their productivity. The more output a given amount of resources can produce each period, the more productive they are.

2. The productivity of labour can be measured by the average volume of output or the average value of output produced by each worker in a given period of time.
That is, the average product of labour = total output per period/total number of workers.
Alternatively, the average revenue per worker = total revenue per period/total number of employees.

3. Two other ways a firm can increase the productivity of its workforce include (choose two): increasing specialization or the division of labour in production; training to improve existing skills and to teach employees new skills and production techniques; offering workers performance-related payments and bonuses if they improve their productivity; giving employees shares in the ownership of their company so that they are encouraged to improve its profits by increasing productivity;

improving working conditions and job satisfaction, which can help to motivate workers to achieve higher levels of productivity; replacing old machinery with new, more advanced and efficient equipment; introducing new production processes and working practices designed to reduce wasted time and materials in the production process.

**E** The first thing to do is to investigate the possible cause(s) of low productivity in your firm. Once you know these you can introduce changes designed to overcome them. For example, is the machinery and equipment in the firm old and out of date? Does it keep breaking down and holding up production? Do workers have the right skills to use the machines and equipment? If so, replacing the machinery and equipment and training workers to use it will be sensible. Other causes may be lack of job satisfaction, low levels of pay, a poor working environment, out of date working practices, poor time management, high levels of waste, and so on. Refer to question 3 for possible ideas.

## 3.6.2 Labour-intensive and capital-intensive production
## 3.6.3 Demand for factors of production

1. Labour-intensive production refers to a process of production that employs a higher proportion of labour than capital equipment and machinery. In contrast, capital-intensive production refers to a process of production that employs a higher proportion of capital equipment and machinery than labour. Many of the individual tasks in the production process will be automated.

2. Changes in the demand for factors of production may occur because of changes in demand for the goods and services they produce. This is because demand for factor inputs is a derived demand. If consumer demand for certain products is rising, firms producing those products will tend to increase their demand for all factors of production in order to increase output. Initially they may employ more labour; for example, by paying their existing employees to work overtime or by expanding their workforces. However, if the increase in demand continues, firms may also invest in additional capital equipment, plant and machinery but only if it is profitable to do so. Firms may also increase their factor demand if factor prices fall and/or factor productivity rises. A fall in wages, raw material costs and equipment costs will reduce production costs and improve profitability. Similarly, an increase in productivity will increase output faster than costs. Average costs should fall and profit margins will increase.

Changes in relative factor prices may, however, result in factor substitution. For example, firms may increase their demand for labour and reduce their demand for new capital equipment if wages fall relative to new equipment costs. This may also occur if labour is more abundant than new capital equipment; for example, if there is shortage of new equipment making it difficult to get hold of.

3. Factor substitution refers to the replacement of one factor of production with another in a production process; in this case, the substitution of capital equipment, plant and machinery for labour. This may occur if the price of capital equipment falls relative to wages and other employment costs. It may also occur if new capital equipment is more productive than labour, is more accurate and results in less waste. A shortage of skilled labour may also result in firms using more capital intensive production methods, especially if demand for their products is rising enabling them to mass produce their items for sale.

**E** 'Small Firms Association argues increase in legal minimum wage will hurt economy': may reduce demand for labour, notably for the low wage unskilled or semi-skilled workers the legal minimum wage is designed to benefit.

'Real wages are falling as inflation accelerates while wage growth stagnates': this means that real wages will be falling. As a result this could increase the demand for labour.

'Increase in government subsidies to help firms invest in new equipment': this will reduce the fixed costs of capital equipment. As a result, demand for capital will increase and possibly at the expense of a reduced demand for labour.

'Government announces 2% increase in payroll taxes on employers': this will increase the cost of employing labour, resulting in a fall in demand for labour.

'Profits slump as consumer spending continues to fall': firms may reduce output in response. Demand for labour and natural resources may fall initially, followed by a fall in demand for capital as firms delay or cut investments in additional capacity. Demand for all factors of production will also fall if some firms are forced to close.

'New smart technologies boost productivity': this is likely to increase demand for new capital equipment and machinery, possibly being substituted for labour in production processes.

# 3.7 Firm's costs, revenues and objectives

## 3.7.1–2 Definition and calculation of costs of production

## 3.7.3–4 Definition and calculation of revenues

1. A fixed cost of production does not vary with the amount produced. For example, factory rent, machinery hire charges, insurance premiums and the costs of running an office do not depend on the volume of goods and services produced or sold. In contrast, variable costs such as the costs of materials and components used in the production of other goods and services and the electricity used to run production machinery, vary directly with the volume of goods and services produced.

2. The total cost of producing a given level of output will consist of the total fixed costs of the producer and the total variable costs of producing that level of output. For example, if a firm has fixed costs of $200 per week and variable costs of $1 per item, then the total cost of producing 100 items or units of output each week will be $300 (i.e. $200 plus $1 × 100). The average cost of producing each one of those items will therefore be equal to $3, i.e. the total costs of $300 divided by the 100 units produced.

| | (a) | (b) | (c) | (d) | (e) | (f) |
|---|---|---|---|---|---|---|
| Total output (units per week) | Total fixed costs ($) | Total variable costs ($) | Total cost ($) | Average cost per unit ($) | Total revenue ($) | Profit or loss ($) |
| 0 | 3,000 | 0 | 3,000 | – | 0 | –3,000 |
| 1,000 | 3,000 | 4,000 | 7,000 | 7 | 5,000 | –2,000 |
| 2,000 | 3,000 | 8,000 | 11,000 | 5.5 | 10,000 | –1,000 |
| 3,000 | 3,000 | 12,000 | 15,000 | 5 | 15,000 | 0 |
| 4,000 | 3,000 | 16,000 | 19,000 | 4.75 | 20,000 | 1,000 |
| 5,000 | 3,000 | 20,000 | 23,000 | 4.6 | 22,500 | –500 |

4. The new firm will have to pay its fixed costs of $3,000 per month regardless of how many cases for sunglasses it produces each month, even if its total output is zero. This is because fixed costs do not depend on the amount produced.

6. The average cost of producing each case will fall as output is increased. If the firm produces 1,000 units each month its total costs will be $7,000, so the average cost of producing each case will be $7 (that is, $7,000/1,000 units). However, if the firm produces 5,000 cases each months its total costs will be $23,000 and the cost per unit just $4.60. This is because its fixed costs of $3,000 per month remain unchanged as output rises.

9. a) Average revenue per item sold = total revenue from sales/total number of items sold. If the firm sells 4,000 cases at $5 each then its total revenue will be $20,000 and the average revenue from each sale will be $5. However, if the firm sells 5,000 units and total revenue from their sale is $22,500, then the average revenue from each case sold will be $4.50.

   b) Average revenue has fallen because the market price of cases for sunglasses has fallen as their supply has increased.

11. a) Biggest loss at 1,000 units per month.

    b) Biggest profit at 4,000 units per month.

    c) The firm will break even if it produces and sells 3,000 units each month.

## 3.7.5 Objectives of firms

1. Profit is a reward for enterprise. A business owner that has taken the risk to start a business will earn a profit if the business is successful and sells its products at prices that exceed their cost of production.

2. Profit is made when the revenue earned by a firm from the sale of its products exceeds their costs of production. Profit maximization is a goal pursued by most private sector firms. It therefore involves aiming to maximize the difference between total revenues and total costs.

3. Not all organizations always aim to maximize their profits. Some may aim to increase their sales and market share by cutting prices and increasing spending on advertising. This can reduce total revenues and increase costs in the short run but in the long run it may help these firms to increase their profits.

   Other firms may adopt social and environmental goals; for example, increasing the number of disabled people they employ and reducing pollution. Although these aims may increase their costs and reduce their profits achieving them can improve the reputation of these firms with consumers which in turn may help them to generate more sales and profits in the long run.

   However, profit is not a goal for some business organizations. Many government-owned enterprises provide free or affordable public services to people in need of them. Many charities aim to help as many disadvantaged people or animals as they can or aim to protect the natural environment. Any surplus they make from donations and sales of gifts over their costs they will invest in expanding and improving the services and care they offer.

   Many cooperatives, mutual societies and clubs are not-for-profit enterprises. They are run for the mutual benefit of their members and any surplus they make from their revenues exceeding their costs will be invested in making improvements or lowering the prices or fees they charge.

   **E** Boeing aims to increase both its revenues and profits long-term by increasing its efficiency and expanding its after-sales and parts businesses.

   Border biscuits aims to grow through investment in a new production line and by increasing its international sales and market share.

## Key words

| 1 P | 2 E | 3 C | 4 N | 5 J | 6 A | 7 B | 8 O | 9 G | 10 M |
|-----|-----|-----|-----|-----|-----|-----|-----|-----|------|
| 11 F | 12 D | 13 K | 14 H | 15 L | 16 I | | | | |

## Revision summary

| 1. increasing; lower | 2. labour | 3. capital | 4. labour-intensive | 5. increase; falls |
|---|---|---|---|---|
| 6. fixed; variable | 7. revenue; loss | 8. break-even | 9. long-run | 10. profits |

# 3.8 Market structure
## 3.8.1 Competitive markets
## 3.8.2 Monopoly markets

1. In economics, the term market structure is used to distinguish between different types of market according to their characteristics, notably the number of firms that supply the market, the extent to which they differentiate their products from each other, the degree of competition or collusion between them and how easy it is for other firms to enter the market to compete with existing firms

2. a) highly or perfectly competitive market / perfect competition;

   b) monopoly.

3. Because there are a large number of firms competing to supply a perfectly competitive market, no one firm is able to have any influence over the equilibrium price established in that market where market demand is equal to market supply. That is, all firms supplying the market are price takers because they can only sell their products at the market price. If a firm attempts to increase the price of its products its sales will fall to zero as consumers switch to other firms in the market selling the same products at the lower market price.

4. a) To avoid a price war with its major competitors, a firm may adopt a price matching strategy. So called 'follow the leader' pricing involves each firm in a market setting its price or prices equal to those of its closest rivals. The firm with the largest market share will usually be the price leader. If the price leader raises its prices, then all other firms in the market will do the same. Similarly, if the price leader cuts its prices, all other firms will reduce theirs.

   b) A monopoly that risks losing sales and profits to new competitors seeking to enter its market may deploy a competitive pricing strategy called destruction pricing. It involves the monopoly lowering its prices to significantly below the average costs of its new competitors in order to 'destroy' their sales, inflict losses and force them out of the market. If it is successful it can then raise its prices again and recover any losses it may have made.

5. Firms in a competitive market supplying the same or very similar products as each other are individually likely to have very little or no influence over the market price of the product they supply. In contrast, a pure monopoly controls the total supply of a product to a market and is therefore able to influence the market price at which it sells its product. For example, by restricting its supply a monopoly can force the market price to increase so that it is able to earn an excess or abnormal profit. Further, a monopoly may create barriers to entry to stop firms entering its market and competing away its sales and profits. As a result the monopoly may fail to control its

costs compared to firms that have to compete with each other for customers. Under these conditions the market price in a monopoly is likely to be much higher than the market price for the same product if it was instead supplied by a large number of firms in a competitive market.

However, because the monopoly will supply the entire market it may enjoy many cost advantages compared to smaller firms due to its much larger scale of production. It may therefore be able to sell its product at a lower price than firms in perfectly competitive market and still make a large profit. The firm may also be a natural monopoly. This means the most efficient size of the firm will be one that supplies the entire market. Production in smaller firms will therefore be less efficient and average costs will be higher.

If, in addition, the market is contestable because entry barriers are low and new firms are able to enter the market easily, then the monopoly will have to price its product competitively or it will risk losing its sales and profits to rivals.

**E** A government can use competition policy measures to prevent or stop a monopoly from restricting competition and earning abnormal profits. These measures may include capping or regulating the price(s) the monopoly can charge; setting minimum service levels the monopoly must meet; forcing the monopoly to break-up into smaller competing firms; imposing fines on a monopoly that uses its market power to restrict competition.

## 3.8.2 Monopoly markets

1. Barriers to entry benefit existing firms in a market. This is because they restrict competition from supplying a market by making it difficult and more costly for new firms to enter. If the existing firms are much larger and/or more efficient than new, smaller firms due to economies of scale, then the barriers are 'natural'. In contrast, artificial barriers to entry are created by the existing firms precisely to deter new competition.

2. Two examples of artificial barriers to entry are (choose two from the following): a monopoly may use predatory or destruction pricing when it is threatened by a new competitor. This involves setting the price of the product low so that the new firm will be unable to make any profit from its sale, especially if it has higher average costs than the monopoly; the monopoly may be big and powerful enough to prevent its suppliers from supplying materials, components and/or services to new competitors by threatening to stop buying supplies from them if they do; a monopoly may prevent retailers from stocking and selling competing products. If sales of the monopoly's product accounts for a large proportion of their total sales and profits, then the retailers will not want to risk the monopoly refusing to supply its product to them; a monopoly can make it

difficult for new firms to compete by creating a strong brand for its product(s) through heavy advertising and marketing. This can be expensive but large monopolies will be able to spread these costs over a much larger output than new competitors who are also likely to lack the capital they will need to promote their products.

3. Two potential disadvantages of monopolies for consumers are (choose from the following): they may restrict competition and consumer choice by creating artificial barriers to entry. These are designed to block potential entrants from entering the market profitably; a monopoly may restrict the market supply in order to force up price. If the product is an essential item, then consumers will have no choice but to pay the higher price; product quality may be poor if competition is low because the monopoly does not have to compete for sales against rival products. A monopoly may even reduce product quality to reduce its costs and boost its profits further; a monopoly may make little effort to control its costs and use its resources in the most efficient way because it does not have to compete for sales and profits with other firms. This is called x-inefficiency. It refers to 'organizational slack' which can often develop in firms that face little or no competition.

**E** Advantages may include: the monopoly may benefit from economies of scale and some of these cost savings may be passed on to consumers as lower fares; the monopoly may invest more in making service improvements and innovations that will benefit consumers because there is no longer a risk that profits from service improvements will be competed away;

Disadvantages may include: the lack of competition may result in less choice and higher fares; it may also result in cuts to services and service quality as the monopoly attempts to reduce its costs to boost its profits; the new combined firm may be managed less efficiently than the two firms were, again because it no longer has to compete on costs, services or fares. As a result, its costs may be higher and it will be able to pass these on to consumers in higher fares.

## Key words

| 1 L | 2 M | 3 H | 4 A | 5 P | 6 N | 7 E | 8 O | 9 I | 10 F |
|-----|-----|-----|-----|-----|-----|-----|-----|-----|------|
| 11 J | 12 G | 13 K | 14 D | 15 B | 16 C | | | | |

## Revision summary

| 1. structure | 2. takers | 3. monopoly; higher | 4. lower | 5. competitive |
|---|---|---|---|---|
| 6. increase; abnormal | 7. barriers (to) entry; predatory | 8. natural monopoly | 9. abnormal | 10. contestable; low |

## Working with data and diagrams

1.

| Output per month | Total fixed costs ($) | Total variable costs ($) | Total cost ($) | Total revenue ($) | Profit or loss ($) |
|---|---|---|---|---|---|
| 0 | 4,000 | 0 | 4,000 | 0 | –4,000 |
| 2000 | 4,000 | 20,000 | 24,000 | 24,000 | 0 |
| 4000 | 4,000 | 40,000 | 44,000 | 48,000 | 4,000 |
| 6000 | 4,000 | 60,000 | 64,000 | 72,000 | 8,000 |
| 8000 | 4,000 | 80,000 | 84,000 | 96,000 | 12,000 |

2, 3

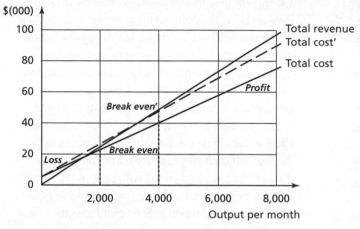

## Multiple choice questions

| 1 A | 2 B | 3 A | 4 C | 5 C | 6 B | 7 A | 8 B | 9 A | 10 A |
|---|---|---|---|---|---|---|---|---|---|
| 11 D | 12 B | 13 C | 14 A | 15 D | 16 A | 17 C | 18 D | 19 D | 20 D |

## Structured questions

1.  a)  Disposable income is the amount of income that households have available for spending and saving as they wish after income taxes have been deducted or paid.

    b)  Two functions, other than taking decisions on interest rates, that a central bank may take could include the following (explain two): It issues notes and coins for the nation's currency. It manages payments to and from the government. It manages the national debt. It supervises the banking system, regulating the conduct of banks, holding their deposits and transferring funds between them. It is the lender of last resort to the banking system. It manages the nation's gold and foreign currency reserves.

    c)  Inflation can affect each of the four functions of money. A particularly high rate of inflation could negatively affect money as a medium of exchange because if its purchasing power was dramatically reduced, it may be less generally acceptable as a medium of exchange. The function of money as a measure of value or unit of account could be negatively affected by inflation because it will make money less accurate as a measurement of value over a period of time. The function of money as a store of value will be particularly badly affected by inflation, because when the general level of prices is rising rapidly in an economy, the real value of money will be falling. This will also affect the ability of money to act as a standard for deferred payment. Every day payment for goods or services is deferred, the amount to be paid will fall in real terms. Suppliers are therefore less likely to offer the sale of products to customers on credit terms, i.e. 'buy now, pay later', when inflation is high or rising.

    d)  People have many different motives for saving that will be influenced by their income, age, family circumstances, economic conditions and taste. Saving allows a person to delay spending and consumption; for example, to purchase an expensive product such as a car or to fund their retirement from work. Saving for retirement will tend to involve long-term saving over a person's working life. Many people also save as a precaution, for example against possible future unemployment and medical bills. Income is a major determinant in saving decisions. People on higher incomes will tend to save a larger proportion of their incomes than people on lower incomes. People on low incomes will tend to spend most of their income on meeting their needs, that is, spending money on food and accommodation. They will have little left over to save to fund future consumption. Young people tend to earn lower incomes and will spend more and save less than middle-aged people. Older people may also have low incomes and will fund their spending from any savings they have made over time. Middle-aged people are more likely to earn more income but also save more to fund large purchases in the future, such as a new car or home, and to fund their retirement or to pay for their children's education.

    e)  Workers supply their labour to firms to undertake productive activities in return for wages, usually paid per period of time or in some cases per unit of output produced. In general, the higher the wage rate for a job the more labour workers will be willing to supply, in the form of increased hours and/or because more workers overall are attracted to the occupation.
    If the supply of labour to an occupation greatly exceeds the demand for that labour, then the market wage rate is likely to be quite low. However, even at a relatively low wage, some workers would fill the available jobs. This is likely to be because they are relatively low skilled with low levels of productivity and would be unable to command higher wages in alternative occupations. Some workers may also be geographically immobile and unable to move from areas where wages tend to be low to areas where

average wages are much higher. For example, this could occur because they cannot afford to move or because of family ties to the area they currently live in. However, in choosing between occupations, workers will also consider the occupations' net advantages in addition to any differences in wage rates. For example, they will compare such factors as when and how long they are required to work each day or week, holiday entitlements, promotion prospects, job security, and any non-wage benefits such as free medical insurance, subsidized canteens, or the provision of a company car or free travel. So, for example, a worker may choose a job that offers a relatively low wage over another job with a higher wage because it offers more holidays, greater job security, and other benefits which more than offset the wage differential in their preferences.

Some people also work for relatively low wages in charities that help people and animals in need because of the job satisfaction it gives them.

f) As interest rates rise, households tend to save more of their disposable incomes and borrow less to buy expensive items such as new cars, homes or holidays. As a result, household spending tends to fall. However, there are many other factors that affect the spending decisions of households.

For example, if price inflation is high or rising, household spending may increase in order to purchase items before their prices rise. If the rate of inflation is higher than the rate of interest, then the incentive to save is also reduced because the real value of savings including any interest will be falling. Households may even increase their borrowing because the real value of interest charges and loan repayments will also be falling if the interest rate is less than the rate at which prices are rising.

Spending on goods and services required to satisfy human needs for food and shelter, for example, is also unlikely to be affected by changes in interest rates. Similarly, small everyday cash purchases, such as the purchase of a newspaper or cup of coffee, are also likely to be unaffected.

Spending levels will also depend on disposable incomes and personal wealth. If both these are rising then spending is also likely to increase even if interest rates are also rising. Reductions in taxes on incomes and wealth are also likely to boost spending.

2. a) A trade union can be defined as an organization of labour that promotes and protects the interests of its members, such as in relation to the improvement of wages and working conditions.

b) 'Collective bargaining' refers to the process of negotiation that takes place between representatives of workers and representatives of employers. Sometimes one trade union will represent all of the workers and in other situations the negotiations will involve a number of trade unions. Collective bargaining is in contrast to a situation where each employee bargains individually with the employer. Workers support collective bargaining because a trade union would normally be able to negotiate better pay and working conditions than if workers bargained individually. Employers support collective bargaining because they would rather negotiate an agreement with all employees than with each employee individually.

c) A firm may respond in a number of ways to a request by its workers to increase their wages. It may refuse or it can agree. Or it could agree to enter into negotiations to consider alternative options, such as increasing holiday entitlement or increasing non-financial rewards instead, which may be less expensive for the firm than increasing wages.

If wage rates are rising across the industry then the firm may have no option but to increase its own wages in order to retain its existing workers and to attract new ones when positions become available. If it did not raise wages, its experienced workers may move to other firms offering higher wage rates.

Refusing to increase wages may also result in its workers losing motivation. Their productivity and output may fall thereby increasing average costs. They may also take disruptive industrial actions, such as strike action. To avoid this, the firm may have to meet their demands for higher wages.

However, much will depend on how profitable the firm is and whether it can afford to pay higher wages. If the firm is making a loss then higher wages will increase its loss and may result in its closure. In contrast, even if it is profitable will the owners of the firm be willing to take less profit? Or will they be able to pass on their increased costs to consumers through higher prices without a loss of sales and profits? This will depend on how responsive consumer demand is for their products. If demand is inelastic, the fall in demand will be proportionately less than the increase in price and so revenues will increase thereby allowing the firm to fund the wage increase.

The firm may also agree to pay higher wages but may reduce its demand for labour as a result, choosing instead to replace some or all of its workers with cheaper, more productive capital equipment. However, not all labour tasks can be replaced with machinery and it can also be expensive to do so. The firm may not have sufficient funds of its own to buy more equipment and may have to borrow the money instead, which will also mean having to repay its loan with interest charges.

d) Workers doing the same job in the same country might be in different locations and therefore subject to different regional or local labour market conditions. As a result, their market wage rates could differ. For example, one may work in an area of the country where there are labour shortages, perhaps because there are poor transport links or because housing costs are high. Wages may need to be higher in this area to compensate for these factors and to attract a supply of labour.

They may also receive different wage rates because they have different levels of experience and skill. One may be more productive than the other and receive a higher wage rate to reflect this. It is also possible that one worker is not in a trade union while the other may belong to a trade union that has successfully negotiated higher wages for its members.

The firms they work for may also pay different wage rates because they reward their workers in different ways. For example, one worker may receive a lower wage rate than the other because he or she also receives free medical insurance, free travel, company shares and other non-financial rewards. Firms that do not offer these additional benefits may have to pay a higher wage rate to attract workers.

Wage rates may also differ because of discrimination. For example, female workers who are as skilled and productive as male workers doing exactly the same job may be paid less simply because they are discriminated against unlawfully by their employers. However, even if the two workers are paid exactly the same wage rate, their take-home pay or earnings may differ because their hours of work may differ. One may be contracted to work fewer hours each week than the other or one worker may choose to work more overtime than the other.

3. **a)** A market structure is defined as how a market is characterized by certain features, especially the number of firms that compete in the particular market, the degree of competition and the method of competition. Market structures can also be contrasted in terms of the price and output decisions of firms in a market.

**b)** Features of a highly competitive market may include aggressive price and non-price competition between rival firms – prices, product features and promotions may change frequently; there may be a large number of firms competing to supply the market; each firm acting alone will have little or no influence over the market price; products and brand images may be highly differentiated; market shares and profits are likely to change over time; barriers to new market entry are low. If the market is perfectly competitive, all firms have perfect knowledge, will supply identical products and be price takers. There are no barriers to new market entry.

**c)** There are different types of merger, but it is usually the case that firms that merge with others operate in the same industry, although this may be at different stages of the production process. However, sometimes firms from different industries decide to merge in what is called lateral or conglomerate integration. There are many different possible reasons to explain such mergers. The main reason is one of diversification, i.e. it is a risk-spreading economy where a firm has interests in many different industries. It is unlikely that there will be a fall in demand for all of a firm's products in different sectors and so lateral or conglomerate merger has as an objective the aim of balancing the increases and decreases of demand in different sectors. Another reason for such integration is that the profit made in one industry can be used to finance development in other aspects of a firm's business interests. A very large firm, brought about as a result of lateral merger, is likely to be in a better position when negotiating a loan with a financial institution, and so benefiting from financial economies of scale. It is also possible that such a large firm is able to benefit from distribution economies of scale, because although different products may be produced by the firm, the transportation of these products could be arranged to benefit from the large scale of operations.

**d)** A monopoly is often seen as operating against the interests of consumers. Price is higher and output lower than would be the case in perfect competition. Consumers have a restricted choice of products to choose from. The supernormal profit that a monopoly makes in both the short run and the long run may not be ploughed back into the firm. A monopoly is both productively and allocatively inefficient.

However, there are potential advantages of a monopoly. If the supernormal profit is used to invest in new products, consumers will benefit. They will also benefit if the supernormal profits are used to keep down the prices that consumers are required to pay. The economies of scale that a monopoly can benefit from, given its large size, will not only lead to a lower average cost of production, but possibly to lower prices.

In conclusion, it can therefore be seen that a monopoly is not always against the interests of consumers and there can be benefits as well as drawbacks.

4. **a)** A social enterprise is a private sector firm engaged in the production and sale of goods or services to customers that aims to improve social or environmental welfare rather than maximizing profits for its owners. Profits are usually reinvested in the firm to fund social or environmental projects.

b) Labour-intensive production methods require more labour inputs than capital. These methods are common in many service industries where it is difficult to replicate and replace human efforts and interactions with machinery and other capital equipment. In contrast, capital-intensive production methods require more capital inputs than labour. Capital-intensive production processes are usually semi- or fully automated and used to mass-produce goods for large consumer markets.

c) Not all firms aim to or are able to maximize their profits in the short run. For example, developing and testing a new aircraft or medicine can take many years and cost many billions of dollars before their manufacturers are able to start selling them to earn a profit.

New firms in any industrial sector can also be expensive to start up and it will often take time for them to build-up sales and market share, especially if the market is highly competitive. As well as the fixed costs of acquiring premises and equipment, a new firm may also have to spend a lot of money on promoting its products and, in addition, may have to set its prices low to attract new customers and generate sales. All of these actions will reduce its profits. It may even operate a loss initially. However, if successful and the new firm is able to survive and expand its sales and output, it may be able to maximize its profits in the long run.

Expanding the productive scale of a firm through merger or internal growth can also be expensive. The cost of acquiring larger or additional premises, machinery and equipment, will all reduce profits but, longer term, as output expands average production costs will tend to fall. Larger firms may additionally enjoy economies of large scale of production that will reduce their costs and expand their profits further.

In contrast, some firms do not even try to maximize their profits even in the long run. Some entrepreneurs are happy to just to make a satisfactory level of profit that provides them with enough income to enjoy a relatively good standard of living without having to work too hard to do so.

Some firms, including charities and social enterprises, do not aim to make any profit. They have social or environmental welfare objectives and will usually reinvest any surplus revenue in expanding the provision of their goods and services.

Similarly, some firms are state-owned enterprises required to deliver merit goods and other public services to people who may not be able to afford to pay the full cost of their provision.

d) The average cost of producing each unit of output tends to fall as output increases as fixed costs, such as rents, insurance, loan repayments and machinery hire charges, are spread over a larger volume of units. In the short run, a firm can increase output by employing more labour; for example, to work overtime. However, longer term a firm can only expand its scale of production through merger with another firm or through internal growth by investing in new premises, machinery and equipment. Larger firms will often benefit from additional cost savings not available to smaller firms. For example, to encourage large firms to place bulk orders, suppliers will often offer them generous price discounts. Larger firms may also be able to borrow money from banks at lower rates of interest than smaller firms and can also reduce business risks by selling their products into different foreign markets. These and other economies of large-scale production will further help larger firms to reduce their average costs of production.

If a firm has a natural monopoly it will produce and control the entire market supply of its product because doing so is the most efficient scale of production. That is, the average cost per unit of output will be at its lowest at the point at which output is equal to the total market supply. Rail, gas pipeline and electricity grid network operators are examples of natural monopolies because it would be far more costly to have two or more suppliers competing to provide each network to customers because of the huge infrastructure costs involved building them.

However, most firms do not have natural monopolies and may see their average costs begin to rise if they attempt to expand their scale of production too far and too quickly. For example, controlling and coordinating production in a large firm can be difficult especially if it produces and sells a wide variety of products in many different locations. A large firm can have many thousands of employees and many different layers of management and this can cause communication problems and disagreements.

Very large firms may also experience labour shortages and may have to increase wages to attract the workers they need. They may face shortages of the materials and components they need to continue production from their usual suppliers. They may have to buy-in more materials from expensive suppliers or risk production hold-ups.

Labour disputes can also disrupt production. These may become more common in large firms that employ highly capital-intensive mass production methods. As a result, jobs may be uninteresting for many workers who may feel that their skills are being undervalued.

These problems are diseconomies of large-scale production and will result in rising average costs of production in firms that have grown too large.

# 4.1 The role of government
# 4.2 The macroeconomic aims of government
## 4.1.1 The role of government
## 4.2.1 The macroeconomic aims of government

1. A government can act as a producer of goods and services in an economy in a variety of ways. Nationalization creates a situation of state control where goods are produced and services provided by the government or by state agencies, especially where it is believed that such provision can be in the public interest. For example, public goods can be provided in situations where it is unlikely that they would be provided by firms in the private sector. Examples of public goods include defence, the police and street lighting. Governments may also provide merit goods, which are goods that could be provided by the private sector, but which are likely to be underconsumed and underproduced, so the government intervenes in the market to ensure that they are made available to the people. Examples of merit goods include education and health care.

2. A government can act as an employer in an economy in a number of ways. The provision of public goods and merit goods gives rise to the employment of many people who work in the armed forces, the police, the education service and the health sector. It is, in fact, possible to divide employees of a government into three categories. Firstly, there are employees of national, regional and local government authorities and their administrative departments and offices. Secondly, there are employees of the government agencies that are responsible for the delivery of public services, such as a food standards agency, a health authority or a law enforcement agency. Thirdly, there are employees of public corporations, such as the people who are responsible for the day-to-day running of nationalized industries.

3. Public sector current expenditure involves recurrent spending, including the payment of wages of public sector workers and the running costs of government departments and offices. In contrast, capital expenditures by the public sector in an economy are investments in long-lived assets, such as new roads, railways, hospital buildings, and other infrastructure.

4. The four macroeconomic aims of government are: economic growth; full employment or low unemployment; low and stable price inflation or to maintain a long-term inflation target; stability in the balance of payments.

5. Two other possible government objectives are to reduce poverty/to reduce inequalities in incomes and wealth; to protect the natural environment and achieve more sustainable economic growth.

## 4.2.2 Possible conflicts between macroeconomic aims

1. Many governments aim to achieve full employment and low, stable inflation. Higher levels of employment can be encouraged by reducing taxes and increasing public spending using an expansionary fiscal policy, and by lowering interest rates and increasing the money supply, using an expansionary monetary policy. These policies will expand total demand in the economy, boosting both output and employment. However, there is a risk that total demand increases at a faster rate than total supply, causing price inflation to accelerate.

2. A government may have the aim of redistributing income while encouraging economic growth. A more equal distribution of income could be achieved by making income tax more progressive so that rates of tax payable increase with income. For example, a government might decide to tax incomes below $20,000 a year at a rate of 20%, any additional income over $20,000 but less than $50,000 per year at a rate of 40% and any income above $50,000 per year at 60%. However, while this may help to bring about a more equal distribution of after-tax income in an economy, there is risk that some of the high-earners might emigrate to work in countries where income tax rates are lower. The loss of some of the most productive, innovative and highly skilled workers and entrepreneurs from the economy could have a major detrimental impact on future economic growth. The productive capacity and total output of the economy is likely to fall as a result.

 The fiscal and monetary policy measures to expand total demand may help to reduce unemployment, but if total output fails to expand at the same rate as demand then market prices are likely to rise. That is, the expansionary policies may result in an acceleration in the rate of price inflation.

## Key words

| 1 D | 2 E | 3 H | 4 G | 5 F |
|-----|-----|-----|-----|-----|
| 6 A | 7 B | 8 I | 9 C |     |

## Revision summary

| 1 consumer; regulates; failures | 2 macroeconomic; full; inflation |
|---|---|
| 3 policy; interest rates | 4 demand; supply; economic; unemployment |

# 4.3 Fiscal policy
## 4.3.1 Definition of the budget
## 4.3.2 Reasons for government spending

1. A government will use the budget to set out its plans and forecasts for total public sector spending and public revenues for the next year and beyond. It will include detailed plans for changes in public sector spending

on different items, projects or objectives and detailed plans for changes in different tax rates and allowances including for the introduction of any new taxes.

2. If a government plans for total public sector spending to exceed the amount of public revenue it expects to raise over the same period, the budget will be in deficit. However, the government will be unable to spend more than it receives in public revenue unless it borrows the extra money it needs to fund its spending plans from private sector individuals or organizations including banks or from foreign governments.

3. Explain four of the following reasons for public sector spending in a mixed economy: to provide goods and services that are socially and economically desirable including public goods, such as street lighting and national defence, and merit goods, such as education and healthcare, that would otherwise be underprovided and underconsumed without direct public sector provision; to invest in social and economic infrastructure to support human and economic development; to support agriculture and other key industries by subsidizing their production and/or supporting investment in their productive capacity; to reduce inequalities in incomes and help vulnerable people; for example, through the provision of low-cost housing and welfare payments; to manage the macroeconomy; for example, by increasing public sector spending to boost jobs and economic growth or cutting it to reduce inflationary pressures.

**E**

| Country | Public expenditure | Public revenue | Budget balance |
|---------|--------------------|----------------|-----------------------|
| A | $520 billion | $560 billion | $40 billion (surplus) |
| B | $140 billion | $105 billion | $35 billion (deficit) |
| C | $350 billion | $350 billion | $0 (balanced budget) |

A government could reduce a budget deficit by raising taxes; cutting public sector spending; introducing measures to reduce tax avoidance and evasion so it is able to collect more tax revenue from existing taxes; boosting economic growth so that incomes and therefore tax revenues rise; refinancing the national debt at lower interest rates so that debt interest costs are lower.

## 4.3.3 Taxation
## 4.3.4 Principles of taxation

1. The tax burden is the proportion of the total national income of a country or macroeconomy that is collected in taxes.

2. Two characteristics of a good tax are (choose two from the following): a good tax should be fair, so that the ability of people and firms to pay a tax should be taken into account; it should not distort economic behaviour, for example, a tax that was so high it discouraged people

from working would not be a good tax; a good tax should provide certainty, in that those paying the tax should know when it should be paid and how much the amount will be; it should be convenient for people and firms to pay a tax; it should be relatively simple and easy to understand; finally, a tax should be relatively inexpensive and easy to collect.

3. A government may impose taxes for a number of reasons (any two of the following): to finance public expenditures, including public services such as healthcare and education, welfare payments and the armed forces; taxation is also an important instrument of fiscal policy. Taxes may be reduced with the aim of stimulating total demand, output and employment in the economy or they may be raised to reduce a demand pull inflation; progressive taxes can be used to bring about a more equal distribution of disposable incomes in an economy; taxes, such as tariffs and excise duties, may be used to raise the prices of imported goods in order to contract demand for them, thereby helping to reduce a trade (or current account) deficit in the balance of international payments; taxes may be imposed on harmful or demerit goods, such as cigarettes and alcohol, to reduce their consumption; taxes may also be imposed on goods that cause pollution or damage to the natural environment so as to discourage their consumption and therefore reduce their negative impacts or external costs.

**E** 'Major hike in taxes expected as government announces boost in healthcare spending': taxes are being used to fund an increase in public expenditures.

'New plastics tax on the way': to reduce plastic waste and the external costs it imposes on the environment. The tax will increase the costs and reduce the profits of firms using non-recyclable plastic to package their products. Firms will be able to avoid the tax if they use other, more environmentally friendly, packaging materials.

'Chinese government announced mix of tax cuts and spending increases': taxes are being used to manage total demand in the Chinese economy and to achieve the macroeconomic aim of stronger economic growth.

'Government prepares to cut the lowest rate of income tax': tax cut intended to reduce inequality in incomes after tax and to encourage people who are out of work and in receipt of unemployment benefits or welfare payments to seek paid employment. This in turn should help to reduce government spending on these transfer payments while greater numbers of people in work will help to boost tax revenues.

## 4.3.5 Classification of taxes
## 4.3.6 Impact of taxation

1. A progressive tax increases as a proportion of income as income rises. That is, the percentage of income taken in tax from a high income will be greater than the

percentage of tax taken from a lower income. In contrast, a regressive tax reduces as a proportion of income as income rises.

2. A direct tax is collected directly from the incomes or wealth of individuals or organizations. For example, corporation tax is tax imposed on company profits. Other examples include income taxes and inheritance taxes. In contrast, an indirect tax is imposed on goods and services. They include sales taxes and excise duties. The producers or suppliers of the taxed products are responsible for paying these taxes and will therefore pass on as much of their burden as they can to consumers by raising the prices of their products. Consumers therefore usually end up paying an indirect tax when they buy taxed products.

3. Advantages of direct taxes are: their cost of collection is low compared to the amount of revenue collected from them; because they are levied on personal and business incomes, a government will have a reasonably good idea of how much money it will be able to collect from them and this helps it to plan its fiscal policies; where a direct tax is progressive, it can help to bring about greater equality in the distribution of income and wealth in an economy; a direct tax will usually take into account a person's, or a firm's, ability to pay the tax.

4. Disadvantages of direct taxes are: people may be less inclined to work hard or seek employment if they have to pay high rates of income tax on their earnings; similarly, high rates of tax on the profits of companies may discourage entrepreneurs from starting new businesses; high rates of tax may encourage tax evasion and government's will have to use up more resources trying to catch those individuals or businesses who evade their tax liabilities.

5. **(a)** 30% **(b)** 16% ($7,999.70 tax /$50,000 income)

6. Advantages of indirect taxes are: they are relatively cheap and easy to collect because the task of collecting them and paying them to the government normally falls to the producers or suppliers of the goods and services to which indirect taxes have been applied; indirect taxes are paid by anyone who buys goods or services and not just those people in work or business who earn incomes; they can be levied on products which are harmful and over-consumed, such as cigarettes and alcohol, to discourage their consumption; it is relatively easier and quicker for governments to change indirect taxes than direct taxes, so they are regarded as being more flexible.

7. Disadvantages of indirect taxes are: they are inflationary because they increase the prices of the goods and services on which they are levied; they are regressive because they take a higher proportion of a low income than a high income; the amount of revenue received from indirect taxes is usually more difficult to predict than revenue from direct taxes, making it more difficult for a government to plan its future spending; high indirect taxes can encourage the smuggling of goods

from countries with lower or no indirect taxes and cash payments to avoid paying VAT or sales taxes on services received.

**E** Tax A is regressive; Tax B is proportional; Tax C is progressive.

## 4.3.7 Definition of fiscal policy
## 4.3.8 Fiscal policy measures
## 4.3.9 Effects of fiscal policy on government macroeconomic aims

1. Fiscal policy refers to the use of total public expenditures and taxation by a central government to manage total demand in an economy in an attempt to achieve its macroeconomic aims.

2. An expansionary fiscal policy involves increasing public spending and/or reducing taxes to increase total demand in the economy in order to boost output, jobs and incomes. In contrast, a contractionary fiscal policy aims to contract total demand in an economy, for example to reduce inflationary pressures, by cutting public expenditures and/or raising taxes.

3. An increase in government spending can affect total demand in a number of ways. The government is a major consumer of goods and services in most economies and so any increase in its spending on consumable items will directly benefit those firms supplying them, generating more revenue and encouraging them to respond by increasing output and employment opportunities. Cutting public spending on consumable items will have the reverse effect.

   Alternatively, a government can increase welfare payments such as unemployment benefits, disability allowances and state pensions. This will increase the income of many people who in turn may increase their spending on goods and services.

   Similarly, changes to direct taxes will have a direct impact on household disposable incomes and therefore the amount they are able to spend and save. Raising taxes will reduce their disposable incomes and levels of spending, which may be necessary to reduce the rate at which prices are rising in the economy. Cutting direct taxes will instead increase disposable incomes. However, it is possible that households simply save the increase rather than increase their spending.

   Increases in government spending may also fail to expand total demand if it crowds out or reduces private sector spending instead. This may happen if the government has to increase taxes or borrow more from the private sector to finance the increase in public spending.

   It is also difficult for a government to accurately calculate by how much total demand in an economy needs to be increased or decreased to achieve its desired objective. If it cuts taxes or increases public spending by too much it may create a spending boom resulting in rising price inflation. Similarly, steep increases in taxes or deep cuts to public spending to reduce inflation may risk plunging the economy into recession. High taxes can also be a disincentive to people to work and to run businesses. Some skilled employees and entrepreneurs may also move to other countries where taxes are lower.

 'Government cuts corporation tax': expansionary measure; will increase a budget deficit/reduce a budget surplus.

'Increase in top rate of income tax': contractionary measure; will reduce a budget deficit/increase a budget surplus.

'Increase in welfare payments to be paid for by increase in indirect taxes': should be budget neutral and leave budget balance unchanged.

'Boost in infrastructure spending': expansionary; will increase budget deficit/reduce budget surplus.

## 4.4 Monetary policy

### 4.4.1 Definition of monetary policy

### 4.4.2 Monetary policy measures

### 4.4.3 Effects of monetary policy measures on government macroeconomic aims

1. Monetary policy refers to use of interest rates and the money supply to influence levels of consumer spending and total demand in an economy.

2. An expansionary monetary policy aims to expand total demand in an economy through reductions in interest rates or by expanding the money supply; for example, using quantitative easing to increase the amount of money banks have available to lend. In contrast, a contractionary monetary policy aims to contract total demand by increasing interest rates or reducing the money supply.

3. Changing interest rates in an economy will affect the cost at which consumers and firms can borrow money and also the return they will receive on any savings. Raising the cost of borrowing should therefore reduce the total amount consumers and firms are willing and able to borrow and repay over time. Raising the reward for saving may also persuade them to save more from their incomes by reducing or delaying some of their current consumption. Increasing the interest rate could therefore prove effective in reducing demand during a period of high or rising inflation. However, it may not have this effect if the rate of inflation exceeds the rate of interest because this will reduce the real cost of loans and the real value of saving, in which case it makes more sense for consumers and firms to continue borrowing and to reduce their savings.

Similarly, cutting interest rates to boost demand during a deep economic recession may also prove ineffective. Consumers and firms may not respond to a reduction in

interest rates if unemployment is high and they are not confident that future economic conditions will improve. That said, it is also possible that borrowing and thereafter spending expands faster than total supply can respond, resulting an increase in inflation. An expansion in the money supply may have a similar impact on the economy.

 'Reserve bank of India has raised key interest rates': a contractionary measure designed to reduce inflationary pressures by increasing the cost of loans and reward for saving, therefore reducing total spending in the economy.

'Indonesia's central bank cuts its benchmark interest rate': an expansionary measure designed to boost total spending by reducing the cost of loans and the reward to saving. If successful, the policy should encourage firms increase output and employment.

'Japanese central bank doubles money supply': expansionary measure designed to boost consumer spending, investment and growth in the Japanese economy which had all fallen due to recession and deflation in the economy.

## 4.5 Supply-side policy

### 4.5.1 Definition of supply-side policy

### 4.5.2 Supply-side policy measures

### 4.5.3 Effects of supply-side policy measures on government macroeconomic aims

1. Four supply-side policy instruments are (choose four from the following): selective tax reductions or incentives; for example, cutting income taxes to Increase the reward from work or cutting taxes on profits to encourage new business start-ups; the use of subsidies to encourage the research and development of new products and production processes or to support new training initiatives; expanding and/or improving education to improve future workforce skills; labour market reforms to curb the power of trade unions to restrict the supply of labour and force up wages; reducing unemployment benefits to encourage more people to seek employment; removing barriers to international trade and competition; breaking up or restricting the power of monopoly firms so that they cannot restrict market supply and competition; transferring public sector functions and activities to the private sector which may be able to provide them more efficiently; deregulation to remove or reform complex and out-of-date regulations in order to reduce costs on business activity.

2. There are a great many ways a government could use regulations to control the behaviour of private firms, for example (explain two):
   - Regulations can be used to restrict or outlaw certain activities, such as placing limits on working hours, waste and pollution or outlawing the production of harmful products. Firms that fail to comply with regulations may have to pay substantial fines.

- They can be used to set standards for certain products and for hygiene and safety in work places. This can increase costs of production in some firms but may also benefit those firms able to demonstrate that they have met or exceeded regulated standards. Consumers are more likely to buy products that are made to high standards and employees are more likely to be attracted to those firms that offer good working conditions.

- Regulations can also stop firms from misleading consumers about their products and prices. They can prevent powerful monopolies from restricting competition and consumer choice and from charging high prices in order to earn excess profits.

- Employment-related regulations can specify the minimum wages firms should pay their workers and their entitlements to rest periods, holidays and sick leave and pay. They can also ensure firms take measures to protect the health and safety of their employees even if this imposes additional costs on firms.

3. Supply-side policies can be used to influence the level of aggregate supply in an economy. For example, training and retraining schemes can increase the skill levels and productivity of workers and make them more employable. Competition could be increased in an industry, such as through a privatization initiative, and this could to lead to higher levels of efficiency and productivity. Disincentives to work could be reduced, for example by reducing the benefits paid to unemployed workers and by reducing the basic rate of income tax.

However, there are potentially some disadvantages of supply-side policies. For example, privatization could lead to greater efficiency and productivity, but if a firm moves from the public sector to the private sector, there is no guarantee that it will survive if it makes losses. If the firm fails, jobs may be lost leading to an increase in the level of unemployment. Even with firms that do survive in the private sector, it may become necessary to make people redundant if the firm is to survive and increase its profitability, again contributing to an increase in the level of unemployment.

In addition, some supply-side policies, such as expanding education and training to increase the skills of the future workforce, can be expensive and may also take many years to have their desired effect.

**E** Main benefits are likely to be an increase in the supply of basic food items, a reduction in their price and increase in their affordability to people on low incomes and a reduction in levels of malnutrition as a result. Main drawbacks are likely to be the cost of the subsidies. The government may have to raise taxes, increase borrowing or cut other worthwhile public expenditures to pay for the subsidies. Farmers may also get used to receiving subsidies from government and reduce their efforts to improve their own efficiency and reduce their

costs of production. It may also be cheaper to import basic foods from farmers in other countries with lower production costs.

## Key words

| 1 O | 2 E | 3 N | 4 I | 5 C | 6 M | 7 J | 8 K |
|-----|-----|-----|-----|-----|-----|-----|-----|
| 9 F | 10 A | 11 G | 12 L | 13 P | 14 D | 15 H | 16 B |

## Revision summary

| | |
|---|---|
| 1. more; less | 6. fiscal; demand |
| 2. tax | 7. contractionary; taxes |
| 3. progressive; regressive | 8. monetary; increase; reduce |
| 4. direct; direct; reduce | 9. expansionary |
| 5. indirect | 10. supply-side |

# 4.6 Economic growth

## 4.6.1 Measurement of economic growth

1. The term 'Gross Domestic Product' can be defined as the total value of all final goods and services produced within the geographical boundaries of an economy by its factors of production in a given period of time.

2. There are three different methods used to calculate the Gross Domestic Product of an economy (select one).

Firstly, there is the output method. The value of the final output produced in an economy is added up (by adding up the value of the final output produced, the problem of double counting is avoided); that is, the value added by each firm at each stage of production is added.

Secondly, there is the income method. This measures the total income earned from the production of a country's output, i.e. it includes rent, wages and salaries, interest and profit. It is only earned incomes that are included; unearned incomes, such as transfer payments (transfer payments could include pensions, unemployment benefits and child benefits), are excluded.

Thirdly, there is the expenditure method. This measures the total amount of money that is spent on what has been produced in the country. This includes spending by households, firms and the government, as well as money spent abroad on buying a country's exports; spending on imported goods from other countries is deducted from the total.

3. It is important to distinguish between nominal GDP and real GDP. Nominal GDP refers to a figure that has not been adjusted to take into account the effect of inflation. Real GDP, on the other hand, refers to a figure that has been adjusted to take into account the effect of inflation. Inflation can distort GDP figures and so a real figure is one that has been adjusted for inflation.

4. GDP statistics can be useful for a number of reasons and in a number of ways (describe two). Economics is about the allocation of scarce resources in an economy and the need to make that allocation as efficient as possible. GDP

statistics can make people better informed and so it is likely that the decisions taken will be better, taking into account the relevant data. This is particularly the case for a government; for example, a government could use the data to take appropriate fiscal decisions. The GDP statistics also allow comparisons to be made with earlier periods to see if there has been economic growth and an improvement in standards of living. They also allow comparisons to be made with other countries in terms of economic growth and standards of living. Economic growth is usually measured through changes in GDP and standards of living are usually compared through changes in GDP per head/per capita.

**(E)** (a) B (b) C (c) D (d) A

## 4.6.2 Definition of economic growth
## 4.6.3 Causes of economic growth

1. Economic growth usually refers to an increase in a country's output over a period of time, usually one year, measured through changes in real GDP. It can be represented on a country's production possibility curve (PPC) or frontier (PPF) by an outward shift of the curve. The PPC is usually shown with consumer goods on one axis and capital goods on the other axis and if there is a shift outwards of the curve, then it is possible for a country to produce more of both goods, i.e. there has been an increase in the productive capacity or capability of an economy.

2. Economic growth can be caused by a number of possible factors and these can be broadly divided into supply-side and demand-side factors (select two).

   Supply-side factors can include the discovery of more natural resources, e.g. oil and gas. It can also come about through increased investment in capital goods, supporting a move from labour-intensive to capital-intensive production. Investment could also be in terms of infrastructure projects, such as the building of additional runways, new airports, motorways and improved rail links, such as through the development of high-speed trains. Infrastructure development in the provision of gas and electricity would also be helpful to growth. Economic growth can come about as a result of technical progress, with various inventions and innovations pushing out the PPC. It is also likely to come from increased commitment to research and development. The development of a sophisticated financial sector is also likely to enhance growth, making it possibly easier to raise required capital. Economic growth could be the result of an increase in the quantity and/or quality of human resources. The quality of the labour force could be enhanced through education and training, making workers more productive, and the quantity of the labour force could be increased as a result of migration of people into a country. The reallocation of resources in an economy from one sector to another could also stimulate growth, as resources are moved away from the less productive sectors of an economy to the more productive sectors.

   Demand-side factors arise from increases in consumer spending, leading to an increase in output by firms to satisfy the increase in demand. This is likely to be particularly the case in those countries experiencing a rapid increase in population.

3. An increase in government spending will increase total demand in an economy, which can encourage firms to hire more workers and expand their output. In turn, the increase in incomes this generates can have a multiplier effect as the increase is spent on other goods and services. This can create new business opportunities and may also encourage firms to invest in new plants and equipment which will expand the productive potential of the economy.

   If the government spends more on education, it can increase the productive potential of the future workforce. Similarly, government investments in new roads and other infrastructure can also raise the productive potential of an economy while also providing jobs and incomes for many people.

   Increasing government subsidies to firms will reduce their costs of production encourages firms to produce more.

   However, raising taxes to pay for increased government spending may have a negative impact on demand and work incentives, while increasing government borrowing instead may push up interest rates. As a result people and firms may borrow less and private sector spending may fall.

**(E)** The PPC has shifted outwards, indicating there has been economic growth / and increase in the productive potential of the economy. Total output has increased from point X to Y. This growth may be the result of discoveries of additional natural resources, expansion of the labour force (for example, due to net inward migration), investments in new capital equipment and/or in education and training to improve workforce skills, or technical progress.

## 4.6.4 Causes and consequences of recession

1. The aim of governments is to achieve an increase in the real GDP of their economies. However, real GDP growth can vary considerably over time, even becoming negative during some periods. The business cycle or economic cycle refers to the pattern cyclical changes or fluctuations in real GDP growth rates that occur in many economies over a period of several years. The typical economic cycle passes through four stages. Firstly, there is growth or expansion when an economy's output is growing rapidly. Secondly, there is a boom or peak where the growth in an economy's output is most significant; this stage is often associated with a relatively high rate of inflation.

Thirdly, there is a recession or downturn when there is negative growth; that is, output actually falls. This stage of the cycle is usually associated with an increase in unemployment. Finally, there is a recovery or upturn in an economy when confidence starts to recover and the economy starts to expand again, leading to a fall in the level of unemployment.

2. A 'recession' is defined as a period of two successive quarters (that is, a period of six months) when there is negative economic growth, i.e. when total GDP falls or shrinks.

3. Economists are concerned by the prospect of a recession because results in falling output, employment and living standards. A deep and prolonged recession may also result in deflation. Falling prices in the economy deter people from spending causing total demand, output and employment to fall further. Many businesses may also be forced to close.

4. A 'U-shaped recession' is one in which there is a prolonged slump in an economy. Negative growth can occur over a number of years. A 'V-shaped recession' is one in which the slump in an economy does not last for a long period of time. Negative growth is relatively short-lived and is followed by a rapid and sustained economic recovery.

**E** (a) 2009 (b) 2010–11

## 4.6.5 Consequences of economic growth
## 4.6.6 Policies to promote economic growth

1. An increase in real GDP can be of benefit in the following ways (explain two of the following): it increases the volume of goods and services produced satisfy more consumers' needs and wants, which in turn can improve living standards and economic welfare; there are likely to be increased employment opportunities and this can increase incomes and reduce poverty; tax revenues will increase without the need to raise tax rates, thereby providing a government with more funds to spend which it may choose to invest in improvements in education, healthcare and the national infrastructure; it can boost the profits of existing firms and create new business opportunities; it can help to reduce inflationary pressures in the economy if total output expands at a faster rate than aggregate demand.

2. Economic growth may not always be beneficial to all groups or organizations in an economy. For example, an increase in output could increase pollution, damage to the environment and the rate at which natural resources are depleted. It is also possible that economic growth is associated with a growing divide between the rich and poor if the proceeds of growth only benefit those people who are already rich. If growth is the result of technical progress and a move towards capital-intensive production, it may result in higher levels of unemployment and poverty. The benefits of growth may

also depend on what type of goods and services are produced in greater volume. For example, increasing the output of military equipment at the expense of many consumer goods or increasing the output of cigarettes and other harmful goods may increase external costs. It is therefore necessary to stress that economic growth, especially a high rate of economic growth, has an opportunity cost. This is why many economists argue the need for economic growth to be more sustainable. That is, growth should not be achieved at the expense of creating irreversible damage to the environment and economic problems for future generations.

3. Two policies governments could use to promote economic growth are (explain any two of the following):

• A government may use fiscal policy to boost total demand by cutting direct taxes and increasing public expenditures. Lower income tax will increase disposable income and encourage consumer spending. Increased spending on welfare payments will also encourage consumer spending while increased spending on capital projects, such as new road constructions, will help create new jobs by increasing business and household incomes. However, a fiscal policy stimulus could cause inflation to increase and growth to slow again as a result.

• Monetary policy may also be used to reduce interest rates to encourage higher levels of borrowing and therefore spending in the economy to promote growth. If lower interest rates fail to boost demand, the government may also instruct the central bank to use measures such as quantitative easing to increase the money supply in the economy. However, boosting total demand will do very little to expand the productive potential of the economy and its rate of long run growth. This requires supply-side policies.

• Supply-side policies can be used to boost the long-run productive capacity of an economy by reducing or removing barriers to improvements in productivity and enterprise; for example: increased investment in education and training, to increase the skills, knowledge and occupational mobility of the current and future workforce; supporting investments in the research and development (R&D) of new, innovative products, technologies, production processes and materials that can be used to produce more and better goods and services; public investments in modernizing existing, and building new, economic infrastructure, such as new power generation and distribution systems, mobile and broadband communications networks, roads, airports and ports, all of which will directly benefit many firms, the process of production and the movement of people, goods and services within an economy; giving tax cuts and subsidies to new firms to encourage people to start new businesses; encouraging multinationals to locate and invest in the economy thereby boosting output and providing additional jobs; other measures aimed at improving resource efficiency including privatization, deregulation, lowering income taxes to improve work incentives and labour market reforms.

 The articles illustrate the following potential problems with economic growth:

- the need for workers to retrain and update their skills more often as technology advances or risk becoming unemployed;
- an increase in pollution and waste from increased levels of production and consumption;
- there may be a failure to distribute the benefits of growth across populations to help reduce poverty and to improve the living standards of the many rather than the few.

## Key words

| 1 E | 2 N | 3 K | 4 A | 5 H | 6 I | 7 J |
|-----|-----|-----|-----|-----|-----|-----|
| 8 M | 9 F | 10 L | 11 G | 12 C | 13 B | 14 D |

## Revision summary

| 1. expenditure; nominal; real | 5. negative; quarters |
|---|---|
| 2. production; possibility | 6. expansionary |
| 3. trade; growth; boom; downturn; recovery | 7. long-run; supply |
| 4. progress; development; patents | |

# 4.7 Employment and unemployment
## 4.7.1 Definition of employment, unemployment and full employment
## 4.7.2 Changing patterns and level of employment
## 4.7.3 Measurement of unemployment

1. If there is full employment in an economy, most people who are willing and able to work will be in employment. That is, there is a high and stable level of employment and relatively little unemployment. Unemployment occurs when people who are willing and able to work cannot find paid employment. Full employment does not therefore mean there is no or zero unemployment in an economy. Some people may be unemployed for short periods as they change jobs or because their jobs are seasonal. Some people may also choose not to work, for example, because they need to care for their children or because unemployment benefits exceed the wages they

could earn in work, while some other people may instead work voluntarily without pay for charities and other organizations.

2. There are a number of factors that can affect the participation rate in a country (select two). These can include the birth rate, the number of people in education (which will be affected by a country's school leaving age), the retirement age (in many countries, the retirement age has been increasing as people on average live longer than in the past), the social security system and the extent to which people can live on the various benefits and transfer payments, the social attitudes towards work (this can be particularly important in relation to the proportion of women who are employed) and the availability of child care (this will affect the extent to which parents are able to go to work).

3. There have been a number of changes in the pattern of employment in many economies over the last 50 years. One of these is the change in the industrial structure with the proportion employed in the primary and secondary sectors declining and the proportion employed in the tertiary sector increasing (in some countries, the proportion employed in the tertiary sector is over 70%). In some countries, a number of people are only employed as part-time workers, and this often tends to be women. In many countries, a supportive enterprise culture has encouraged more people to become self-employed.

## 4.7.4 Causes and types of unemployment
## 4.7.5 Consequences of unemployment

1. The term 'unemployment rate' can be defined as the percentage of a country's labour force that is officially registered as unemployed. It does not include those people who would like to be employed but who are not registered as being unemployed.

2. There are a number of different possible causes of unemployment in an economy. One cause is when the level of aggregate demand in an economy is not enough to consume all that has been produced and so people lose their jobs. This is known as demand deficient unemployment. It is often associated with trade cycles which affect many countries and if there is a recession, the level of unemployment in a country will rise; this is known as cyclical unemployment. Unemployment could be caused by trade unions using their power to push wages higher than firms are able to pay, leading to workers losing their jobs. Structural unemployment is where there has been a change in the industrial structure of an economy and some workers find that there is no longer the same demand for workers; this is especially the case with workers in the primary and secondary sectors. This form of unemployment can be a problem in particular areas of a country, when it can be called

regional unemployment. In some countries, employment can be closely related to the seasons and at certain times of the year there can be seasonal unemployment; this can be a particular problem in agriculture and tourism. Some people have lost their jobs because of a move from labour-intensive production to capital-intensive production, a situation known as technological unemployment. Some people may be out of work when the number of people unemployed is being calculated, i.e. they are between jobs; this is known as frictional or search unemployment. Some people may not actually be capable of keeping a job for a variety of reasons, a situation known as residual unemployment.

3. The question refers to a fall in the unemployment rate. This may be the result of a fall in the number of people unemployed in an economy or an increase in the labour force; for example, due to net inward migration. If the labour force increases, the rate of unemployment will fall, but there may be no change in the number of people unemployed. Unemployment could even be higher than before.

   If there is a reduction in the number of people unemployed it can benefit an economy in a number of ways. If more people are in work, more can be produced and more people will be earning an income. These in turn can help to improve living standards and reduce poverty. Increasing output can also help to reduce inflationary pressures in the economy and, if some is sold overseas, it can also improve the trade balance.

   Public spending on unemployment benefits will fall as revenues from income taxes rise because more people are in paid employment. In turn a government can cut income and corporation tax rates to encourage higher levels of productivity and enterprise and/or increase spending on education and healthcare. This can also improve living standards while also creating a more skilled and productive workforce.

   However, falling unemployment may also create labour shortages and this in turn can push up wages. Increasing wage costs can reduce profits and may be passed onto consumers by firms in higher prices.

**E** Change in demand linked to weather conditions = seasonal unemployment; substitution of labour for capital = technological unemployment; falling demand for exports = could be cyclical or structural (if long term decline) unemployment; people changing jobs = frictional unemployment.

## Key words

| 1 G | 2 J | 3 M | 4 B | 5 L | 6 I | 7 C | 8 F | 9 E |
|-----|-----|-----|-----|-----|-----|-----|-----|-----|
| 10 P | 11 N | 12 Q | 13 H | 14 K | 15 D | 16 A | 17 O | |

## Revision summary

| 1. structural; regional; seasonal | 6. voluntary; involuntary |
|---|---|
| 2. demand; deficient; cyclical | 7. minimum |
| 3. technological; frictional | 8. occupational; geographical |
| 4. working; actively | 9. supply; cyclical; structural |
| 5. negative/downward; multiplier | |

# 4.8 Price inflation
## 4.8.1 Definition of inflation
## 4.8.2 Measurement of inflation

1. If the rate of inflation in an economy is increasing, this means the general level of prices is rising more rapidly than in previous periods.

2. Inflation is an increase in the general level of prices in an economy per period of time. The inflation rate will vary from one country to another, and within one country from one year to another. Most governments aim to keep the rate of inflation low and stable in their economies. However, sometimes the rate of price inflation can accelerate so much that average prices double, treble or more within just a few months, weeks or even days such that money becomes almost worthless. This is called hyperinflation.

3. There are a number of stages involved in the calculation of a consumer prices index. Firstly, a number of goods and services are chosen to be included in the index to be representative of a typical budget. The actual number of goods and services included will vary from country to country, but many indices use between 600 and 700 different goods and services. Secondly, any price changes in these goods and services are monitored and recorded over a period of time. Thirdly, the different goods and services are given weights in the index to indicate their relative importance in the spending of people, that is, items such as food and housing are usually very important in the spending of most households so this spending is given a higher weighting than for other products. Fourthly, a base year is chosen and given the value of 100. Finally, to create a weighted price index, the price index for each product is multiplied by its weight and these figures are added up. The total figure is then divided by the total number of weights to produce the price index.

4. A consumer prices index may be used in the following ways (explain two): it is widely used as a measure of price inflation faced by households and therefore as a measure of changes in the cost of living in an economy; it may be used by workers and trade unions to set their wage demands, seeking increases that match or exceed the increase in the cost of living measured by the increase

in the index; the CPI will also be used by entrepreneurs in making business decisions concerning their purchases and the setting of wages and prices; inflation reduces the real value of money - a CPI is therefore used to deflate various economic series to calculate their real or inflation-free values, such as changes in real GDP or in the real value of incomes and welfare payments; a government may increase the value of certain welfare payments, such as state pensions and disability allowances, by the increase in the CPI so that their real value is unchanged and people in receipt of these payments are not made worse off as a result of rising prices; similarly, income tax allowances may be 'indexed' – increased in line with the change in the CPI – so that people do not end up paying more tax from their nominal incomes while the real value of their incomes may be unchanged or falling.

**E** (a) 2008 (b) 2012 (c) At the end of 2016.

## 4.8.3 Causes of inflation

1. Inflation is caused by 'too much money chasing too few goods' meaning that market prices are continually rising because consumers and firms are increasing their spending on goods and services at a faster rate than their supply can expand. This can only occur if consumers and firms have more money to spend, either because wages and other factor rewards are rising or because they are able to borrow more from banks. Factor rewards and bank lending can only be increased if there is more money in the economy to fund them. Therefore, total demand cannot increase unless the supply of money increases.

2. Inflation can be caused by a number of factors, but the causes are usually divided into demand-pull and cost-push explanations. Demand-pull inflation is a situation in which the aggregate demand in an economy is greater than the aggregate supply, and so there is excess demand. Monetarists argue that an important aspect of this demand-pull inflation is that it is caused by excessive increases in a country's money supply. This situation is often described as one where too much money is chasing after too few goods. Monetarists will often state that inflation is everywhere a monetary phenomenon.

3. Cost-push inflation is a situation in which instead of the general level of prices in an economy being pulled up by excess demand, they are in fact pushed up by increases in the costs of production. These increased costs could be in the form of more expensive raw materials, more expensive costs of land and increases in the wages and salaries paid to workers. Changes in a country's exchange rate can have an impact on the rate of inflation, because if the exchange rate loses value against other currencies, a situation known as a depreciation in the value of a currency, the cost of imports will now be relatively more expensive, and if firms rely on imported raw materials or component parts, this will put up their costs of production. This situation is known as imported inflation.

**E** 'Increase in fuel prices': cost-push inflation; 'CPI in lowest rise for 17 years': disinflation due to falling import prices; 'Indonesian inflation': demand-pull inflation.

## 4.8.4 Consequences of inflation
## 4.8.5 Policies to control inflation

1. Price inflation will reduce the purchasing power or real value of money. As prices rise, each dollar or unit of money is able to buy fewer products.

2. Maintaining low and stable inflation is an important goal for many governments and central banks because a high or rising inflation can create significant social and economic problems. High inflation will erode the real value of money and create hardship for many people, especially those on low and fixed incomes. Firm's costs will also rise, squeezing profits and their ability and incentives to invest. They may also suffer from declining sales of their products in international markets and at home if prices are rising in the economy at a faster rate than in others making their products less competitive. As a result, inflation can also create unemployment and reduce economic growth.

   Maintaining a low and stable rate of inflation therefore avoids these problems. It avoids lenders, workers with low bargaining power and people with low and fixed incomes from experiencing a fall in their purchasing power. The real value of savings will also be protected if interest rates are at or above a low rate of inflation.

   A low and stable rate of inflation also creates greater economic certainty, allowing consumers and firms to plan their future expenditures with greater confidence. The international competitiveness of domestically produced goods will also improve if prices are rising at a slower rate than prices in other countries. This can help to increase demand for home produced goods and services, thereby helping to boost output and employment opportunities and also improving the balance of international trade.

3. Governments may use a variety of demand-side and supply-side measures in an attempt to maintain a low and stable rate of inflation in their economies. If inflation is high or rising, a government may deploy demand-side measures to reduce total demand in the economy or the rate at which it is rising. Contractionary fiscal policy involves making cuts to public spending and raising taxes. However, increasing direct taxes and cutting welfare payments will reduce disposable incomes and consumer spending but may cause hardship for people, especially those on low incomes. Increasing indirect taxes on goods and services will also squeeze household budgets because they are inflationary.

   Increasing taxes on businesses will reduce their profits and may therefore result in a contraction in output and higher unemployment. Cutting back the public sector workforce will reduce public spending on wages and salaries but will also increase unemployment. Other cuts to public spending, such as reductions in capital expenditures on the construction of new roads and school buildings, will also reduce revenues for private sector firms undertaking the work.

Alternatively, a government could tighten monetary policy by raising interest rates. This will increase the cost of borrowing as well as the reward for saving. As a result, consumers and firms may reduce their borrowing and therefore spending, and people may be encouraged to save a greater proportion of their disposable incomes and reduce the proportion they spend. However, people who have existing loans may find it more difficult to repay them. Some people may even lose their homes if they cannot afford to repay their mortgages. Some firms may also struggle to repay increased interest charges on their existing loans and may have to cut back other costs. including wages, by reducing their workforces. Firms will also cut back borrowing to fund investments in new plants and machinery. This may reduce future economic growth.

In contrast, supply-side policies aim to expand the productive capacity and total output of an economy. Inflationary pressures in the economy will fall if total supply is able to increase at the same or a faster rate than total demand. Doing so will also help to reduce unemployment and boost economic growth in the economy at the same time. Supply-side policies can therefore avoid many of the policy conflicts that arise using demand-side policies. However, they can be expensive and may take some time to have their desired effect. For example, the benefits in terms of increased workforce skills and productivity from expanding and improving education will only be released once students have completed their education. Cutting taxes on incomes and profits to boost incentives to work and enterprise and increasing subsidies to help firms expand output and to undertake more research and development, will require the government to cut other public expenditures to pay for them or increase borrowing. Both of these actions may result in crowding out private sector spending instead.

**E** Beneficiaries of inflation include people and firms who have borrowed money. This is because inflation will reduce the real value of their loans.

Lenders and people on fixed incomes, such as old age pensioners, will lose out due to inflation. This is because it will erode the real value of loans (that is, money repaid at a later date will be worth less than when it was first loaned) and will reduce the purchasing power or real value of incomes.

## 4.8.6 Deflation

1. Deflation is defined as a fall in the general level of prices in an economy over a period of time. Deflation will therefore increase the real value of money over time. In contrast, disinflation means the rate of increase in the general level of prices is falling. That is, average prices are continuing to rise by at a slower rate each period. The real value of money will still be eroded if there is disinflation.

2. Deflation may be caused by a number of factors (explain two): total demand may be falling due to firms cutting back their investments and consumers increasing saving; the money supply in the economy may be falling; for example, as banks reduce lending which in turn may be causing the fall in total demand; total supply in the economy could be expanding at a faster rate than total demand causing market prices to fall; competition between firms may have increased, causing them to lower their prices to compete more aggressively for sales; total supply may be expanding at a faster rate than total demand because of technological progress and increasing labour and capital productivity, reducing average production costs.

3. If prices are falling in an economy, the purchasing power or real value of money will be rising. People will be able to buy more goods and services, satisfy more of their wants and enjoy a higher standard of living. Falling prices may be a sign of increased competition and of increased productivity and advancing technology, which have reduced average costs and expanded total output. These are beneficial for an economy and will boost economic growth.

However, if the general price level continues to fall over a prolonged period time, the causes and effects are unlikely to be beneficial. This is because consumers will delay many spending decisions as they wait for prices to fall further. Stocks of unsold goods will therefore accumulate so firms are likely to cut their prices further, reducing their profits and incentive to invest. As firms cut production, they will reduce the size of their workforces. Household incomes will fall as unemployment rises, further reducing demand for goods and services. The value of debts held by people and firms will rise in real terms as prices fall and this increases the burden of making loan repayments. Eventually the economy goes into a deep recession as demand, output, the demand for labour, and incomes continue to fall. Many firms may go out of business because they are unable to make any profit no matter how much they cut their prices by as consumers simply continue to delay their spending further. The real cost of public spending will also be rising but tax revenues will fall as economic activity slumps. This means the government must borrow more money despite the rising real cost of doing so. These are the negative consequences of a prolonged or malign deflation in the general level of prices in an economy.

**E** Deflation occurred in 2015.

## Key words

| 1 M | 2 D | 3 G | 4 F | 5 H | 6 I | 7 B | 8 N |
|-----|-----|-----|-----|-----|-----|-----|-----|
| 9 L | 10 A | 11 C | 12 O | 13 J | 14 K | 15 E | |

## Revision summary

| 1. prices index; base | 7. money |
|---|---|
| 2. basket; weighting/weight | 8. less |
| 3. inflation; hyperinflation | 9. target |
| 4. disinflation; deflation; | 10. contract; demand-pull |
| 5. indexation | 11. malign |
| 6. demand pull; cost push | |

## Working with data and diagrams

1. The weighted price index has to be calculated for each of the four product categories, remembering that the base year = 100. For food, this is 5 × 120 = 600. For clothing, this is 2 × 110 = 220. For transport, this is 2 × 110 = 220. For other products, this is 1 × 120 = 120. The four figures need to be added together (600 + 220 + 220 + 120) = 1,160. This figure of 1160 needs to be divided by the total number of weights (10) = 116. Given that the base year is 100, the rate of inflation in the country is 16%.

2. The real GDP growth rate of a country is calculated by subtracting the rate of inflation from the rate of increase of nominal GDP. In this case, it is 4.75% - 2.15% = 2.60%.

3.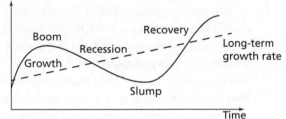

4. **(a)** Qatar  **(b)** Slovenia  **(c)** Libya

## Multiple choice questions

| 1 C | 2 D | 3 C | 4 A | 5 A | 6 D | 7 C | 8 C | 9 D | 10 C |
|-----|-----|-----|-----|-----|-----|-----|-----|-----|------|
| 11 A | 12 C | 13 D | 14 B | 15 A | 16 B | 17 C | 18 D | 19 B | 20 D |

## Structured questions

1  a) The 'real' rate of growth of output in the country over the past year, i.e. the rate of growth after taking the effects of inflation into account, is calculated by subtracting the rate of inflation from the increase in output. In this case, this is 8.7% - 7.8% = 0.9%.

   b) The term 'hyperinflation' is defined as a particularly high rate of inflation which can lead to a collapse of confidence in a country's currency as money becomes almost worthless. There is no agreed point at which inflation becomes hyperinflation, although Germany in the early 1920s is often given as an example of hyperinflation because at that time the rate of inflation rose to 24,000%.

   c) The government would be concerned about the consequences of a high rate of inflation for a number of reasons. Inflation causes the purchasing power of money to fall, i.e. if the general level of prices in the economy is rising, then a given sum of money will be able to buy less. Inflation discourages people from saving money because if money is saved for a number of years it will be able to buy less than it would have been able to do if there had been no inflation. Of course, the extent to which this happens depends on the rate of interest that is paid on savings accounts by financial institutions. Those people who are on fixed incomes, or whose incomes only rise a little each year, will be worse off because their income is not keeping pace with inflation. Inflation also creates a situation of uncertainty about the future and this can make planning by individuals and firms much more difficult than would otherwise be the case. It will reduce the competitiveness of a country's exports, if the rate of inflation is higher than in other countries, and this could lead to a worsening of a country's trade balance.

   d) It is important to distinguish between the causes of frictional unemployment and of seasonal unemployment. Frictional unemployment comes about as a result of changes in an economy. In a dynamic economy, it is likely that there will be some sectors of an economy that are growing and some sectors that are declining and so it is inevitable that some workers will move from sector to another. Frictional unemployment, in this sense, is actually a sign of a healthy and dynamic economy. The actual extent of frictional unemployment in an economy will depend on particular factors. For example, in this country, it is stated that people are taking much longer between leaving one job and obtaining another, partly because of the relatively high level of transfer payments paid to the unemployed and partly because of the lack of information about job vacancies in different parts of the country. If the government wanted to reduce the extent of frictional unemployment in the economy, it could substantially lower the transfer payments paid to the unemployed, or stop them altogether, and improve the availability of information about job vacancies in different parts of the country, such as through establishing information centres and information websites, to make the unemployed better aware of what jobs are available.

   Seasonal unemployment is different from frictional unemployment because it refers to a situation where the rate of unemployment is not even throughout the year and is much higher at certain times of the year. This situation is caused by seasonal variations in the pattern of demand for certain types of workers. The examples given are agriculture and tourism. Both of these industries are affected by differences in the weather.

e) The government is concerned about the consequences of a high rate of unemployment for a number of reasons. For individuals, unemployment means that people have been denied a basic human right, i.e. the right to work. Employment gives workers a sense of self-worth and satisfaction; if they do not have a job, there is a chance that this could have a negative effect on them, leading to depression.

The consequences of unemployment can also be seen in terms of the economy. Unemployed people represent a waste of a scarce resource, with the result that output will be lower than would otherwise be the case. There is likely to be a negative multiplier effect, with lower incomes leading to lower spending and so other firms will be affected by a rise in the level of unemployment. This can lead to an increase in social problems and possibly an increase in the crime rate.

Unemployment can also have an effect on the government. If fewer people are working, fewer people will be paying income tax. If people have lower incomes, they are likely to reduce their spending and so the revenue from indirect taxes on expenditure is likely to fall. Also, if more people are unemployed, there are more people that the government will need to give transfer payments to. If public expenditure on transfer payments in increasing and public revenue from taxation is declining, this will impact on a government's fiscal policy, making it more likely that the government will have a budget deficit and less likely that it will have a balanced budget.

f) The term 'recession' can be defined as a situation when a country experiences negative growth, i.e. output is actually falling, over two successive quarters.

g) A low rate of inflation can benefit an economy in a number of ways. It may mean that domestic products become more internationally competitive. As a result, the balance of trade may improve as demand for exports may increase while demand for imports to the country may fall in favour of buying more domestic products. In turn, these changes may encourage producers to increase output and take on more employees, thereby reducing unemployment.

It will also help firms to control their costs and plan ahead without worrying that costs may rise rapidly in the near future. Wage demands by trade unions and workers may also be relatively low if prices are only rising slowly in the economy. In turn, this may mean

they are not dragged into higher marginal income tax bands. This may occur if they have to increase their wages substantially to keep up with a high and rising inflation. A low inflation can therefore boost confidence and encourage firms to invest in new plant and equipment and expansion. This will boost the productive capacity of the economy.

Savers and lenders will also benefit if interest rates are above the rate of inflation.

However, the downside of keeping inflation low may be higher unemployment and slower economic growth in the economy, if low inflation can only be achieved by the government raising interest rates, cutting public spending or raising taxes. There is also a risk the economy may slip into a prolonged economic recession during which prices may fall. A prolonged period of deflation can discourage consumption and investment. It will also reduce government tax revenues to spend on the achievement of other objectives, such as better education and healthcare.

Despite being low, the rate of inflation may still be higher than inflation rates in other countries; in which case, there will be no improvement in the balance of trade. On the contrary, it is likely to worsen because imports may be better value than domestically produced goods and demand for exports falls.

A low inflation may not be welcome to borrowers who might prefer a higher rate of inflation to erode the real value of their debts.

2. a) Inflation is defined as a persistent and sustained increase in the general level of prices or average prices in an economy over a particular period of time, usually one year.

b) An increase in aggregate demand in an economy could lead to inflation when the level of demand is greater than the aggregate supply, i.e. there is a situation of excess demand. This is sometimes referred to as too much money chasing too few goods. Monetarist economists, in particular, argue that an important aspect of this demand-pull inflation is that it is caused by excessive increases in a country's money supply. Monetarists will often state that inflation is everywhere a monetary phenomenon. This situation of demand-pull inflation is particularly likely to happen in an economy that is experiencing full employment and so an increase in demand cannot be met by an increase in output because the economy is operating at full capacity. There is thus an output gap, known as an inflationary gap.

c) A government can take a number of different measures to influence the patterns and levels of employment in an economy. It could provide financial support to families to help them pay care for childcare, and this would be useful in encouraging parents to work knowing that their children were being looked after. A government could also take the initiative in persuading employers to be more flexible in their approach to workers, encouraging them to allow workers, where possible, to have flexible working hours or to allow workers to work part-time rather than full-time. Employers could also be encouraged to allow workers to job-share wherever possible. A government could encourage the development of an enterprise culture, such as through a variety of education and training schemes, so that more workers were able to become self-employed. Investment in education and training schemes would lead to a more skilled workforce and this would be useful in allowing workers to move from one sector of industry to another, encouraging the occupational mobility of labour. A government could also make information about job vacancies more available, and possibly provide some form of financial assistance for those workers who moved from one region of a country to another. This would be extremely useful in terms of improving the geographical mobility of labour.

d) Deflation refers to a situation where the general level of prices in an economy is falling over a period of time. A government will be concerned about the consequences of deflation for a number of reasons. If prices are falling, many people may decide to postpone consumption of some products in the expectation that the prices may continue to fall. This situation could be worrying for firms who may decide to reduce the number of people they employ until demand picks up again. If the general level of prices is falling, this may have a negative effect on the profitability of firms, making them reluctant to invest. If employment does fall, and people become unemployed, this will further reduce aggregate demand in an economy. It may also have an effect on a government's fiscal policy because if more people become unemployed, the government may need to give out unemployment benefits to more people. Not only could public expenditure rise as a result of the increase in the level of unemployment, but revenue is likely to fall if fewer people are paying tax, both direct and indirect. The worry is that this could lead to a situation of recession for a country when there is negative growth, i.e. the output of an economy actually falls.

However, a government will not always be concerned about the consequences of deflation. There is one advantage of deflation and that is when the general level of prices in an economy is falling, it will mean that the purchasing power of a given sum of money will increase in terms of what it can buy. This means that the real income of people will rise and this could lead to an improvement in their standard of living. It is also the case that if a country is experiencing a fall in the general level of prices, it will make its exports more price competitive (the actual effect will depend

on how one country's rate of inflation compares with that of another country's) and this could lead to an improvement in a country's balance of trade position. Of course, the degree to which demand will change in response to price changes will depend on the price elasticity of demand.

Therefore, in conclusion, a government will often be concerned about the consequences of deflation, but there may well be some situations in which a short period of deflation could have advantages for an economy, especially when it is the result of improvements in productivity and advances in technology.

3. a) Gross Domestic Product is defined as the total output that is produced in an economy over a particular period of time, usually one year, by the factors of production that operate within the geographical boundaries of a country, irrespective of the ownership of them.

b) During an economic recession, an economy will experience negative economic growth as total demand contracts and firms cut output and jobs in response. Unemployment will therefore tend to rise during an economic recession. As more people lose their jobs, incomes will fall and revenues from direct taxes on incomes will also fall. Revenue from indirect taxes will also tend to decline as consumer spending falls. Corporation tax receipts will also fall as company profits shrink.

A government may also cut tax rates in an attempt to boost total demand and lift the economy out of recession. This will further reduce tax revenues during a recession but should help to boost private sector spending.

c) A government or central bank in an economy may increase interest rates to reduce inflationary pressures in an economy. Doing so will increase the cost of borrowing for both consumers and firms. Those with existing loans will see their repayments rise, leaving them with less money to spend on other goods and services. The increased cost of interest charges on loans will reduce firms' profits.

The rise in interest rates will also reduce demand for new loans, resulting in a further reduction in spending in the economy. In response to falling demand and profits, firms are therefore likely to cut back production and wage costs by making some of their employees redundant. As a result unemployment will increase.

Consumers may also respond by increasing saving as a proportion of their incomes, resulting in their total spending declining further, causing firms to cut back more and forcing some into closure. Lay-offs of workers are therefore likely to increase further. However, if the rate of interest remains below the rate of inflation in the economy, the real value of both loans and savings will be falling over time. This will discourage saving and encourage borrowing. Total spending on goods and services in the economy and levels of output and employment, may therefore be unaffected.

That said, spending on exports from the country may fall following an increase in interest rates. This is because higher interest rates will tend to increase the value of the national currency on the global foreign exchange market. This will make exports more expensive to buy but will also reduce the cost of goods imported from other countries. As a result, consumers in the economy may switch from buying domestically produced products to buying cheaper imports instead. Domestic producers facing a fall in demand for their goods and services at home and in other countries may therefore react by cutting output and employment.

**d)** Economic growth is regarded as an important aim of governments and this is because the gains of growth can be positive for an economy. It can lead to improvements in health welfare services and in education, leading to a rise in living standards and a better quality of life. Economic growth represents increased output in an economy and so there will be a greater availability of goods and services to satisfy the needs and wants of consumers, leading to an increase in the standard of living of people. There are likely to be increased employment opportunities and there are also likely to be increases in income. The increase in income is likely to lead to an increase in tax revenue for the government, giving it the necessary funds to spend on further improvements in education, health care and the infrastructure. Business opportunities are likely to be enhanced, raising the profitability of firms in the economy. If the increase in supply stays ahead of the increase in demand, a country is likely to experience a relatively low rate of inflation and so there would be no conflict between aims of economic growth and low inflation.

However, the consequences of economic growth for an economy may not always be positive and it is also necessary to consider the possible negative impact of economic growth. For example, an increase in a country's output could lead to a rise in the level of pollution, damaging the quality of a country's environment. It is also possible that economic growth is associated with a growing divide between the rich and poor, i.e. the distribution of income and wealth becomes less equal. The growth in output could be as a result of technical progress and a move towards capital-intensive production with the result that some people may lose their jobs. It is also possible that economic growth uses up a country's scarce resources

at a faster rate than would otherwise be the case. Therefore, the consequences of economic growth may not always be positive and economists, especially 'green' economists, will often stress that economic growth, especially a high rate of economic growth, has an opportunity cost in terms of the alternatives foregone. This is why many economists have stressed the need for economic growth to be sustainable, i.e. any improvements in the welfare of the present generation should not be at the expense of the welfare of future generations.

**4. a)** Economic growth can be defined as the increase in a country's output, as measured by the change in Gross Domestic Product, over a given period of time. It is the increase in output that comes about from the factors of production that are located within a country's geographical borders, irrespective of the ownership of these factors of production.

**b)** A merit good is a product that has potential benefits not only for an individual but also for the wider society. It is likely to be underproduced and underconsumed if left to the private sector, because of information failure on the part of consumers; that is, they do not have sufficient information to appreciate the true value of a merit good. A government would therefore want to encourage the consumption of merit goods, such as education and healthcare, because a better educated and healthier workforce is not only good for the individuals concerned, but is also good for the wider society. For example, a well-educated and healthy workforce is likely to be more efficient and more productive than would otherwise be the case.

**c)** A variety of fiscal policy measures could be used to control the rate of inflation in an economy. For example, if the inflation is caused by aggregate demand being greater than aggregate supply, that is, it is demand-pull inflation, fiscal policy measures could be used to reduce the level of aggregate demand. Public expenditure could be cut and/ or taxation could be increased, giving rise to a contractionary policy, which would reduce the level of demand. A limitation, however, is that it is not always easy to bring in such measures; for example, much public expenditure is committed many years in advance, and also such measures can take a long time to have an effect.

**d)** There may be conflicts between different government economic aims. For example, if measures are taken to stimulate the level of aggregate demand in an economy, so as to reduce the level of unemployment or to increase the rate of economic growth, demand could go up too much, especially if it is in excess of aggregate supply, and such a situation could lead to inflation with the excess demand 'pulling up' the general level of prices in an economy. If aggregate demand is greater than the ability of the domestic economy to satisfy it, it may lead to an increase in the level of imports, causing a deficit in the current account of the balance of payments. If measures are taken to try to bring about a more equitable distribution of income, such as through making income tax very progressive, this could have the effect of contributing to a 'brain drain' where highly skilled and highly qualified workers migrate to other countries because of the disincentive effects of the tax. However, it is not necessarily the case that there will always be a conflict between government economic aims. If a government takes into account all of the aims that it has, it may be able to achieve a balance between all of them. It would certainly help if a government had reliable, up-to-date, information about the economy so that the decisions that it took were more likely to balance these different objectives. For example, if a government intends to increase the level of aggregate demand in an economy, it needs to avoid increasing this by too much because of the danger of the possible inflationary consequences of such an action, so reliable information will help the government to increase the level of aggregate demand by just the right amount without it leading to an increase in the rate of inflation.

# 5.1 Differences in economic development between countries

## 5.1.1 Differences in economic development between countries

1. Economic development refers to more than economic growth. It refers not just to an increase in the productive capacity of a country, but to an increase in the economic welfare or well-being of the people of that country. In addition to the increase in output, it also includes improvements in the standards of education and heath care, investment in the social and economic infrastructure and wider social and economic choice.

2. There are a number of important characteristics of a developing economy (select two): they usually have a high level of infant mortality, a high rate of population growth (although that is not the case with all developing economies), relatively poor levels of education and health care, a relatively poor infrastructure (especially in terms of transportation and communication), relatively poor sanitation, poor housing conditions, a problem of access to clean water, a relatively low level of productivity and often a reliance on the primary sector of production, especially agriculture, where much of the farming is subsistence farming.

3. There are a number of possible reasons for the relatively low economic development of some countries (select three): there is an overdependence on agriculture in many developing countries to provide employment and incomes, and the yield from agricultural crops have fallen in many countries. It is also the case that many developing countries have suffered in international trade from the relatively low prices of agricultural commodities. Many of the developing countries suffer from a lack of capital, which means that they do not have the funds to invest in production and infrastructure and as a result of this lack of capital, many developing countries have to borrow money from other governments and/or international agencies, often at very high rates of interest. In many of these countries, there has been a lack of investment in education, training, health care and infrastructure. Many developing countries have a very high rate of population growth which means that increases in output need to be quite significant to maintain the same level of GDP per head. In some of these countries, there has been a great deal of corruption which has meant that any funds received in aid have not always reached the areas intended. Also, in some parts of the world, developing countries have suffered from attacks from other countries and also from civil war.

**E** As the economy of a country develops, it is likely that the secondary sector of manufacturing and construction, and then the tertiary sector, will grow in importance both in terms of their contribution of employment and output. The output of the agricultural and extractive industries sector may grow, but will fall as a proportion of total output as the secondary and tertiary sectors expand. Mechanization of the agricultural sector and other extractive industries, including mining, will increase productivity but will also displace labour from these industries. There may be an absolute as well as relative decline in employment in the primary sector as a result.

The manufacturing and construction sectors are normally the first to expand. Low wages attract investment in basic manufacturing industries and urban areas expand as workers are attracted from farming communities to towns and cities to work in the growing number of factories. However, how much manufacturing grows and what types of goods are produced will often depend on what resources are available in the economy. For example, a rich source of iron ore will enable a country to develop an iron and steel industry and, if it has access to the sea, a major shipbuilding sector that uses locally produced steel.

As national output and incomes rise, the choice and availability of different goods and services will then tend to expand, particularly through and expansion of retailing but then also banking, hospitality and leisure sectors as incomes continue to rise and people start to save more and spend their money on healthcare, education, leisure and entertainment.

## 5.2 Living standards
### 5.2.1 Indicators of living standards
### 5.2.2 Comparing living standards and income distribution

1. GDP per capita is average output or income per head. It is calculated by dividing the total GDP of a country by its population.

2. In addition to GDP per capita the Human Development Index (HDI) also includes levels of education, measured by how many years on average a person aged 25 will have spent in education and how many years a young child entering school now can be expected to spend in education during his or her life; and health, healthcare and the achievement of healthy lifestyles, measured by average life expectancy from birth.

3. An increase in the GDP of a country is measured by the increase in the total money value of all incomes or total output. However, people may be no better off if GDP increases simply because prices have increased. In fact, many people could become worse off if prices rise faster than their individual incomes.

   Changes in real GDP per head over time therefore provide a much better measure of how living standards are changing in a country because it excludes the impact of rising prices on incomes and also divides the total GDP by the population to calculate the average income per person. An increase in total output will increase real GDP and should therefore increase average incomes and reduce poverty.

   However (explain two or three of the following counter arguments):

   • If the distribution of income is very unequal the increase in real GDP may only benefit a small number of relatively well-off people leaving the incomes of the rest of the population, and therefore levels of absolute poverty, unchanged.

   • If the population of the country is expanding at a faster rate than real GDP, then real GDP per capita will be falling and poverty could become more widespread.

   • Real GDP per head may increase if a country produces more capital goods to expand the future productive potential of the economy. However, most people will be no better off and may even experience a fall in their living standards if the increase in the production of capital goods reduces the supply and increases the prices of consumer goods in the short run.

   • Real GDP per head doesn't take account of other important aspects of living standards such as the amount of political and cultural freedom people have, levels of education and healthcare, and availability of good quality housing. Many of these aspects of living standards may have declined despite an increase in real GDP per head.

• The increase in real GDP may have been achieved by a substitution of capital for labour in production leaving more people unemployed and without incomes, thereby increasing poverty.

**E**

| Development Indicator | Developed economy | Least developed economy |
|---|---|---|
| GDP per capita ($) | HIGH | LOW |
| Population living on less than $2 per day | LOW | HIGH |
| Life expectancy from birth (years) | HIGH | LOW |
| Adult literacy rate (%) | HIGH | LOW |
| Children completing primary education (%) | HIGH | LOW |
| Population without access to safe water supplies (%) | HIGH | LOW |
| Prevalence of underweight children under 5 (%) | LOW | HIGH |
| Fertility rate (total births per female 15 – 44 years) | LOW | HIGH |
| Hospital beds (per 1,000 people) | HIGH | LOW |
| Access to electricity (% of population) | HIGH | LOW |
| Secure internet servers (per 1 million people) | HIGH | LOW |

## 5.3 Poverty
### 5.3.1 Definition of absolute and relative poverty
### 5.3.2 The causes of poverty

1. Absolute poverty can be defined as a standard of living which fails to provide the basic necessities of life. These include such essential things as food, water, basic clothing and shelter.

2. Relative poverty can be defined as a standard of living where a number of people in a country are not able to enjoy all the products that would be available to people with a greater income.

3. The amount of income people have to spend and the amount of goods and services available to them are key determinants of their living standards. GDP per head takes account of both because it divides the total output or income of a country in a given period by its population. Data on national income, output and population is also readily available in most countries.

   However, because it measures average income per person GDP per head does not take account of potentially wide disparities in the distribution of incomes between people in some countries. GDP per head may appear high because some people may be very rich while most others are poor.

   The cost of living can also vary greatly between different countries. GDP per head may appear high in some countries because their inflation rates are high causing the prices of their goods and services to increase rapidly and making them unaffordable for people on low incomes. GDP per head also fails to take into account other aspects of living standards, including the quality of drinking water, education, healthcare and housing. Additional measures, such as life expectancy, adult literacy rates, access to safe water supplies , levels of subsistence farming and malnutrition should also be used to compare living standards.

 The article describes an increase in absolute poverty because it refers to increasing numbers of people unable to meet their basic needs and living on less than $1 per day.

## 5.3.3 Policies to alleviate poverty and redistribute income

1. There are a number of different policies which could be taken to alleviate poverty in a country. One way is for a government to support a higher rate of economic growth in a country, which will lead to higher output; all people will benefit from this, including those in poverty. For example, tax cuts would leave people with a higher disposable income, while an increase in public expenditure, such as on infrastructure projects, would be likely to lead to greater employment, creating a multiplier effect in the economy. Sometimes policy measures could be targeted at the poor, such as through providing employment opportunities in particular areas of a country where the extent of poverty is greatest, e.g. special development areas could be established as part of a regional policy to attract firms to move to certain areas, such as by giving tax incentives. Taxation could be made more progressive, e.g. income tax bands could be changed to take more money from the higher-income workers and this could be used to finance greater expenditure on transfer payments to the poor, such as various kinds of income support and child benefit. A government could also spend money on widening education and training schemes to make people more employable and so more able to earn an income through work. For example, schemes could be provided to improve the level of literacy of people. A government could also decide to subsidize certain products, such as particular food items, to make them more affordable for the poor. Subsidies could also be used to help make housing more affordable. If a country did not have a minimum wage, this could be introduced; this would have the effect of raising the wages of many of the poorest people in a country. If a country already had a minimum wage, then this wage level could be substantially increased.

2. There are a number of benefits of aid as a way of reducing the extent of poverty in a country. Sometimes this aid will involve providing developing countries with food aid, improving the standard of living of the people. Financial aid is another approach, where money is given to developing countries in the form of a loan to help the country improve its infrastructure. Technological aid is another example of aid where a developed country may provide a developing country with certain equipment and machinery.

However, there are a number of drawbacks to aid. For example, food aid may be detrimental to the farmers of a developing country if fewer people buy their produce, lowering their income. Financial aid can often come with strings and conditions attached. For example, it may specify particular firms that will need to be involved in an infrastructure project, often from the developed countries. If a government is provided with a loan, that government may often be required to carry out particular economic policies, such as reducing the size of a budget deficit. This is often the case with loans from the International Monetary Fund and the World Bank, restricting the freedom of action of a government to carry out particular economic policies. It can sometimes happen that a government is unable to pay back the money it has borrowed, when the interest payments are taken into account, a situation experienced by Mexico and Argentina. Sometimes, however, it is possible that some external debt repayments have been cancelled. Technological aid often involves the need for extensive training of people to be able to use the more advanced equipment and machinery. Also, advanced equipment may only require relatively few workers, so it does not help if the aim is to significantly reduce the extent of unemployment in a country. Corruption by some officials in some countries can stop aid from reaching those it is intended for.

**E** Country A has the lowest GDP per head of just $760 and has a relatively low average life expectancy and, on average, its population only receives seven years of schooling each. In contrast, Country B has the highest GDP per person of $3,175. However, life expectancy and the average number of years each person spends in education is higher in country A, which has a slightly lower GDP per head of $3,000. It is not clear therefore which of these countries has the highest standard of living using these measures alone. Other indicators worth comparing might include the distribution of income within each country; the percentage of their populations with access to safe drinking water; political freedoms; adult literacy rates; the number of doctors and hospital beds available per 1,000 people; birth and death rates; access to electricity; the proportions of their populations in absolute or relative poverty; air quality; etc.

## Key words

| 1 E | 2 G | 3 H | 4 K | 5 A | 6 J | 7 C |
|-----|-----|-----|-----|-----|-----|-----|
| 8 I | 9 B | 10 M | 11 F | 12 D | 13 L | |

| 1. high, developing, low | 2. GDP per capita, income | 3. low, high | 4. agriculture, capital, investment | 5. literacy, expectancy, ownership, lower |
|---|---|---|---|---|
| 6. absolute, relative | 7. progressive | 8. human, economic, overseas | 9. debt | |

## 5.4 Population

### 5.4.1 The factors that affect population growth

### 5.4.2 Reasons for different rates of population growth in different countries

1. Birth rate is defined as the number of live births for every 1,000 people in the population of a country over a given period of time, usually a year.

2. Death (or mortality) rate is defined as the number of deaths for every 1,000 people in the population of a country over a given period of time, usually a year.

3. Net migration is defined as the difference between immigration, i.e. the movement of people into a country, and emigration, i.e. the movement of people out of a country, in a particular region or country over a period of time, usually a year.

4. The natural rate of increase in a population is the difference between the birth rate and the death rate. In most countries birth rates exceed death rates so populations are growing.

5. The rate of population growth in one country may be different to that of another country for a number of reasons. One reason is because of the natural increase in population. This is as a result of the difference between the birth rate and the death rate. Birth rate varies a great deal between one country and another. For example, Niger has a birth rate of 50.54 while Monaco has a birth rate of only 6.94. These differences in birth rate can be explained by a number of factors, such as differences in living standards, differences in information about, and availability of, contraception, different customs, religious beliefs, such as in relation to the use of contraception, changes in female employment and the age at which people get married in different countries. Death rate also varies a great deal between one country and another. For example, Angola has a death rate of 23.40 while the United Arab Emirates has a death rate of only 2.06. These differences in death rate can be explained by a number of factors, such as differences in living standards, advances in medicine, the quality of healthcare provision and the existence of natural disasters and wars. These differences help to explain why some countries have a much higher average life expectancy at birth than others. For example, Monaco has an average life expectancy at birth of 89.73

while Angola has an average life expectancy at birth of 38.76.

The other reason to explain the different rates of population growth in various countries is the net migration rate. This is the difference between immigration into, and emigration out of, a country. Net migration rates vary a great deal between one country and another. This can be explained by a number of factors, such as the level of development in different countries, differences in standards of living and quality of life, differences in employment opportunities and wage levels, differences in the availability and quality of housing, differences in the standards of education and healthcare and differences in the extent of political and religious freedom.

### 5.4.3 The effects of changes in the size and structure of population on different countries

1. a) Changes likely to occur in the occupational structure of a population in a country as it becomes more developed include (explain one in detail or list two): a fall in the percentage of people employed in the primary sector, followed by growth in the number of people employed in secondary sector industries and thereafter an increase in employment in the tertiary sector as the secondary sector contracts (or fewer people working on farms, more people working in factories and in construction and then more people working in services); economic growth; increasing incomes and living standards/improved human and economic development.

   b) Changes likely to occur in the geographic distribution of the population of a country as it becomes more developed include: migration from rural to urban communities; increased employment opportunities in the secondary and tertiary sector; these in turn are likely to increase living standards but can also lead to overcrowding and pollution in urban areas and the decline of rural communities.

2. There are likely to be a number of problems and consequences of population change for developing countries. They are likely to experience rapid increases in population, with some developing countries increasing their population size by 30 or even 40% over a period of 10 years. This is likely to have a significant effect on the standard of living and quality of life in such countries because of the demand of people for services. This is likely to have a profound effect on economies where the scarce resources are already stretched. It is possible that such countries could experience famine, the rapid spread of disease, high and rising unemployment, an increasingly unsustainable use of natural resources, overcrowding, especially where there is increasing urbanization when people move from rural to urban areas, and a limited access to basic amenities.

3. An ageing population occurs in a country when people are, on average, living longer and therefore the average age of the country's population is rising. It is regarded as a problem because it brings about a change in the ratio of the working population to the dependent population, i.e. the ratio becomes lower. It can also have an impact in terms of the money that will need to be found to finance expenditure on healthcare and pensions. The effect of this is that many countries have increased the age of retirement to reduce the pressure on pensions. For example, in the UK, the retirement age is gradually being increased from 65 to 68 over a number of years.

**E** The average age of the population of Finland is higher than that of Vietnam which has proportionally more children than it does adults over 60 years of age. It is likely that Finland has an ageing population. Proportionally more people live in rural areas in Vietnam than in Finland and are employed in its agricultural sector. In contrast, the vast majority of Finnish people live in urban areas and are likely to be employed in tertiary or service industries.

## Key words

| 1 I | 2 G | 3 D | 4 C | 5 A | 6 E | 7 L |
|---|---|---|---|---|---|---|
| 8 N | 9 F | 10 P | 11 M | 12 B | 13 Q | 14 K |
| 15 H | 16 J | 17 O | | | | |

## Revision summary

| 1. birth, falling, devloping | 2. over-populated | 3. working, depend-ent, birth, death, developed | 4. birth, death | 5. devel-oping, de-veloped, female |
|---|---|---|---|---|
| 6. increased | 7. inward migartion | 8. geographic | 9. rural, ur-banization, industrial-ized | |

## Working with data and diagrams

1. To calculate the change in the population of this country, the number of deaths needs to be subtracted from the number of live births to give the natural change in population (2,423,864 − 1,896,452 = 527,412). Then, the number of emigrants needs to be subtracted from the number of immigrants (665,890 − 431, 892 = 233,998) to give the net migration. The change in population of this country is the natural change in population plus the net migration. In this case, this is 527,412 + 233,998 = 761,410.

2. To calculate the annual population growth of this country, it is necessary to take the difference in population (in this case, 5 million), divide this figure by the population at the start of the year (in this case, 50 million) and then multiply this figure by 100 to get the percentage figure for the population change. So it is 5/50 x 100/1 = 10%.

3.

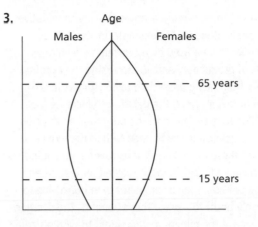

## Multiple choice questions

| 1 B | 2 B | 3 A | 4 A | 5 C | 6 A | 7 D | 8 D |
|---|---|---|---|---|---|---|---|

## Structured questions

1.  a) A 'developing economy', or less developed country, is defined as one which is relatively poor. These economies are mostly in the southern hemisphere in Asia, Africa and South America.

    b) A developing economy is characterized by a number of characteristics. These include relatively low average incomes, relatively low levels of investment, poor quality of infrastructure, high levels of poverty and a great deal of deprivation. They are often dependent on primary products with a relatively high proportion of workers employed in agriculture, forestry and fishing, and with a much smaller proportion of workers employed in the secondary and tertiary sectors, although the occupational distribution can vary a lot from one developing country to another. Such countries can often have a severe debt problem, largely due to the reliance on a great deal of foreign aid.

    c) The term 'absolute poverty' refers to a situation of extreme poverty in a country that can be defined in relation to a particular standard, such as US$1.00 or US$1.25 a day. It usually refers to a lack of basic necessities, such as food, water, basic clothing and shelter.

    d) The government's policy initiatives to reduce poverty may well be effective. Subsidies, in the form of financial assistance, will be given to a number of producers, especially in the agriculture industry, as a way of keeping down the prices of essential food items. This could well prove effective in keeping prices of such items lower than they would otherwise be, making them more affordable to the poor. Also, the decision of the government to increase the benefits that are given to poorer people may well be effective, raising the income levels of the poor. The government has also decided to increase the minimum wage that is paid to workers and this will have the effect of increasing the incomes of those in work.

However, there is no guarantee that these initiatives will prove effective. For example, in some cases, subsidies can be used by producers to keep down the costs of production, and so increasing their profits, rather than being passed on to consumers in the form of lower prices. The decision to increase the benefits that are given to the poor may be effective, but the government will need to find the money to pay for these benefits out of its revenue and if it does not have sufficient funds, it may either lead to an increase in taxation or an increase in borrowing (or possibly both) to pay for these benefits. The decision to increase the minimum wage paid to workers could also be effective in making workers on relatively low incomes better off, but there is the chance that firms will not be able to afford to pay these higher wages, leading to an increase in unemployment.

Therefore, in conclusion, while there are clearly some potential benefits of these initiatives, there are also a number of possible drawbacks and limitations of the measures proposed.

e) The term 'net migration' refers to the difference between the number of people coming into a country, called immigrants, and the number of people leaving a country, called emigrants. The figure will usually be for a particular period of time, usually one year.

f) The term 'optimum size' refers to the size of a country's population in relation to the resources of a particular country. It is in this sense that an optimum population can be described as the best population given the availability of resources, i.e. a country is neither underpopulated nor overpopulated. In this particular case, the government is concerned that the size of the country's population is above its optimum size. This means that the rate of growth of the population is such that the population size is greater than the available resources to sustain that population, suggesting that the country has become overpopulated.

g) There are a number of measures that a government could take to try to make it easier for workers to move from one sector of the economy to another. For example, a government could introduce a number of training and education schemes to improve the skills of workers (this will be especially helpful if these skills are transferable, i.e. they can be used in different types of work and are not specific to particular jobs); this should help to make unemployed workers, or those that choose to move from job to another, more employable. A government could also improve the availability of information in different parts of the country. If the movement of labour from one occupation to another involves moving from one part of a country to another, a government could help improve the geographical mobility of labour by offering an element of financial support to those moving.

h) It is stated that a number of workers have moved from rural to urban areas and this is likely to create a number of possible problems. This process of urbanization is likely to stretch the resources there. This can be seen in relation to the different services that the people need access to. One of these is housing and it is possible, and even likely, that the housing stock of a town or city will not be sufficient to satisfy the needs of all those moving to the urban areas. This could lead to overcrowding, and with the level of demand for housing being greater than the available supply of housing, it is likely to lead to an increase in the cost of housing. Not everybody moving to the urban areas will be able to afford this high cost of housing and some may resort to sleeping on the streets. There is also the possibility that although many people have moved to the towns and cities, there is no guarantee that all of them will be able to find work. This could therefore lead to a situation of high levels of unemployment in the urban areas. If the level of unemployment in the urban areas is relatively high, there is the possibility of this being associated with a high crime rate and this may then lead to police and law and order resources being stretched.

2. a) Birth rate is defined as the number of live births per 1,000 of a country's population over a given period of time, usually one year.

b) People may migrate from one country to another for a number of different possible reasons. It could be as a result of the level of development in different countries, with people leaving relatively poorer countries to move to more developed countries. In these countries, the standard of living and quality of life will be better. There may be more employment opportunities than in their own country and the wage levels may be higher than where they migrated from, especially if the more developed country has a minimum wage in place and the less developed country does not. Migration from one country to another may also be because the more developed country has a greater availability, and a better quality, of housing. The more developed country may also have better standards of education and healthcare. People may migrate out of a country to escape war, civil strife and possibly political and religious repression, whereas in the more developed country there may be a greater extent of political and religious freedom.

c) An ageing population can be defined as one in which the average age of people in a country is increasing. Many countries are experiencing an ageing population because of improvements in living conditions, especially in terms of sanitation, access to clean drinking water and the availability of vaccinations against diseases. Improvements in health care and the treatment of the old have meant that people have, on average, been able to live longer. The average life expectancy of people at birth has been increasing in many countries and people in Monaco, for example, can expect to live for about 90 years.

d) The consequences of an ageing population are usually seen as negative. For example, there will be an increase in the dependency ratio of a country, i.e. there will be fewer people working and paying taxes and they will be required to support an increasing number of elderly people who will be receiving a state pension. There will therefore be more pressure on the working population. There will be a need for the government of a country to allocate more funds to spending on healthcare and pensions. This could force a government to raise taxes to pay for this increase in spending and an increase in income taxes could have a disincentive effect on those at work. It could be the case that a country begins to experience a shortage of workers, leading to higher wages and this may have an effect on a country's inflation rate.

However, it is not necessarily the case that an ageing population will always be seen as negative. For example, older people could be regarded as an economic asset to a country because of all the experience that they have gained during their working lives. Some firms tend to employ a relatively high proportion of older people and stress this in their marketing material, such as in terms of the quality of service that customers will receive. In terms of the burden of paying for state pensions, a government could decide to respond to an ageing population by increasing the retirement age, making older people work for longer before they are eligible to a pension.

Therefore, in conclusion, although the negative consequences of an ageing population tend to be frequently stressed, it may not be as much of an economic problem as is sometimes suggested and there can even be benefits arising from the employment of older workers.

3. a) Relative poverty can be defined as that level of poverty in a country where some people are significantly worse off than others in that society, i.e. their standard of living is significantly lower than that of the average person in that society.

b) Economic development refers to a process whereby a country is able to benefit from an increase in output and an increased access to a variety of goods and services. It is a wider concept than economic growth and as well as including an increase in output, it also includes improvements in a range of services, especially access to education and healthcare. The process of economic development can be measured by a range of indicators, including standard of living and average life expectancy at birth. Economic development, at its widest, can include sustenance, i.e. the ability to meet such basic needs as food, basic clothing and shelter, self-esteem, i.e. a sense of worth and self-respect, and freedom, i.e. freedom from oppression and from environmental disasters.

c) Standards of living are often compared between countries, but it is also useful to compare standards of living within a country. In all countries, there will be some degree of inequality in the distribution of income and wealth and so although there will be a per capita GDP figure for every country, this will only be an average and will disguise inequalities in the distribution of a country's income and wealth. Some people in an economy will earn much more than others because of the particular skills that they have, i.e. the supply of such workers is relatively inelastic. In this situation, workers are paid more because of the high proportion of economic rent in their payment, i.e. payment over and above the transfer payments that they could earn in alternative employment. Some people will have a great deal of income and wealth, not as a result of earned income but because it has been inherited. Standards of living within a country may also vary from one region to another. For example, economic activity may be concentrated in certain regions of a country and these areas are likely to be better off than other areas. In many countries, the region in which the capital city is located is often economically more prosperous than other regions, with higher levels of employment and higher than average wages and salaries. It is possible to obtain figures for per capita GDP not only for a particular country, but for regions within that country.

d) An increase in a country's standard of living will often lead to an increase in its quality of life. Standard of living is often expressed in terms of GDP per capita and this will refer to the output of a country divided by its population. If a country experiences an increase in output, it means that there will be a greater number of products produced in the country, giving people a wider range of goods and services to choose from.

However, an increase in a country's standard of living may not necessarily lead to an increase in its quality of life. For example, the increase in output may have come about as a result of an increase in working hours and it is possible that this may have a detrimental effect on the work–life balance of many people in a country. This could lead to increased levels of stress and if people spend less time with their families, there could be a number of consequences, such as increase in the divorce rate. It is also often the case that those countries with the highest standards of living have very high suicide rates. High living standards can also be associated with certain illnesses, such as diabetes and heart disease. It is also possible that at least part of the increase in output is due to an increase in the production of demerit goods, such as alcohol and tobacco. An increase in the consumption of such goods could be damaging to health. It is also possible that some of the increase in output is in terms of the production of military weapons to be used in war. An increase in output could also lead to a greater level of pollution and there could therefore be a detrimental effect on the environment which would not lead to an improvement in the quality of life.

Therefore, in conclusion, although an increase in a country's standard of living can often have beneficial effects, leading to an increase in the quality of life, it is also possible that such an increase could have a number of drawbacks with the result that there is a decrease in at least some of the elements that make up a country's quality of life.

# 6.1 International specialization
## 6.1.1 Definition of globalization
## 6.1.2 Specialization at a national level
## 6.1.3 Advantages and disadvantages of specialization at a national level

1. National or regional specialization occurs when a national economy or regions within an economy use their scarce resources to produce a limited range of goods and/ or services. For example, Saudi Arabia has vast natural oil reserves allowing it to specialize in the production and export of oil while Germany's specialist engineering skills has helped it become the world's biggest exporter of cars.

2. A country that specializes in the production of a limited range of products will improve its efficiency and produce a surplus that it can trade with other countries to obtain those goods and services it is unable to produce. This increases consumer choice. The production, sale and transportation of exports also provides additional business and employment opportunities which in turn can boost economic growth. Through international trade, firms gain access to overseas markets, which allows them to grow bigger and to benefit from economies of scale.

3. Overspecialization is excessive specialization and occurs when a firm or an entire economy produces just one product or a narrow a range of products leaving it vulnerable to falling demand for its products.

4. Overspecialization in a country makes it overdependent on one or more other countries for vital resources. Political, economic or other changes in these countries may halt the supply of goods or services it needs. A country may also experience high levels of persistent structural unemployment and negative economic growth if global demand for its narrow range of products falls.

**E** You can find examples of international specialization by looking at statistics on the output and exports of different types of goods and services by country. For example, use the internet to find out the world's largest producer of cheese and the world's largest exporter of cheese. You may be surprised to learn that in 2017 the largest producer of cheese in the world was the United States but Germany exported more cheese than any other country. Germany also exported the most cars that year but more cars were produced in China than in other country.

# 6.2 Globalization, free trade and protection
## 6.2.1 The role of multinational companies (MNCs)

1. A multinational is a business organization that has business operations in more than one country, but it will usually have its headquarters in its country of origin. A multinational is usually a public limited company. When a multinational locates its business operations in another country, this is an example of foreign direct investment (FDI) into that country. A multinational is essentially a firm that produces in more than one country.

2. A government might try to persuade a multinational to locate in its country for a number of possible reasons. It may do so in order to provide jobs and so reduce the level of unemployment in the country. As more people earn an income, there will be more spending and this could create a positive multiplier effect. Workers will be able to learn new skills. There will be inward investment into the economy in the form of factories, machinery and equipment. They will also pay taxes on the profits earned.

3. Two problems the location of a foreign multinational might create in an economy are (choose any two): it may force competing firms in the economy out of business to establish a monopoly position in the economy; if employment laws are weak it may exploit workers by making them work long hours for low wages; it may increase the rate at which natural resources are depleted and may cause environmental damage; the national government may offer the multinational generous tax concessions and subsidies to attract it to locate operations in the economy, which will mean other public expenditures may have to be cut or taxes on other businesses and employees have to be raised; it may transfer its profits overseas to avoid paying taxes in the economy.

**E** Advantages: multinationals can provide jobs and incomes; they can help to boost exports and economic growth. Disadvantages: they may exploit the local workforce and the natural environment when employment laws and environmental regulations are weak or absent.

## 6.2.2 The benefits of free trade

1. Free trade involves the exchange of goods, services and money across international borders without the imposition of restrictions or barriers such as tariffs, quotas and duties.

2. Choose any two from the following: Free trade means a country does not have to be self-sufficient. This means a country can specialize in the production of those goods and services it is best able to produce with its scarce resources. This allows it produce those goods and services at volume and benefit from economies of scale. Free trade provides access to the cheapest and best natural, labour and human-made resources available globally. Consumer choice is increased because they can consume a wider variety of goods and services. Domestic monopolies will have to compete with producers in other countries forcing them to cut prices and improve their efficiency. Trade provides additional business and employment opportunities and can boost economic growth.

3. Increasing global trade and competition, especially from rapidly growing economies, is threatening many established businesses in developed economies and new, small businesses trying to grow in many less-developed economies. Established businesses may lose market share and may even be forced to close if they cannot compete with larger overseas businesses or new businesses in low-cost economies. Small businesses in less-developed economies may also be unable to grow if consumers in their countries are able to buy imported products far more cheaply than locally made products.

   The free movement of capital internationally has made it easy for multinational firms to shift their production from countries where wages and other costs are high, to less-developed countries where wages, land prices and taxes on profits are lower. This shift, some people argue, has not only increased the unemployment rate in many developed economies, but in some cases has also led to the exploitation of workers in less-developed economies where health and safety laws may be more relaxed or easier to ignore. In some cases it has also resulted in environmental damage in less-developed countries where environmental protection laws are weak or their governments choose not to enforce them.

   Increasing international trade may also have widened the gap between rich and poor countries. Many developed and rapidly developing economies dominate the global demand for many natural resources from smaller less-developed countries, including foodstuffs, timber, zinc, tin, copper and other ores, and use their purchasing power to force down global prices. This has reduced revenues for producers of natural resources in these economies.

    The articles highlight the following potential gains from free trade:

- Increasing production of goods and services for export can create new jobs and incomes and boost economic growth and living standards.
- Similarly, foreign direct investment can boost output, jobs and economic growth.
- Free trade can increase consumer choice and because trade increases competition, it can reduce prices and incentivize firms to reduce their costs and improve product quality.

## 6.2.3 Methods of protection
## 6.2.4 Reasons for protection
## 6.2.5 Consequences of protection

1. A tariff imposes an indirect tax on an imported good. This will raise the price of the imported good making it more expensive for consumers to buy. If demand for the imported good is price elastic then demand for it should fall significantly.

2. Choose any two of the following: to protect infant, sunset and strategically important industries in their economies from the impact international competition can have on their sales, output and employment; to protect its industries from dumping when producers in another country floods it with cheap, subsidized products with the aim of forcing its domestic producers out of business; to protect infant industries with significant growth potential from larger and cheaper foreign competitors to provide them with the time and chance to grow and become more globally competitive; to help slow the rate of decline in a sunset industry allowing time for new industries to grow to provide alternative employment opportunities in the economy; to protect a strategically important industry such as energy or agriculture from international competition so that the country does not become dependent on other countries for the supply of important items; to prevent overspecialization by maintaining a wider range of industries, some of which may otherwise have been forced out of business by international competition.

3. An international trade agreement will usually allow countries to that agreement to trade freely with each other but will use trade barriers, such as tariffs and quotas, to restrict imports and competition from producers in other countries. This is to protect indigenous industries and jobs from competition from more efficient or heavily subsidized producers overseas. Trade restrictions will allow new firms to develop, grow and hopefully become globally competitive with the potential to provide many more jobs and incomes in the future. They may not otherwise get the chance to develop and grow if they are quickly eliminated by overseas competition. The danger is that growing industries may continue to require protection from cheaper imports even when they have become established. Trade barriers will

also restrict consumer choice and other countries may also retaliate with trade barriers of their own which can harm the industries the country is trying to protect: they will be unable to sell their exports overseas and this will restrict their economic growth. As the question suggests, therefore, many economists prefer free trade.

This is because international trade enables economies to specialize in the production of those goods and services their natural, human and human-made resources are best able to produce because they have an absolute or comparative cost advantage over producers in other countries. They can then trade their surplus output with other countries to obtain the other goods and services they need and want. Through specialization and trade, therefore, output, incomes and living standards will be much higher.

Reducing or removing trading restrictions should therefore help to increase international trade by lowering the cost of trade and improving market access. A developing country may immediately see an increase in its visible exports to other countries and this will improve its balance of trade. Wages and salaries are still relatively low in many developing economies and this enables many of their firms to produce goods and services far cheaper than those in more developed economies. An increase in demand for their products in international markets will therefore improve revenues and, as a result, exporting firms are likely to expand their production. Output, employment and national income are likely to rise, thereby helping to boost domestic consumer demand for goods and services. However, some of the increase in consumer spending may be on imports. The lifting of trade restrictions will increase consumer choice in developing countries and allow them to access a wider variety of goods and services. The threat of competition from overseas producers will also provide domestic firms with the incentive to improve their own efficiency to keep their costs and prices low. If they were protected too much from overseas competition they might become inefficient and, as a result, their costs and prices would be higher and their product quality lower than they would be in a more competitive market.

**E** There are many examples of trading blocs. Some examples are the Association of Southeast Asian Nations (ASEAN), the East African Community (EAC), the European Union Customs Union (EUCU), the North American Free Trade Area (NAFTA).

Members of a free trade area remove tariffs and other restrictions on trade between them. They will continue to apply their own individual tariffs, quotas and other measures on trade with non-members.

Members of a customs union also remove tariffs and other restrictions on trade between them but apply common external tariffs, quotas and other measures to imports from non-member countries.

## Key words

| 1 Q | 2 D | 3 J | 4 M | 5 L | 6 P | 7 G | 8 H | 9 I | 10 E |
|---|---|---|---|---|---|---|---|---|---|
| 11 K | 12 O | 13 F | 14 A | 15 B | 16 C | 17 N | | | |

## Revision summary

| 1. specialization | 2. surplus | 3. international trade | 4. wants; markets |
|---|---|---|---|
| 5. depleted | 6. multinational; developed; developing | 7. trade barriers; tariffs; quotas | 8. infant |
| 9. sunset | 10. dumping | 11. overspecialization | 12. efficient; increase |

# 6.3 Foreign exchange rates
## 6.3.1 Definition of a foreign exchange rate
## 6.3.2 Determination of foreign exchange rates in the global foreign exchange market

1. The price of one currency in terms of another – or the rate at which one unit of a currency can be traded for another currency on the global foreign exchange market.

2. 10 Canadian dollars would have bought approximately 7.5 US dollars.

3.

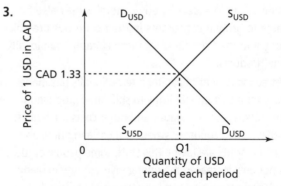

4. Reasons include (choose and explain at least three): to pay for goods and services supplied by firms in other countries; to save money in banks located in other countries; to buy shares in the ownership of foreign companies; to invest in premises and equipment to start and run business operations in other countries; to pay wages to employees or pensions to retired employees located in other countries; to give financial aid or make charitable donations to organizations located in other countries; to lend money to people, firms or governments in other countries; to change foreign currencies received, for example, from the sale of exports, into national currency; to buy and sell the national currency in order maintain a fixed exchange rate.

**E** The owner of a small company trading on the internet may require foreign exchange, including to pay for goods or services he or she imports from other countries; to pay the wages of any employees based in other countries; to make purchases when the owner is on holiday or business trips in other countries; to change into his or her national currency any monies received in foreign currencies from sales to residents of other countries; to make investments in other countries.

## 6.3.3 Causes of foreign exchange rate fluctuations

1. **a)** The US dollar appreciated against the euro. This means its value against the euro increased. One US dollar could be exchanged for more euros than it could a week earlier.

   **b)** Demand for US dollars from Eurozone countries could have increased, for example if residents of European countries are buying more US imports; and/or the supply of US dollars could have fallen, for example if US residents are spending less on exports from Eurozone countries or reducing their investments in Eurozone countries.

2. **a)**

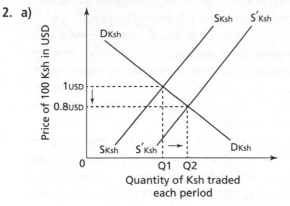

   **b)** If residents of Kenya are buying more imports from the US or imports from other countries priced in US dollars, then they will need to 'buy' more US dollars to pay for them. To do so they must supply more Kenyan shillings. The increase in the supply of Kenyan shillings on the forex market in return for US dollars will reduce the value of the Kenyan shilling against the US dollar.

   **(E)** An increase in interest rates in India may increase the external value of the rupee. Demand for rupees may increase as international investors are attracted by the higher interest rates.

   A worsening trade deficit may reduce the external value of the rupee. India will have to sell more rupees to buy foreign currencies to pay for its imports.

   A fall in the Indian inflation rate relative to inflation in other countries may make the prices of its goods more competitive in international markets. Any increase in demand for its exports will increase demand for rupees and boost its external value.

   If a slowdown in growth in the US 'threatens' the Indian economy, then it suggests the US is a major destination for Indian exports. A fall in demand for

Indian goods in the US may increase India's trade deficit and weaken its economy. As a result, India will have to sell more rupees to pay for its imports. International investors may also withdraw their investments from India. The sale of rupees combined with falling demand for rupees on the forex market will cause its value to depreciate.

## 6.3.4 Consequences of foreign exchange rate fluctuations

1. Floating exchange rates fluctuate or change over time due to changes in the demand for and/or supply of currencies on the global foreign exchange market. An increase in demand for a currency will tend to push up its value against other currencies while an increase in the supply of a currency will tend to reduce its value.

2. If 1 euro = 1,000 won, then a South Korean television priced at 500,000 won will cost a Spanish importer 500 euros (i.e. 500,000 won/1,000). If the won depreciates against the euro to 1 euro = 1,250 won, then a South Korean television priced at 500,000 won will cost a Spanish importer 800 euros (i.e. 500,000 won/1,250).

3. A depreciation in the exchange rate of country will reduce the external value of its currency, making exports from that country cheaper and imports more expensive. If demand for both exports and imports is price elastic then demand for exports should increase and spending on imports should fall. This should help to correct the trade deficit. However, if demand for exports and imports is price inelastic then the trade deficit could increase.

**(E)** A fall in the external value of the UK currency will make UK goods cheaper on international markets. If demand for UK goods by residents of other countries is price elastic, then the fall in their price will result in an increase in demand for exports and export revenues. However, the fall in the UK pound will also make imports to the UK dearer for UK consumers and firms to buy. UK manufacturers may therefore be forced to raise the prices of the goods they make for domestic and international markets, especially if the imported content of their goods is high. This is because they will have to pay more for the raw materials and component parts they import from suppliers in other countries.

## 6.3.5 Floating and fixed exchange rates

1. A floating exchange rate is determined on the global foreign exchange market through supply and demand conditions for that currency relative to other currencies. In a fixed exchange rate system, the rate at which a national currency can be exchanged for another currency is set and maintained by the government or central bank of that country.

2. Fluctuations in exchange rates can create uncertainty for firms engaged in international trade because they affect the prices of exports and imports. A fall in the external value of a currency will reduce export prices on international markets but increase the prices of imports. This can increase costs for many firms and consumers. A government may therefore fix its exchange rate to control the prices of its exports and imports. This will reduce price uncertainty for exporters and keep imported inflation under control.

In a fixed exchange rate system, firms must also keep their costs under control so they can price their exports competitively in international markets. This is because their government will not allow the exchange rate of their currency to depreciate to help make exports cheaper overseas to boost demand for them.

3. It can become increasingly difficult and expensive for a government to maintain a fixed exchange rate as global economic conditions change. For example, there will be pressure on the currency exchange rate of a country to fall if it has a growing trade deficit. In a floating system the exchange rate would fall, helping to make exports cheaper in international markets and increasing the cost of imports. However, if the exchange rate is fixed, the government will have to prevent its value from falling by buying up supplies of its currency on the foreign exchange market to hold up its value and it could soon run out of gold and foreign currency reserves doing this. Fixing the exchange rate of its currency against other currencies at a lower level is called devaluation and doing this can therefore prevent the government running out of reserves and may also help to correct the trade deficit by reducing export prices and raising import prices.

**E** The article illustrates two key disadvantages of fixed exchange rate systems:

(i) Foreign currency reserves may be used up very quickly attempting to prop up the external value of the currency as economic and trading conditions change. For example, as demand for imports increases, a country will have to supply more of its currency to buy foreign currencies in order to pay for more imports. Other things unchanged this will normally cause the external value of the currency to fall. However, if the government maintains a fixed exchange rate, it must prevent this from happening by using its reserves to buy up its own national currency on the forex market. Over time its reserves will become depleted.

(ii) A floating exchange rate can help to correct a trade imbalance. For example, a falling exchange rate can improve the competitiveness of exports on international markets while increasing the prices of imports. This will help to close a trade deficit if, in response, demand for exports increases and demand for imports falls. However, this adjustment mechanism is not present if the exchange rate is fixed

and not allowed to fall in value. The government of a country with a trade deficit and a fixed exchange rate will have to use up more of its reserves of gold and foreign currencies, buying up its own national currency to maintain its fixed value over time on the global forex market.

## 6.4 Current account of the balance of payments

### 6.4.1 Structure of the current account of the balance of payments

1. Exports involve the sale of goods and services to residents of other countries. Revenue from the sale of exports is recorded as credits to the current account. Physical goods sold to other countries are recorded as credits to the section on trade in goods, while revenues from services sold to residents of other countries are recorded as credits to the section on trade in services.

Imports involve the purchase of goods and services from other countries. Payments for imports are therefore recorded as debits from the current account. Physical goods purchased from other countries are recorded as debits in the section on trade in goods, while payments for services provided by residents of other countries are recorded as debits in the section on trade in services.

2. In year 1 the sum of balances on the current account of the balance of payments produced a deficit of $60bn. By year 5 the deficit on the current account had been reduced to $43bn largely because of the improvement in the balance of trade in services and the secondary income balance.

3. Choose any two from the following: the balance of trade in goods is the value of physical exports less the value of physical imports; the balance of trade in services is calculated from the sum of credits or revenue from the sale of services to overseas residents less debits for purchases of services from producers in other countries; the balance of income or primary income balance is the difference between international receipts and payments of wages, salaries and investment incomes; net current transfers or the secondary income balance is the measure of international transfers between a country and the rest of the world for which no goods or services are exchanged including gifts, pensions and charitable donations.

4. A deficit on the current account of the balance of payments will occur if the total sum of money paid out by a country to other countries in a given period of time for its imports of goods and services and income debits exceeds the total amount received by that country from the sale of its exports and from income credits in the same period.

## 6.4.2 Causes of a current account deficit and surplus

## 6.4.3 Consequences of current account deficits and surpluses

## 6.4.4 Policies to achieve balance of payments stability

1. A trade deficit represents a net outflow of money from an economy as the value of its imports exceeds its exports. This may have the following consequences for an economy (choose any two): the net outflow will reduce the amount of money in the country available to spend on goods and services. This could reduce demand for many products resulting in falling output and employment; the country will have to borrow money from other countries to finance its deficit. Taxes may have to rise to repay the debt and interest charges. This will reduce disposable incomes and further increase net outflows from the country; the country will need to supply more of its currency to buy other currencies to pay for its imports. This will cause its exchange rate to depreciate which in turn will make imports more expensive. There will be imported inflation and if demand for imports is price inelastic then net outflows from the country will increase further.

2. A government could try to reduce a trade deficit by (choose any four of the following): introducing trade barriers to restrict imports; raising interest rates to reduce consumer borrowing which otherwise have been spent on imports; reducing government spending and raise taxes to reduce aggregate demand including for imports; subsidizing exporters so they can reduce the prices of their goods; devaluing the national currency if it operates a fixed exchange rate system.

3. A surplus on the current account of the balance of payments represents a net inflow of money to a country from foreign markets. This is likely to occur if exports of goods and services exceed the value of imports. This may be the result of placing restrictions on imports, such as tariffs and quotas, to reduce demand for them. Fixing a low external value of the exchange rate can have a similar effect because it will raise the cost of imports and make exports cheaper to buy in other countries.

4. A large trade surplus will boost the income of the country that may result in an excess demand and rising prices (i.e. a demand-pull inflation) as it is spent. Trading partners may introduce trade restrictions in an attempt to reduce their trade deficits with the country. This will reduce sales of exports and in response exporting firms in the country may cut production and reduce their workforces resulting in unemployment and a slowdown in economic growth.

### Key words

| 1 M | 2 E | 3 K | 4 L | 5 C | 6 F | 7 G | 8 A | 9 S | 10 N |
|-----|-----|-----|-----|-----|-----|-----|-----|-----|------|
| 11 H | 12 P | 13 B | 14 R | 15 O | 16 I | 17 D | 18 J | 19 Q | |

### Revision summary

| 1. balance of payments | 2. credit; debit; transfers | 3. exports; imports; exports; imports | 4. foreign exchange; floating |
|---|---|---|---|
| 5. increase; cut | 6. imports; exports | 7. appreciate; increase; fall | 8. increase; reduce |
| 9. depreciate; fall; increase | 10. reduce; increase | 11. raising; contracting; devalue | |

### Working with data and diagrams

1. a) A balance of trade in goods deficit of $75bn
   b) A balance of trade in services surplus of $26bn
   c) A deficit on the primary income balance of $34bn
   d) A deficit on the secondary income balance of $12bn
   e) A current account deficit of $95bn

2.

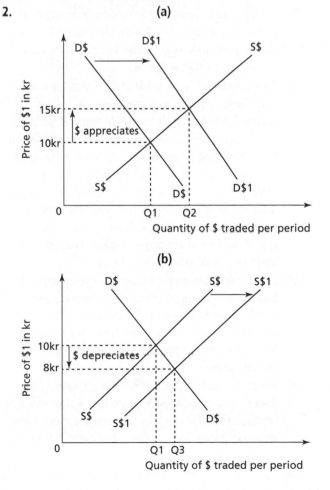

(a)

(b)

3.

| Changing economic conditions | Most likely impact on demand for US dollars? | Most likely impact on the supply of US dollars? | Most likely impact on the US exchange rate? |
|---|---|---|---|
| An increase in the US trade deficit | — | *Increase* | *Decrease* |
| An increase in the US inflation rate | *Decrease* | — | *Decrease* |
| An increase in US interest rates | *Increase* | — | *Increase* |
| Speculation that the value of the US dollar will fall | — | *Increase* | *Decrease* |

## Multiple choice questions

| 1 D | 2 C | 3 B | 4 C | 5 D |
|---|---|---|---|---|
| 6 B | 7 A | 8 D | 9 D | |

## Structured questions

1.  **a)** The extract reports that the government of Switzerland ended its cap on the Swiss franc exchange rate with the euro and that market conditions would determine the exchange rate.

    **b)** The value of a currency in a floating exchange rate system is determined by the global demand for the currency and its supply relative to other currencies on the foreign exchange market.

    **c)** An appreciation in the value of the Swiss franc will make Swiss exports more expensive and imports cheaper. This may result in a fall in demand for Swiss exports. Exporting firms in Switzerland may be forced to cut their output and workforces in response. Other Swiss firms may also suffer from falling sales and profits if Swiss consumers buy more imports instead. If the fall in demand for Swiss products is significant then job losses could follow. Falling demand for exports and rising sending on imports will reduce any trade surplus or increase a trade deficit.

    **d)** The extract refers to the export of large volumes of traditional Swiss products such as chocolate and watches plus major exports of modern mechanical and electrical engineering and chemical products to countries including India, Germany and the United States.

    **e)** Production will be more efficient and total output greater if an economy specializes in a limited range of products than if it attempts to produce a much wider variety of goods and services. It will benefit from

economies of large-scale production and a surplus it can trade with other economies to obtain the other items its consumers need and want.

**f)** If Switzerland has a large, persistent trade surplus then one or more of its trading partners, notably Hong Kong and India, will have trade deficits with the country. There will be a net outflow of money from these countries to Switzerland, reducing income, employment and output in their economies. Their exchange rates may depreciate resulting in imported inflation and, in response, they may introduce trade restrictions.

**g)** A floating exchange rate is determined by market forces. The government will not have to intervene to maintain its value and can therefore focus on its other economic objectives. In contrast, in a fixed exchange rate system the government may have to use up large reserves of foreign currency to maintain the value of its currency on the foreign exchange market, buying it up when its value would otherwise fall. If the government runs out of reserves then it will have to devalue its currency or allow it to float.

To avoid this and to encourage exports, some governments fix their exchange rates at low levels. For example, the value of the Swiss franc was previously kept artificially low against the euro to boost Swiss exports and make imports from the Eurozone less attractive. Doing so restricts free trade and consumer choice and for these reasons, a system of floating exchange rates is preferable.

However, floating exchange rates can fluctuate significantly with changing economic conditions and due to speculation. This can make it difficult for firms engaged in trade to manage their costs and forecast future sales. In contrast, a fixed exchange rate eliminates exchange rate speculation and risks and, therefore, provides greater certainty. This in turn may encourage more trade and investment in the economy.

2.  **a)** Trade protection involves the deliberate use of trade barriers to protect local businesses and jobs from foreign competition, usually by placing limits or restrictions on imports.

    **b)** Choose any two of the following: a tariff is an indirect tax on imported goods; a quota restricts the amount of goods that can be imported; an embargo is a ban on an import; tougher quality controls, standards and regulations, such as labeling requirements, can be applied to imported goods; subsidies can be paid to domestic firms producing goods vulnerable to international competition and to firms producing goods for export.

    **c)** A fall in a country's exchange rate should make its exports cheaper for residents of other countries to buy and its imports more expensive.

If there are no restrictions on trade and demand for its exports is price elastic, then spending on exports will increase which will help to reduce a trade deficit. Similarly, if demand for imports is price elastic, spending on imports will decrease, helping to reduce the deficit further.

However, if demand for exports is price inelastic, the fall in price will reduce export revenues and the trade deficit will widen. Similarly, if demand for imports is price inelastic, total spending on imports will increase and the deficit will increase further.

d) If domestic industries are protected from foreign competition it will restrict consumer choice and may result in less efficient production, higher prices and lower quality. The introduction of trade barriers can also provoke retaliatory measures from trading partners. This could have a major impact on the economy if it is heavily reliant on the production and sale of exports for jobs and incomes.

However, there may be circumstances when some protection may be necessary and justified. For example, if domestic firms are threatened by unfair foreign competition, such as the 'dumping' of cheap subsidized goods from other countries, measures may be needed to safeguard their future output, incomes and employment. This will be especially important for strategic industries such as energy, agriculture and defence equipment so that the country does not become overdependent on other countries for the supply of essential items.

New and growing industries may also need some protection initially from larger, established foreign competitors to provide them with an opportunity to grow in size and benefit from similar economies of scale. Similarly, a sunset or declining industry may need some protection from foreign competition to slow its rate of decline to allow time for new industries to grow to provide alternative employment opportunities in the economy.

3. a) A country will have a trade deficit if the payments it receives from the export of its goods and services to overseas residents are less than the payments it makes to overseas residents in the same period for imports of goods and services.

b) A country will record revenue received from the sale of its exports and services to other countries in the current account of its balance of payments. These will be recorded as credits. It will also record payments made to other countries for imports of goods and services. These will be recorded as debits. In addition it will record credits and debits of incomes and transfers with other countries.

c) A current account deficit may occur if (choose three of the following): there is economic expansion or recovery in the economy as people and firms increase their spending on all goods and services including imports; the exchange rate is too high making export prices high and import prices low; exports are expensive because wages and other production costs in the economy are high relative to other countries; consumers prefer to buy imports because domestically produced goods are more expensive and/or lower quality due to low levels of productivity; inflation in the economy is high relative to other countries making domestic products less competitive than imports; incomes are low or falling in other countries due to economic recession resulting in low or falling demand for the country's exports; other countries use trade barriers to restrict trade making it too difficult or unprofitable to export.

d) A surplus on the current account may be desirable because it represents a net inflow of money that will increase income and boost demand, output and employment in the economy. If, however, demand rises faster than output can expand it could result in rising inflation. Alternatively the inflow of money could be used to make investments in other countries that will return interest, profits or dividends in the future.

A surplus may also be desirable because it increases the foreign exchange reserves of a country. The reserves could be used to pay off any international loans that may have been required in the past to finance a current account deficit.

However, there are many reasons why a surplus may not be desirable. For example, if export growth has been at the expense of producing other goods and services for domestic consumers. The exports may also be non-renewable natural resources that cannot be replaced. This will have an adverse effect on both the natural environment and the future productive potential of the economy.

A surplus can also result in an appreciation in the country's exchange rate making its exports more expensive. If the country is heavily reliant on the production and sale of exports then this could have a significant negative impact on incomes, employment and ultimately living standards in the country. Further, its government may come under significant political and economic pressure from trading partners to reduce its trade surplus so they can reduce their trade deficits.

# OXFORD
## UNIVERSITY PRESS

Great Clarendon Street, Oxford, OX2 6DP, United Kingdom

Oxford University Press is a department of the University of Oxford. It furthers the University's objective of excellence in research, scholarship, and education by publishing worldwide. Oxford is a registered trade mark of Oxford University Press in the UK and in certain other countries

British Library Cataloguing in Publication Data
Data available

978 0 19 842850 3

1 3 5 7 9 10 8 6 4 2

Paper used in the production of this book is a natural, recyclable product made from wood grown in sustainable forests. The manufacturing process conforms to the environmental regulations of the country of origin.

Printed in Great Britain by CPI Group (UK) Ltd., Croydon CR0 4YY

## Acknowledgements

The publishers would like to thank the following for permissions to use copyright material:

**Cover images:** Shutterstock

Artwork by Thomson, Aptara Corp. and OUP.

Although we have made every effort to trace and contact all copyright holders before publication this has not been possible in all cases. If notified, the publisher will rectify any errors or omissions at the earliest opportunity.

Links to third party websites are provided by Oxford in good faith and for information only. Oxford disclaims any responsibility for the materials contained in any third party website referenced in this work.